ROBERT PHILLIP KOLKER

4

BERNARDO BERTOLUCCI

New York
OXFORD UNIVERSITY PRESS
1985

Copyright © 1985 by Robert Phillip Kolker

First published in 1985 in Great Britain
by the British Film Institute, London

First published in 1985 in the United States
by Oxford University Press, Inc.,
200 Madison Avenue, New York, New York 10016

Oxford is the registered trademark of Oxford University Press

Library of Congress Cataloging-in-Publication Data
Kolker, Robert Phillip.
  Bernardo Bertolucci.
  Bibliography: p.   Includes index.
  1. Bertolucci, Bernardo. I. Title.
PN1998.A3B48944   1985   791.43'0233'0924   85-18871
ISBN 0-19-520492-1

Printing (last digit): 9 8 7 6 5 4 3 2 1
Printed in the United States of America

For Doug and Mary Ousley

amici

Contents

Acknowledgments

Many people helped in a variety of ways to make possible a book that turned out to be something of a transatlantic venture. In the US, I wish to acknowledge New Yorker Films, Films Incorporated, and Ladd Pictures/Warner Brothers for making prints available for study.

My research assistants, Maria Marewski and Roberta Penn, along with Martin Farmer, were of invaluable help, as were the motion picture section of the Library of Congress; Harold Mars of 20th Century-Fox; Jeff Berg of International Creative Management; Judith Rice Millon; and Piergiuseppe Bozzetti of the Italian Embassy in Washington.

Colleagues at the University of Maryland were more than gracious with their time. Thanks go especially to Shira Malkin Baker, Vittorio Felaco, Madeleine Cottenet-Hage, Martin Mangold, James Royalty, Joseph Strobel and Robert Swanner.

A Research Support Award from the University of Maryland helped provide funds for travel abroad.

In Britain, I wish to thank Diana Hawkins for helping set up screenings in Rome; and the British Film Institute – Nigel Algar, Liz Heasman and Elaine Burrows in particular. Thanks also to Jim Adams of BFI Education who made the frame enlargements. Very special thanks to David Wilson, my editor and friend.

In Rome, Bertolucci's assistant, Franco Giovalè, and Unitelefilm were gracious in setting up a screening of *La salute è malata o I poveri muoiono prima*, an election film Bertolucci made in 1971. Diana Oliva-Day of 20th Century-Fox, Rome, set up screenings of the full-length *1900* and *Amore e rabbia* at short notice and with good humour and great good will.

Stills by National Film Archive, London. Acknowledgment is made to the distributors of the films illustrated. Acknowledgment is also made to the Civiche raccolte d'arte of Milan for permission to reproduce the painting 'Il Quarto Stato' by Giuseppe Pellizza da Volpedo.

Maria Coughlin prepared the index.

Linda Kolker gave the manuscript its first reading; her time and insight gave it direction and form.

Introduction

L'auteur est mort. Vive l'auteur!

Bernardo Bertolucci is one of the strongest personalities to emerge in
cinema since Jean-Luc Godard. He is a film-maker of international
stature, who (with the exception of one film, *1900*) has been in full
control of his work from inception to completion. His work demonstrates both a powerful consistency and a continual quest for new forms
of expression. When he began film-making in the early 1960s, he
struggled to discover his own style, working through a number of forms
and influences. Once discovered, that style was developed and refined,
changed, reconsidered in a restless attempt to avoid uniformity and
respond to different needs, different currents in film history, different
ideas demanding different forms of expression. The 'content' of
Bertolucci's work manifests a consistent, sometimes obsessive concern
for certain themes and ideas, for the problems of sexual relationships,
for the struggle of children and parents, of generations. Oedipus moves
– often with large feet – through most of Bertolucci's films. At the same
time, he is a committed political film-maker, a communist (in the
Italian style), with a highly developed sense of the connection between
personality and history. Many of his films express the struggle between
bourgeois individualism and collective action.

Such control and consistency, even when it is the consistency of
contradiction, makes Bertolucci the ideal subject for an auteur study.
But at this stage in the development of film criticism, the writing of
such a study runs the risk of appearing hopelessly out of date. *La
politique des auteurs* has served its purpose. It gave the cinema proper
names; it helped create serious film criticism and a school of new
film-makers: the French New Wave, who developed the concept and
then out of it invented themselves. But like quantum physics, each new
critical discovery about the structure of film revealed the need to
develop new structures, new 'particles' to account for the discoveries.
The auteur theory was developed essentially to create a coherence for
the history and form of classic American film, in which, historically, the
director usually played a minor role. Auteurism was a workable myth,

I

an ideology, which provided the base upon which further film theory might develop. From the discovery of personality came the need to forget personalities and discover relationships, links between images and narratives and the viewers who are affected by them. Out of that complex of relationships came discoveries about how the film text operates, how meanings are generated by all the elements of the film within the context of all the other films that make up cinema. Such projects opened further areas of enquiry: the relationship of text and audience to the wider culture that contains both, for example. We now know that film is not the innocent creation of a driving personality who impresses that personality upon a work, communicating meanings to a receptive audience, but a complex array of economic and ideological forces that determine the creator, the creation and the receivers of meaning generated by that creation.

The hows and whys of the complex continue to be investigated. One thing has become certain: we can no longer reduce a film to its 'auteur', no longer account for it by referring to or explaining the 'personality' that creates it. Nevertheless, this is an auteur study, concentrating on the work of one film-maker. In order to incorporate the elements of recent film criticism, I shall attempt to examine 'Bertolucci' not only as an individual, but as a figure who is, in a sense, created by his films and by such peripheral creations as statements made about those films in interviews. Some ideas offered by Michel Foucault are of assistance in this project. He writes:

> A name can group together a number of texts and thus differentiate them from others. A name also establishes different forms of relationships among texts. . . . The author's name characterizes a particular manner of existence of discourse. Discourse that possesses an author's name is not to be immediately consumed and forgotten; neither is it accorded the momentary attention given to ordinary, fleeting words. Rather, its status and its manner of reception are regulated by the culture in which it circulates.

> We can conclude that, unlike a proper name, which moves from the interior of a discourse to the real person outside who produced it, the name of the author remains at the contours of texts − separating one from the other, defining their form, and characterizing their mode of existence. It points to the existence of certain groups of discourse and refers to the status of this discourse within a society and culture. The author's name is not a function of a man's civil status, nor is it fictional; it is situated in the breach, among the discontinuities, which give rise to new groups of discourse and their singular mode of existence. Consequently, we can say that in our

culture, the name of an author is a variable that accompanies only certain texts to the exclusion of others.[1]

The author, Foucault says, is a 'function' of the discourse — that organized narrative with a controlling point of view that makes up the film text.

Such a definition helps remove the romantic subjectivity and cult of personality associated with the auteur theory and provides a means of returning study to the text itself, while at the same time reminding us that texts are produced by individuals and, perhaps even more important, produce individuals — subjects: the creator of the text, who, formed by it, is different from a biographical subject; the reader, who becomes one of the subjects of the text; and the critic, whose analytical structures are initiated by — and may even go beyond — the text. Peter Wollen writes:

> The film is not a communication, but an artefact which is unconsciously structured in a certain way. *Auteur* analysis does not consist of re-tracing a film to its origins, to its creative source. It consists of tracing a structure (not a message) within the work, which can then *post factum* be assigned to an individual, the director, on empirical grounds. It is wrong, in the name of a denial of the traditional idea of creative subjectivity, to deny any status to individuals at all. But Fuller or Hawks or Hitchcock [or Bertolucci], the directors, are quite separate from 'Fuller' or 'Hawks' or 'Hitchcock' [or 'Bertolucci'], the structures named after them, and should not be methodologically confused.[2]

I would take issue with the notion of the film as an 'artefact which is unconsciously structured', for this re-enters the romantic term that modern film theory attempts to suppress (despite the fact that Bertolucci is himself fond of the notion of unconscious structuring). However, Wollen is correct in stating that work and creator ought not to be methodologically confused. As Foucault says, the author becomes a function of his or her texts. The critic must work from the text outwards to the creation of its author.

Bertolucci does not make the task easy. He has given scores of interviews in which he enjoys inserting and asserting his own personality. The allusions to his experience with psychoanalysis, his explanations of sources and influences, his statements of intention, the references to biographical occurrences within his films often make it difficult to separate the personality of the creator from the creation of that personality by the films. At the same time, Bertolucci is anxious to

3

speak of the fact that he shares creative work with a number of individuals: Vittorio Storaro, the cinematographer who worked with him from *The Spider's Stratagem* (the first film in which a distinctive visual style is seen) to *La luna*; Giuseppe Bertolucci, his brother and co-writer on some of the films; Giovanni Bertolucci, his cousin and producer of many of the films; Franco Arcalli, who began as his editor on *The Conformist* and was co-writer of *Last Tango in Paris, 1900*, and *La luna*.

Most often he talks of these figures as extensions of his own creative personality. In other words, Bernardo Bertolucci is quite anxious to be recognized *as* an auteur, an artist whose personal vision and personal life infuses his work. A 'cult of personality' has formed about him, partly through his own doing, partly through the accidents of international fame and his desire to use that fame as a means of asserting 'personal vision'. The resulting clash of personality and work, and of personality created by that work, finally rebounded against him. The phenomenon of *1900*, a film that was intended to be a major political statement but in fact became a battleground between creator, producer and audience, placed Bertolucci at the nadir of his career and has trapped him, perhaps permanently, within the vagaries and tyrannies of current film economics. Personality undid itself and the text suffered. *La luna*, made in the wash of the catastrophe of *1900*, is so overburdened by its author's presence that its form does not survive the weight. When control is regained, when author once again becomes a function of the text in *Tragedy of a Ridiculous Man*, the time of the text and of the author is past. Despite the quality of the film and the remarkable change in style that it signalled, it was largely ignored.

All this makes the desired separation of biographical and textual personality difficult, and this study somewhat impure. The biographical will keep pushing its way in – often in the untidy form of supposition, the critical guess at why Bertolucci may have done one thing or another in a film – and the cliché of 'personal vision' will sometimes be unavoidably present. But as much as possible, the 'Bertolucci' of this book will stand for two things: the nine features made between 1962 and 1981, and the course of modern cinema that period encompasses. Bertolucci is as much a function of contemporary cinema as he is of the films that are part of it. He came to prominence at the time when the modernist movement in European film was reaching its apogee, and is still active at the crucial moment when cinema worldwide seems to be approaching its nadir. He is influenced by this period of film history and in turn influences it. His influence on the visual style of two Italian-American film-makers, Francis Ford Coppola and Martin Scorsese, is marked. Coppola did the best he could to absorb that style by asking Vittorio Storaro to photograph *Apocalypse Now* and *One from the Heart* for him. (Coppola was not the only interested party: Warren Beatty used Storaro as cinematographer on *Reds*.)

Bertolucci is part of that great communal web of cinema that formed in the early 1960s and which each new film-maker felt had to be understood, accounted for and joined. It was a time of consciousness and commitment. The best of the new directors developed a historical and critical faculty that urged them to consider each meaning-producing element in the films they made. In Bertolucci's case, we see this consciousness developing in his first film, *The Grim Reaper* (*La commare secca*). Although it is not the most auspicious first film of someone who would prove to be a major talent, it demonstrates an active trying out of methods and approaches, an awareness of traditions, a conscious seeking after form, if not yet of content.

In his second film, *Before the Revolution*, the critical faculty emerges fully formed. Looking back at that film in 1968, in a prefatory essay to the screenplay published in *L'Avant-scène du cinéma*, entitled 'Ambiguity and Uncertainty in the Mirror', Bertolucci wrote:

> There are two things that I love about the cinema: time and light. The whole life of the Lady O'Haru – youth, maturity and old age, in 3,000 metres. The Germany of the last century (the 20th) in the sublime, mid-length feature of Straub. The unity of time in Ford's *Seven Women*: one or two days, as in tragedy. The atemporal time in the films of Godard.
>
> And light. One does not forget the light of a film. There is a light in *La règle du jeu* that announces the beginning of the war; there is a light in *Voyage to Italy* that announces Antonioni's *L'avventura*, and with that all of modern cinema; and a light in *Breathless* that announces the 60s. And I also believe that, in a certain way, there is a light in *Before the Revolution*. . . .
>
> This is the real question that film-makers must pose: what is the significance of making a film?
>
> One proposition: a law that forbids montage; or at least a law that establishes that there must not be more than twenty cuts in a film. And let us begin (apropos of sound) by saying 'let us *listen* to the images of *Weekend*' and 'let us *see* the soundtrack of Straub's film on Bach' (p. 7, my translation).

These comments are clearly influenced by Godard's terse, aphoristic and synthesizing critical style of the 50s; and like Godard, they show a precision of understanding and a desire to reform cinematic practice.

Bertolucci's connection of *Voyage to Italy, L'avventura, Breathless* and the modernist movement they announced demonstrates a strong awareness of the immediate tradition of which he was to become a part. His theoretical refusal of montage is in line with neo-realist premises and the theories of André Bazin which all self-conscious film-makers were struggling with at the time. His notion of 'listening' to images and 'seeing' the soundtrack indicates an awareness of textual wholeness that would become an integral part of his own film-making.

Embedded in the dialogue of *Before the Revolution* there is further critical commentary about cinema, even more acute than this preface in expressing Bertolucci's awareness of his role as film-maker-critic-historian. The comments have often been quoted out of context, and occasionally attributed to Godard. Fabrizio, the central character of the film, and a friend (played by Gianni Amico, who was Bertolucci's collaborator on the film, and who later became a director with Bertolucci sometimes acting as his co-screenwriter or producer), chat after having seen Godard's *A Woman is a Woman*. Fabrizio, true to his character throughout the film, is distracted by the anxieties of his life. The friend, however, is intoxicated by cinema, and insists on speaking his near delirium. He tells Fabrizio that he has seen *Vertigo* eight times and *Voyage to Italy* fifteen. 'You can live without Hitchcock and Rossellini?' he asks. He says that *A Woman is a Woman* is a more engaged film than those of Lizzani and De Santis, even of Franco Rossi (an interesting extension of the old French argument here: the French claimed that American cinema was better and more important than the French 'Tradition of Quality'; Bertolucci, coming along some years later, states that the new French cinema is better than some post-war Italian cinema). 'Cinema is a matter of style,' the friend says, 'and style is a moral fact. ... A travelling shot, for example, is a matter of style, but this style is a moral fact. I remember a 360 degree circular travelling shot in a Nicholas Ray film, which I swear was one of the most intensely moral and consequently engaged things in the history of cinema.'[3]

That this statement should be attributed to Godard is not surprising, for it expresses the intense interest in the cinema and its forms that obsessed Godard in the 60s. Bertolucci's restatement of such sentiments, his allusion to a Godard film and to Nicholas Ray – a favourite film-maker of Godard – is important not only as a recognition of his relationship to Godard early in his career, but of the intensity of his investigations into the meanings of his own work. The insistence that style is a moral fact – which Bertolucci repeats in an interview given in 1966 – clearly signifies his understanding that content results from its formal expression, and that this expression must be determined with care and commitment.[4] Entering cinema a few years after Godard, Bertolucci had the space to examine and understand the Godardian project – the raising of film to intellectual, analytical consciousness, recognizing its abilities to speak to and about the world, understanding the filmic project as an interrelated complex of imaginative acts, and attempting to recognize the ramifications of rendering the world in cinematic terms.

The first chapter of this book considers the details of Bertolucci's relationship to Godard. But it is important at the outset to stress his sharing of Godard's critical insights in order to point up the fact that throughout his career, and despite his growing differences with Godard, he remained deeply conscious of the critical aspects of his own work and its place in the complex of cinema. As with many of his peers, that consciousness has directed Bertolucci's response both to the tradition of cinema of which he is a part and the cinema he himself makes. In discussing Bertolucci, we are dealing with a film-maker of acute self-consciousness and a powerful sense of purpose and critical understanding, an individual who carefully shapes his work and is, in turn, shaped by it.

But, to repeat, this is not a biography of Bertolucci; rather a critical analysis of his work, with references to events in his life and comments about his work made by him when these seem appropriate. I have never met my subject, although I have spoken with him on the telephone, and he was helpful in getting me access to important material, such as a full-length version of *1900* that I was able to see in Rome. He was adamant about not wanting to talk about his past work at this time, directing me instead to a long career interview by Enzo Ungari, published in Italy in 1982 under the title *Scene madri di Bernardo Bertolucci*, and which was translated for me by Shira Malkin Baker. This and the many other interviews he has given throughout his career have supplied the 'author's perspective' on his work – and some helpful factual information. I must admit, though, to being very selective in my use of quotations. Sometimes the things Bertolucci has to say about his work have little to do with the analysis I am pursuing; sometimes he speaks arrant nonsense. I have felt free to pick and choose.

Freedom, however, is always circumscribed. While it may be easy simply to ignore a personal comment by one's subject because it does not fit or make sense, it is less easy to feel free with one's own desire to avoid biography when dealing with a film-maker who, as I have mentioned, places so much of his life and experience in his work. This is the reason I break my own rules in speculating as to why Bertolucci makes certain aesthetic, formal, thematic choices from one film to another. In the last chapter I discuss a major conflict in his work, that which exists within a bourgeois intellectual – a man of self-consciousness and private angst – who is at the same time a Marxist, committed to a radical analysis of the world by means of a historical, materialist, and collectivist model. I do not know to what degree Bertolucci himself experiences these conflicts; I can only speak of them as they manifest themselves in his work and extrapolate them back and forth upon Bertolucci, the 'function' of that work.

Another element that makes separation of the biographical and the textual difficult is Bertolucci's interest in and textual use of Freud and Freudian analysis. This aspect of his work has been of great interest to American critics, and I hasten to admit that it is neither my special field of knowledge nor my primary concern. I am, for example, unmoved by Bertolucci's defence of *La luna* as a film that emerged from psychoanalysis and dreams of his childhood. From my own critical perspective, *La luna* is more interesting as an indication of Bertolucci's momentary loss of formal and narrative control, as an aesthetic mistake – possibly in reaction to the debacle of *1900* – than as a Freudian exercise. However, the psychoanalytical aspect of his work, particularly his obsession with the Oedipal process, cannot be ignored, especially when he attempts to merge it with a Marxist perspective. Freud – particularly as revised by the French psychiatrist Jacques Lacan – and Marx form a special conjunction in the formal and contextual matter of Bertolucci's films, and as such they will be attended to, though as far as possible through the films rather than through the personality of the film-maker.

This study, then, concentrates as much as possible on close, formal analysis of the films of Bernardo Bertolucci: on their development, on their textual construction and textual relationship with one another, and on the ideological complexes woven by them. Attention will be paid to the ways in which composition, cutting, narrative structure, character gesture and positioning create meaning. I will also explore the extraordinary range of cinematic and extra-cinematic allusion and influence in the work. In interviews Bertolucci is explicit about his use of paintings as models for the visual construction of certain of the films, particularly *The Spider's Stratagem* and *Last Tango in Paris*. The effect of these models needs careful investigation. As does his almost obsessive references to the operas of Verdi – something he rarely mentions in interviews and which is only superficially referred to by American and British critics of his work. Only four of Bertolucci's nine feature films to date are without some allusion to Verdi, either in the form of an opera occurring in a significant part of the narrative, or of a character singing an aria at an equally significant moment. Analysis of the operatic allusions reveals important, often ironic information about the film narrative, and opens out the texts as much as do the cinematic allusions with which they are often filled to overflowing.

Textual analysis creates certain problems for both the writer and the reader. One is a question of where to stop once entry into a text is made. Bertolucci's films are often rich enough to support a shot by shot analysis, a task that a study of this length could not contain and which, even if it could, would quickly tire both writer and reader. I have attempted to solve the problem by forming the analysis around specific questions that set limits to its extent and detail. This means, of course, that certain important sequences will be left out.

Another problem involves the matter of chronology. I have chosen something of a middle course between a chronological and an achronological reading, counterpointing the films, treating first the Godardian influence, particularly as evidenced in *Partner*, before discussing *Before the Revolution*, which came earlier. I move on then to the mature works, using *1900* as a kind of fulcrum, balancing *The Spider's Stratagem, The Conformist, Last Tango* on one side, *La luna* and *Tragedy of a Ridiculous Man* on the other. The last chapter goes back over the films by means of a more contextual analysis, discussing Oedipal patterns, political issues, and ending with an experiment of sorts – looking at the films through a feminist perspective. This organization demands a certain repetition. The same sequences and ideas may be looked at twice, but from different approaches. And, of course, form and content are inseparable. The close analysis of formal structure will always be interpretive rather than merely descriptive; the contextual analysis will refer back to formal matters. My major concern is always how form generates meaning and what meaning is being generated.

Finally, this study is a critical one in all senses of the word. I am a great admirer of Bertolucci's work, but I find some of it imperfect, incomplete, sometimes perfectly wrongheaded. This is another way of saying that what follows is hardly objective or wholly approving. It is often judgmental, though I hope the judgments are made within a context that justifies them. Bertolucci is one of the great reachers in contemporary cinema. Often he catches what he reaches for. Sometimes his reach exceeds his grasp.

1 'Versus Godard'

> *Partner* is the film that has made me suffer the most.
>
> Bernardo Bertolucci

In January 1967, a year before his third feature, *Partner*, appeared, *Cahiers du Cinéma* published an essay by Bertolucci called 'Versus Godard' (the original title is in English).[1] Ostensibly about Godard's most recent bit of bravura, his all but simultaneous filming of *Two or Three Things I Know About Her* and *Made in USA*, the essay expresses the displeasure and the jealousy the young Bertolucci felt about the phenomenon. 'While I was shooting *Partner*,' he said many years later, 'I was terribly jealous of Godard because he had managed to make two, even three, films a year . . .'[2] The language of the essay betrays the emotions of a disturbed lover, someone looking for a way to break the relationship. 'Is everything allowed to those who love?' he begins. 'Spying through Venetian blinds, for example; or searching through the clothes of the loved one for signs of his intimacy, or rummaging in his pockets in order to touch all the things that, as proofs of his treachery, become proofs of his existence . . .?'

What Bertolucci discovers in this spying is what he calls Godard's 'vulgarity': a persistent observation of minutiae which allows him, like the neo-realists, to discover the significance of day to day activity. 'I call "vulgarity" that capacity of his, that aptitude he has of living from day to day, close to things, of inhabiting the world the way journalists inhabit it, knowing how always to arrive the moment events occur and being rewarded by this punctuality with forcibly experiencing the effect, even the most trivial, like the duration of a match flame. This "vulgarity" involves being a little too attentive to everything, and it is in this that we are profoundly grateful to Godard. He risks that for us, because he speaks directly to and for us, in order to help us, the people who exist around him.'

Bertolucci is here expressing an admiration and a debt shared by many film-makers who, consciously or not, came under the influence of Jean-Luc Godard in the 60s. Godard's work constitutes the second and decisive break with cinema's past that occurred after the war. The

Italian neo-realists were the first to confront the form and content of the Hollywood style that, with few exceptions, was the universal film-making style in the 30s and early 40s. For them this style was part of the burden of history and culture they needed to cast off at the end of World War II. The Hollywood style, and its Italian counterpart, the 'white telephone' school of upper middle-class melodrama, was part of the residue of fascism – the political form of evasion and spectacle which the neo-realists saw as the reigning discourse of popular film that had to be destroyed along with the larger politics that had ruled their country for over twenty years.

The neo-realists believed that the way to counter the discourse of melodrama, and its calculated effort at making an audience react to the romantic desires, defeats and victories of middle-class heroes and heroines, was to rid themselves of romance, calculation, heroes and heroines; to develop, in short, another discourse, one that spoke quietly and (they hoped) unobtrusively about the working class and its post-war condition. They would do away with the old codes and signifiers of the traditional film, moving to the streets, making the environment a significant part of their discourse, permitting the audience to observe a world and its inhabitants that was not only barely noted by previous film, but would now be noted by them with a new set of conventions, creating an illusion of quiet, committed and distanced notation.

The neo-realists, in theory at least, would develop a new relationship between camera and subject, and so between audience and film. Their success was only partial, because the one element that most needed to be expunged from the text, sentimentality – the unwarranted, unfulfill-able, irresolvable attachment of viewer to fictional presence – remained. Nevertheless, the neo-realists drew attention to the figure in the environment in such a way as to affect all cinema to come. Bertolucci, with his great admiration for Rossellini, has remained always in their debt.

The French New Wave, and Godard in particular, took the neo-realist premise a few steps further. They agreed that there was a need for a new relationship between camera and subject or, more appro-priately, between the film-maker and his or her creation of the filmic text, along with a new relationship between that text and the audience. But where the neo-realists wished to create the illusion of unmediated observation of the subject by the film-maker and audience, inadver-tently confirming the Hollywood convention of an invisible form of presentation, Godard wished to foreground the presentation, make the signifiers of cinema as important as the content signified, joining ranks with modernist painters, writers and composers by pointing to the primacy of form. For Godard, the primacy of form initially manifested itself in two ways. One was a conscious attention to the artificiality – the cinematic reality – of the image. His use of jump cuts indicated the arbitrary nature of the film-maker's manipulation of time and space. His insistence on creating 90 degree compositions, placing his camera directly in front of the subject, drew attention to the two-dimensional reality of the screen surface. When he worked in colour, he accentuated the primary reds, yellows and blues of the image, reducing the subtle gradations that, in the 60s, were becoming conventional among film-makers who were trying to render colour as 'natural' as possible. He accentuated also the artificiality of narrative form. By drawing attention to the way films told their stories, by focusing upon and deconstructing narrative codes, he encouraged the viewer to understand why and how those stories were told.

The second way Godard manifested the primacy of form was through an investigation of film genres. Unlike the neo-realists, he did not turn away from American film (at least on the generic level) but embraced it with a critic's fervour, analysing its genres not only for what they said, but for the way they said it. Godard started as a film critic, and he continued his criticism in his film-making. Through his 60s films he ran a generic analysis from gangster film *(Breathless)* to musical *(A Woman is a Woman)*, to the film about film-making *(Contempt)*, the 'woman's picture' *(Vivre sa vie, A Married Woman)*, to science fiction *(Alphaville)*, romantic melodrama *(Pierrot le fou)* and spy thriller *(Made in USA)*. In each film he attempted to discover not only how and why the genre operated, but what insights could be gained by examining the machinery. The old forms, re-examined, became revitalized and yielded up new information. Cinema, as Godard advanced his way through it – with all the 'vulgarity' of obsessive observation and analysis – became itself revitalized and yielded up new information. By the mid-60s his films had established one undeniable reality, that the comforting notion of invisible form transmitting unquestioning conventions of human behaviour was no longer tenable. Human behaviour, as rendered by cinema, was the cinematic rendering of human behaviour. This is a tautology that should be self-evident, but it took the work of Godard to make film-makers and some film spectators appreciate its profundity.

There is, of course, another component to Godard's development which is of great matter here, and that is the evolution of the political form and content of his work. In retrospect this evolution was inevitable. To re-examine the form of cinema, and through that re-examination to free both the maker and the viewer from the illusory realism of the classic American mode of viewer manipulation, was itself a political act. Realizing this, Godard went on to pursue other possibilities of developing the political potential of the texts he was creating. Historical events – the Vietnamese war and the aftermath of May 1968 – added an urgency to his pursuit. But above all, his overriding, obsessive concern for the material reality of sound and image, for the ways that essential cinematic material can be moulded and shaped, and the ways the resulting shapes may affect the viewer, guided him into a Marxist reading of history and, especially, of the way history becomes ideology and ideology is transmitted through film and video images.

Ideology, to simplify somewhat a complex phenomenon, is constituted by the images and narratives which a culture and its members create and accept as a means of explaining and rationalizing their lives to themselves and their culture. It is the circuit – often broken – of exchange between the individual and the state, a circuit of shared beliefs and responses, always based on deformed images of historical, political and economic realities.[3] Film and television, along with other apparatuses such as newspapers and schooling, inculcate, infiltrate the individual with images and narratives. In examining the arbitrary nature of sound and image, Godard came to examine the ways in which they form, deform, or reform the culture that attends to them.

I said that many film-makers working in the 60s had to come to terms with Godard's influence. They did not all negotiate the same terms. Many merely assumed some of the more superficial aspects of the Godardian endeavour: location shooting, for example, which started with the neo-realists and became prominent by the late 60s (a phenomenon, particularly in America, that cannot be attributed solely to Godard's and the New Wave's influence, but to the breakdown of the studio system and the resulting lack of cheap accessibility to studio facilities); a more oblique cutting style, by means of which unnecessary transitions were left unstated; a tendency, among a few American film-makers, to begin examining film genres. Some European film-makers, like Jean-Marie Straub and Danièle Huillet, Pier Paolo Pasolini, Rainer Werner Fassbinder, Wim Wenders, and some older directors, like Robert Bresson and Luis Buñuel, as well as the majority of revolutionary film-makers in Latin America, made a conscious attempt to understand, follow, and absorb the more subtle configurations of the Godardian lesson.

No pupil was more eager and more rebellious than Bernardo Bertolucci. His career, almost from its beginning, and certainly up to his most recent film to date, *Tragedy of a Ridiculous Man*, shows an attempt simultaneously to embrace and to throw off, even defy, Godard's influence. The language of the jealous lover that begins his essay on Godard indicates an uneasiness, an anger, the shadow of a doubt falling over the relationship that would soon turn from shadow to substance through a strange attempt to end the relationship by turning influence into imitation in the film *Partner*.

In order to get to that relationship and the attempt to break it, we have to begin from another point and another figure, for in his first feature film, *The Grim Reaper (La commare secca)*, it seemed that Bertolucci would move in a direction very different from Godard's. Bertolucci began his film work as assistant director on Pier Paolo Pasolini's first feature, *Accattone* (1961). In retrospect, it seems almost inevitable that these two would be attracted to one another. Pasolini was a friend of Bertolucci's father, Attilio, a poet and film critic.[4] Older than Bertolucci, Pasolini was himself able to provide paternal guidance, and the two men shared common interests: poetry (Bertolucci had published a prize-winning volume of poems), art history, and politics.

In his own films, Pasolini started as an heir to the neo-realists. *Accattone* is a kind of immediate response to the end of the movement. Pasolini suggests that the film was made out of a certain despair over the closing of the period that made neo-realism possible. 'Neo-realism was the expression in the cinema of the Resistance, of the rediscovery of Italy, with all our hopes for a new kind of society. This lasted until the late 50s. After that neo-realism died because Italy changed: the establishment reconsolidated its position on petit bourgeois and clerical bases. So ... *Accattone* is what it is (apart from the fact that it is what it is because I am made the way I am) for external cultural reasons ... the whole re-establishment of officialdom and hypocrisy. The Italian bourgeoisie had closed one cultural period, the age of neo-realism.'[5] One item needs to be added to this statement. Pasolini neglects to point out that the major neo-realist directors were already heading towards different forms of expression by the time the Italian government changed and began to censor the movement, not only in the broader ideological sense that Pasolini implies, but directly, by publicly condemning it in the late 40s and early 50s.[6]

Accattone, therefore, is a kind of reconsideration of neo-realism, made from a perspective of anger and perversity. Some of the primary signifiers remain: the location shooting, the non-professional actors, the use of environment to define character, a quasi-objective point of view. The sentimentality is there as well, but now covertly articulated within the essential difference between this film and its neo-realist forebears. The characters of interest to Pasolini are not the unemployed working class, looking only for the means – always unattainable – of supporting themselves and their families with some semblance of dignity. Instead, he is fascinated – as he was in his life – by the subproletariat, the self-made and defiantly disenfranchised, who do not wish to work, except perhaps as pimps.

What *Accattone* creates, in effect, is the demonic underside of the neo-realist endeavour, in which sympathy is given to the bedevillers of bourgeois society, those who gleefully, spitefully, smilingly refuse its ideological demands. The character of Accattone – a nickname which literally means 'beggar' – is created as a kind of subproletarian saint, consciously suffering for his sins as he commits them. The music of Bach accompanies his wanderings through the streets (an idea taken, perhaps, from Bresson's *Un Condamné à mort s'est échappé*). He tries to be a labourer but cannot take the work, and is finally killed while escaping the robbery of a food truck. The film is as perverse as its characters, intensely anti-female and anti-humanist, insistent in its demands that, if the viewer does not sympathize with the world and the characters it creates, he should at least understand them and, perhaps, appreciate their energy and agony. I say 'he' for it is difficult to guess what the reaction of a female viewer might be to this film of male camaraderie that uses women as objects of abuse or adoration. (A Catholic subtext, or a homosexual one? It is difficult to determine, particularly given Pasolini's own, somewhat odd Catholicism and declared homosexuality, to which, many years later, after Pasolini's murder, Bertolucci makes a rather back-handed reference in *La luna*, where Franco Citti – who plays Accattone and is a major figure in some of Pasolini's films – plays the character of a homosexual who attempts to pick up Caterina's son in a Roman bar.)

The film is a far cry from Godard's early work. And although later in his career Pasolini picked up a Brechtian influence from Godard, and even made a film strongly influenced by him (*Porcile – Pigsty* – 1969, in which two of Godard's players, Jean-Pierre Léaud and Anne Wiazemsky, have major roles, and which, in its turn, was to influence Bertolucci's *Tragedy of a Ridiculous Man*), his interests centre not upon a Godardian examination of the ways in which cinema can deal with the contemporary world and its conflicting demands upon individual consciousness, but on the mythic, the ribald, with tableaux of social-political-sexual history, culminating in his last film, one of the most transgressive works in modern cinema, *Salò, or the 120 Days of Sodom*.

Accattone is the initial, *direct* influence upon Bertolucci's film-making. As its assistant director he would, obviously, observe Pasolini's methods and absorb some of Pasolini's cinematic view of the world. But in fact there is more than absorption. When, the following year, Bertolucci made his own first feature, it was based on a story written by Pasolini prior to *Accattone*, and which Pasolini wanted to direct before that film.

The Grim Reaper was therefore something of a gift from father to son, a means towards initiation.[7] And the question initially posed to the critic looking at the film in retrospect is what the recipient did with the gift. 'I think more than being influenced by me,' Pasolini said, 'he reacted against me. I was rather like a father to him, and so he reacted against me. In fact when he was shooting a scene he would think to himself "How would Pier Paolo shoot this?" and so he would decide to shoot it a different way.'[8]

The discourse of *The Grim Reaper* is unmistakably Pasolinian, although Bertolucci rewrote the material and says that there developed a strong and for him creative tension between the intentions of Pasolini's original five-page treatment, the script that Bertolucci developed with Sergio Citti, and the strong influence of *Breathless* upon his own direction, an influence not apparent in the finished film.[9] The film speaks of the Roman underworld: a murdered whore, the sub-proletariat, the pimps and petty thieves, the wanderers and the murderer who gather in the late afternoon and evening at a park that is the scene of the crime. The film seems to speak of them (with one exception) dispassionately, inquisitively. Indeed its structure is that of an inquisition. A prostitute is found murdered. The police interrogate various witnesses and suspects: a street punk, who could have stepped straight out of *Accattone*; a pimp who is torn between his love for a respectable young woman and his sordid life as procurer in business with an old hag and her daughter; a soldier; a young boy; and a fair-haired man who is interrogated twice and proves finally to be the murderer. Their 'stories' are told in flashback.

Actually, the word 'structure' is too definitive. In *The Grim Reaper*, Bertolucci searches for a structure, for an identity, in the end without complete success. The film demonstrates the tension with the Pasolinian model, indicating that Bertolucci used it as means for his own initial inquisition into the possibilities of form and expression. He does not find that form here, and the film is essentially about a cinematic talent on the prowl, looking at the films of his time, and the time just preceding, testing ideas and images, ways of seeing, ways of making a visual narrative. *The Grim Reaper* is in no way the equivalent of *Breathless*, for it offers no attack against reigning cinematic practice, and in itself seems to offer little promise. Few things in it would give any notion that *Before the Revolution* would follow, not to mention *The Spider's Stratagem* or *The Conformist*.

The narrative structure of the film – piecing together a story from the perceptions of a number of different characters – harks back, of course, to Kurosawa's *Rashomon* (1950), although I suspect that Bertolucci has an even greater interest in the more complex structural possibilities offered by *Citizen Kane*. Welles proved to be a major influence on Bertolucci's later films, particularly in his use of space and camera movement. In these later films Bertolucci is much more articulate about the process of perception, about the ways in which his characters see their world and how that seeing is communicated to the viewer, who is allowed to see as much as, and more than, the character. These initial experiments with perception, restricted as they are, allow Bertolucci to play with the audience, giving them a visual space for enquiry, a puzzle to be pieced together.

One paradoxical problem with the experiment of *The Grim Reaper* is that it is a little too subtle. One has to see the film twice in order to understand what the film-maker is trying to do. As each of the witnesses tells his part of the story, the viewer is shown, mainly from their perspective, some of the events that occurred, and some of the characters who appeared, during the fateful night when the prostitute was murdered. For example, the first flashback is told by the street punk, Luciano, who admits only to seeing a woman (the prostitute) and some children in the park. What the viewer sees, however, is three people in the far background of the scene he describes. We cannot make them out, and at this early point in the narrative have no idea who they could be. But they are in fact two young boys – one of them Pipito, who will be a witness later in the film – talking with the gay man from whom (we later find out) they are trying to get money to buy a meal for their girlfriends. The homosexual will prove to be a major character in the narrative, for it is he who witnesses the crime. The police ask Luciano about a soldier (again a figure we have not yet been introduced to, and who also will be a witness to some of the events that night), and we can just make out his figure asleep on the park bench. In the succeeding 'testimony' of the other witnesses, we see more and more of the characters in the park who played some role in the night's events; and even though we do not see the actual murder until the final interrogation of the blond man, we do get a notion of what happened during that night in advance of the direct narration of the events themselves.

The second narrational-perceptual structure Bertolucci creates is more interesting. With it, he attempts to provide a device that links together all the characters' stories. The events told by them occur, of course, on the same day and evening. On that afternoon there is a rain storm which interrupts each of their narratives. Each time it rains during one of the character's flashbacks, Bertolucci cuts away from that story to the rain-soaked window of the prostitute who will be the murder victim. Each time the cut is made and the camera pulls back from the window, we see the prostitute preparing for her evening's work: her last evening alive. In the first sequence, we see her getting out of bed and going to the window. During the pimp's testimony, we see her making coffee as the camera tracks to the mirror above her washstand. During the soldier's tale she goes to the mirror, puts on her make-up and then pours her coffee. During the interview with the blond man (the murderer) we do not see the prostitute in her home, only in the park at night. But during the testimony of the young boy, Pipito, Bertolucci picks up her earlier activities at the stove as she gets ready to leave.

Bertolucci refers to the film's perceptual and temporal devices as attempts to capture the poetry of time passing, 'whispered about like a secret, and the whisper is so low that almost no one can hear it'.[10] Not only can they barely be heard, but they seem simply to be there, as ideas Bertolucci had and wished to try out. They are important as experiments in linking the various narrative components, and more important still as a means of providing the viewer with a series of 'privileged moments'. This is particularly true in the treatment of the prostitute, for Bertolucci attempts to go a bit further than would Pasolini in giving her some attention – if not a personality or very much sympathy, at least a presence. He requests that, at the very least, the viewer see her as more than a dead body (which is what we see of her at the beginning of the film), or victim (which is the only way she is observed during her murder as she pathetically raises her arms to her killer in a gesture both of abasement and pleading). She is given a life, rather sad and lonely, but there is not quite enough to allow us to understand her and why she has such a life.

I mention Kurosawa and Welles as influences on *The Grim Reaper*. There are borrowings from other films and film-makers as well: a Godardian gambit and a premonition of the allusive gesture that was to become an important constituent of Bertolucci's work. The very first shot of the film, for example, owes much to the kind of visual experimentation that Antonioni was carrying on at the time. It is a static shot of an enormous bridge, whose structure takes up most of the frame. The sound of a car going by is heard and there is a rustle of papers. The wind blows. The camera pans left and a cut is made to a wall; the papers flutter down. Further cuts and camera movements reveal the prostitute's body. There is a zoom back, revealing a river in the background. This use of urban structures which diminish the human figure owes much to *L'avventura*, *La notte* and *L'eclisse*, the three films Antonioni made between 1960 and 1962, the year of *The Grim Reaper*. With these films, Antonioni made the definitive advance upon neo-realism, defining character not merely within a landscape but *by* the landscape, turning environment into a psychological manifestation of character. Bertolucci does little with this device here, and in fact the Antonioni influence does not appear again in the film. But again it is indicative of his need to try things out, to take what is useful to him from contemporaries other than Pasolini.

One reason the influence of Antonioni is not pursued has precisely to do with the matter of neo-realism. At this moment of his career, Bertolucci apparently did not want to go very far beyond the neo-realist movement – not even as far as Pasolini – but rather to investigate it in order to find what it might hold for him. I have already noted his affection for Roberto Rossellini in the comments made by a character in *Before the Revolution* and in Bertolucci's introduction to that film's published screenplay. In a 1966 interview he makes some further remarks about the 'father' of neo-realism ('I must tell you that the Italian films I love most are those of Rossellini'). He talks of Rossellini's spatial perception: 'Regarding Rossellini's style, there is this capacity of having things never too far away and never too close, the ideal distance that his camera has from things and from characters. It is one of the first cases of a truly open cinema.'[11] In a later interview he says, 'One of Rossellini's great qualities is that he always resolved an authentic moral problem in his choice of distance used to film a sequence.'[12] There is some general influence of neo-realism in *The Grim Reaper*: location shooting, the use of non-professional or little known players. But in one particular sequence, the soldier's narrative, the influence is so marked that it appears Bertolucci consciously used it as an exercise in the neo-realist style and as a homage to Rossellini. In this sequence he pays close attention to the notion of the camera's proximity to or distance from characters and things, to that openness of space that Bertolucci admired in Rossellini and which is apparent in the work of the neo-realists in general.

The sequence is made up of the soldier's wanderings through the streets of Rome, and Bertolucci is content to follow those wanderings, embracing the character (played by an American actor, Allen Midgette, who later had the important role of Agostino in *Before the Revolution* and turned up in small parts in *The Spider's Stratagem* and *1900*) and his surroundings, with affection and with simple pleasure in an observation that attempts to discover the 'ideal distance' between camera and character. The soldier chases women in the streets. He looks in shop windows, goes to the Colosseum where an American guide gives a talk to tourists. He looks at a little black child. (The tour guide at the Colosseum is certainly a passing reference to a sequence in Rossellini's *Voyage to Italy*, where Ingrid Bergman is guided through a museum and various sights in Milan; the brief episode with the black child probably refers to the sequence in *Paisà* involving a black

Neo-realism and the 'ideal distance': the soldier's story in *La commare secca* (Allen Midgette)

American soldier and a Neapolitan child. Bertolucci's admiration for Rossellini is too great for these to be mere coincidence.) Through it all, Bertolucci is content to observe the small, inconsequential gestures of this innocent, who can walk through the streets singing 'Praise to the God of Abraham', adding, as he smiles at the prostitutes standing along the walls, 'who created ... beautiful women'.

A series of shots occurs within this sequence that is not merely a homage to neo-realism, but all but creates an ideal neo-realist episode. The soldier, tired from his wanderings, sits and rubs his feet. Trains can be seen going by in the distance. He gets up and stares through a chain-link fence, putting his fingers between the wires, fingering something. Bertolucci cuts to a wall and another fence; clothes hang on a line. The camera pans down to reveal two children sitting on the street under an umbrella, two street urchins who might have slipped into the film from *Rome, Open City, Germany, Year Zero*, or De Sica's *Bicycle Thieves*. The rain storm that occurs in each of the other flashback sequences begins.

After the insertion of the linking sequence of the prostitute who continues to ready herself for her night's business, Bertolucci returns to the soldier, running through the rain, finding shelter by a wall (neo-realist characters are often photographed by these urban boundaries of their lives). There is a sound as if of thunder and the soldier looks up in surprise, but a cut reveals that it is only a train passing overhead. More prostitutes are seen lingering by the walls, the soldier laughs in the rain, and the camera begins a long, lingering pull back, revealing more prostitutes under the train bridge, the soldier standing in the light in the distance, children playing, dogs barking.

This sequence is of major importance to Bertolucci's development as a film-maker. While he would never again return to such a direct imitation of the neo-realist style (though he uses it as a base from which to work in *The Spider's Stratagem*, refers to it in a sequence toward the end of *The Conformist*, and uses it as the general aesthetic model for *1900*), his knowledge and acknowledgment of the movement would never leave him, no matter how many changes in style there were in his later work. In *The Grim Reaper* he imitates some of its forms without the anger and cynicism of Pasolini in *Accattone*, and it remains part of the textbook aspect of the film, another example of the student doing his exercises.

In sum, the film is a thing of bits and pieces, of good observations, of unassimilated influences and ideas, of unfriendly attitudes toward women and gays (it is left quite ambiguous as to whether 'the grim reaper' of the title is the prostitute's murderer or the homosexual who points him out to the police); yet it demonstrates at least a film-maker anxious to try things out, to show that he is aware of the various possibilities inherent in the act of cinema-making. It is also his debt to his mentor, Pasolini, and, perhaps, an attack. Not only is the homosexual in the film presented as a sinister figure, but the murderer himself comes from Friuli, the province of Pasolini's childhood. Whether payment or attack, once made, it allowed Bertolucci to go on to other things. 'I only had a very general influence on him,' Pasolini said, 'and as regards his style he is completely different from me. His real master is Godard.'[13]

Godard, Rossellini, Pasolini, Visconti, Sternberg, Mizoguchi, Ophuls, Welles. Bertolucci has either mentioned them as influences, or made their influence apparent in his work. But Godard above all. *The Grim Reaper* has diverted us – as it must have diverted its director – from confronting directly the Godardian presence. Bertolucci's second feature, *Before the Revolution (Prima della rivoluzione)*, came somewhat closer to facing Godard. It contains direct reference to a Godard film; a character carries on a conversation about cinema in the Godardian manner. More important, this film in which Bertolucci discovers a more comfortable, 'personal' form of expression than he did in *The Grim Reaper* relies in large part on the rapid, elliptical cutting and the general attack upon classical cinematic forms launched by Godard and his New Wave colleagues. Bertolucci claims that *Breathless* lurked behind the creation of *The Grim Reaper*; but in the struggle of masters, Pasolini won. Godard did not begin to prevail for another two years. Yet the influence of Godard on *Before the Revolution* is somewhat diffuse. The film's form and style bear the weight of the entire New Wave movement, as did so many other films of the time. The Godardian influence is certainly there, but it is a presence almost taken for granted. Bertolucci is using, but not yet confronting the master.

Because *Before the Revolution* is the first definitive statement of Bertolucci's major formal and thematic concerns, I shall defer discussion of it until the next chapter. In order to continue exploring the relationship between Bertolucci and Godard – which is, in effect, the exploration of Bertolucci's place in the cine-modernism of the 60s – I shall move ahead a few years, to the work that culminated in *Partner*, the film in which Bertolucci attempts to become Godard. A task that proved impossible on all counts.

Between *Before the Revolution* and *Partner* Bertolucci made some documentaries on petroleum for Italian television, wrote the initial script for Sergio Leone's meta-Western, *Once Upon a Time in the West*, a script (as Christopher Frayling has noted) so long and so full of references to every Western Bertolucci had ever seen that Leone had to have it rewritten. The resulting film influenced Bertolucci's own style. In 1967, he made a rather strange short film. Originally titled 'Il fico infruttuoso' ('The Barren Figtree'), it was to appear in an anthology film entitled *Vangelo 70*. Retitled 'Agonia', it appeared in another anthology film in 1969, *Amore e rabbia (Love and Anger)*, which also contained contributions by Carlo Lizzani, Pasolini, Godard, and Marco Bellocchio. The film is difficult to find these days, and the print I was able to view only once was unsubtitled and ragged.

This is unfortunate because while none of the contributions represents anything approaching the best work of their directors, the

23

film is an interesting expression of the European left's rage against America and the Vietnamese war in the late 60s (Bellocchio's episode in particular, playful, anarchic and slightly mad as are all his films, expresses acutely the sentiments of the European new left and the politics of '68). Bertolucci's contribution is only tangentially involved in the political struggles of the time, and represents instead another detour from the ideas and forms he was developing in *Before the Revolution*. He seems to have had at the time a speculative interest in theatre, and the theories of Antonin Artaud in particular. Both 'Agonia' and *Partner* give expression to these interests, the first quite directly, as it consists of about twenty-five minutes of somewhat malformed self-expression by Julian Beck and his 'Living Theatre'. All but forgotten now outside Europe, the group was prominent in New York in the late 50s and early 60s, when they did some important productions of Pirandello and Brecht, and then somewhat notorious in the late 60s, when they adopted a free-form, confrontational – indeed Artaud-influenced – style, which was to a large extent based on taking their clothes off in front, or in the middle, of the audience. By the late 60s they had become very popular in Italy.

The Living Theatre, and groups like them in the late 60s, were living out the end of live drama; they were confronting not merely their audience and themselves, but the fact that film (and in particular the work of Godard) was largely taking over the intellectual, political, enquiring elements that were once the driving forces of committed theatre. The adoption of Artaud-influenced techniques of improvisation, 'self-expression', emotional and physical abandon and other elements of 'the theatre of cruelty' were desperate efforts at keeping alive the idea of the theatre, of living beings communicating forcefully with others. The Living Theatre also represented something of the anarchic spirit of the late 60s, throwing off theatrical conventions and niceties, somewhat in the manner of the Dadaists in the 20s, though perhaps without Dada's subtlety and humour. Also, without a sense of form. The Living Theatre may have understood, on some level, Louis Althusser's comment that 'the play itself *is* the spectator's consciousness', but they pursued a false, or misdirected, consciousness which – based on Artaud rather than Brecht – equated revolution with sensation. The structure of their 'happenings' was anti-intellectual, a semiotics of sensual display. Godardian cinema, on the other hand, was creating a semiotics of the image, an analysis of thought, feeling and ideology which did not confront, but enquired, which respected the spectator's consciousness as it attempted to clarify it.

For whatever reasons, Bertolucci was attracted to The Living Theatre, and they to the cinematic attention he gave them. He wrote a

24

piece about his experience for *Cahiers du Cinéma*, and Beck wrote of his experiences with Bertolucci in the same issue. Bertolucci's essay is called 'Le Monde entier dans une chambre' ('The Whole World in a Room'), a title with interesting presentiments of *Last Tango in Paris*. The film 'Agonia', alas, has no such presentiments. On a bed, in a room with white walls, a man (Beck) lays dying. Around him, the Living Theatre troupe appears in the form of various 'visions', various poses and ritualized movements. They make statements: political ones about the war, personal ones about their lives. Formally, the piece gave Bertolucci an excellent opportunity to experiment with camera movement and cutting, using the restricted environment to rehearse the tracking shots and the careful arrangements of figures in the frame that would be refined, expanded and articulated in his later work. It is his first film in colour and wide screen (not counting the very brief colour segment in *Before the Revolution* and a twelve-minute document-ary, *Il canale*), and he does well in contrasting the whiteness of the environment and the various costumes worn by the troupe. Unfortuna-tely, as a coherent text, 'Agonia' only exists as a formal experiment, and a dead-end experiment at that.

'Agonia' is the film that Jacob, the central character(s) of *Partner*, might have made, had he survived the struggle with his double. For Jacob is a theatre teacher and director; he wants his troupe to do political improvisations, not in a room, but in the streets. He would have them take over a power plant, control the lighting of the city, turn all Rome into a theatre (just as, with much greater and more deadly effect, Athos Magnani Sr turns the little town of Tara into a theatre in *The Spider's Stratagem*, the film that follows *Partner*). But Jacob has no success in his plans; as little success as Bertolucci has in depicting them, though for different reasons that emerge both from the film's execution and its subject.

Partner is derived from an early Dostoevsky novel, *The Double*, though it might just as easily have come from Poe's 'William Wilson', or Conrad's *The Secret Sharer*, or any of the literature or cinema – such as *The Student of Prague* – concerning that archetypal theme, the man and his Other. Here the mild-mannered intellectual theatre teacher, Jacob, meets and must deal with his wild, anarchic, murderous double (both played with considerable energy by Pierre Clementi, the threatening and anarchic actor of many late 60s and early 70s films, who turns up again as the chauffeur in *The Conformist*). Their confrontations and theatrical experiments make up the film's narrative, whose thematic contains most of the codes of the literary archetype. The double manifests the main character's unconscious, his desire and his fear, the release of his repressed energies; the doomed fantasy of the imprisoned self come to life, battling its oppressor which is both itself and the superego of society.

But the fantasy here is doubly doomed. In the literary convention that charges the film, the doubles either do not survive, or the once repressed component of the personality gains control and destroys his former prisoner. In *Partner*, they reach an impasse. Bertolucci, however, is more interested in the formal construction of his work than in its narrative movement, and both are undone by another double – Jean-Luc Godard. *Partner* is a film that Godard might have made in the early 60s, had he not the intellect and inquisitiveness to make the films he did. Like *A Woman is a Woman* and *Contempt*, like the later 60s films, *Pierrot le fou, Made in USA* and *Two or Three Things I Know About Her*, it is filmed in colour and wide screen (with the exception of 'Agonia' it is the only anamorphic film Bertolucci has made). This might appear a minor technical point, were it not for the fact that Bertolucci uses the 'scope ratio precisely the way Godard does: he consistently frames his characters in 90 degree compositions. That is, he photographs them straight on, using the width of the frame to emphasize the two-dimensionality of the screen space.

Like Godard, Bertolucci composes his characters against a poster or painting on a wall (or the artificial backdrop of painted furniture in Jacob's flat). In the first sequence, in which Jacob II reads Lotte Eisner's book on Murnau and does an imitation of Max Schreck in *Nosferatu*, the character is in a café by a pinball machine – a favourite Godard place and composition, replete with cinematic allusions. In dialogue sequences (the two Jacobs speak French, everyone else Italian) Bertolucci tends to use either very long, static shots, of the kind Godard had refined during the early 60s, or shots that pan and track from one participant in the dialogue to the other – a device which sometimes lends itself to un-Godardian trickery when the movement of the camera encompasses both Jacobs, each played by the same actor. When not tracking between characters, Bertolucci, like Godard, will often move his camera away from a character to an empty space – a wall splotched with paint – or avoid character altogether, as in one sequence where he pans from one bridge across the Tiber to another, changing aperture settings so that the image goes from dark to light and then to dark again.

Bertolucci often uses the same, spare primary colours to which Godard was attracted because of their artificiality; although at times, particularly in night sequences, the cameraman Ugo Piccone brings out the pastels of Italian walls that were to become so prominent in the later films. Other Godardian devices appear: Jacob and his double, like so many Godard characters, love to stare into the camera and tell stories which are tangential to the action but provide insight into their perceptions and desires. Bertolucci borrows, without subtlety, Godard's 60s satire of consumerism. In one sequence Jacob the double entertains, and subsequently kills in a washing machine overflowing with suds, a young woman who sells soap powder. The character, incidentally, has eyes painted on her eyelids, so that when her eyes are closed they look open. The effect is both an allusion to Cocteau's *The Testament of Orpheus* and to Godard's *Contempt*, in which there appear Greek statues with painted eyes – an allusion to which Bertolucci will return, to better effect, in *The Spider's Stratagem*.

In one sequence Bertolucci and Godard seem, perhaps unconsciously, to copy one another. Godard's film *Le gai savoir*, made in the winter of 1967–8, contains a sequence in which the Jean-Pierre Léaud character teaches the making of a Molotov cocktail. In *Partner*, made in 1968, there is a sequence in which Jacob (I or II – there is a point in the film after which it becomes difficult to tell the one from the Other) gives his theatre class instruction on how to make a Molotov cocktail. I do not know whether Bertolucci saw Godard's film before its commercial release and took the idea from him (they did know each other during this period), or whether both film-makers were independently playing on the radical energies flowing at the time.

There are further borrowings and influences here. At the end of the Molotov cocktail sequence in *Partner*, Bertolucci attaches the bomb to the camera apparatus so that, as the camera pans round the room, the bottle appears to float before the figures in the background. This device is used by Sergio Leone in *Once Upon a Time in the West* when, in a gunfight sequence, he mounts one of his characters in front of the camera dolly and then pans so that the attached figure appears stationary as the background moves behind him. Bertolucci himself uses the device again in *The Spider's Stratagem*, in which the statue of Athos Magnani's father, its eye sockets painted white, floats across the background as if unattached to its base. Finally, even the music track for *Partner* is constructed in Godardian fashion. Ennio Morricone's score is cut into short, incomplete phrases that deny resolution, a denial often echoed in the images as well. Like Godard, Bertolucci interrupts the flow of the narrative with strips of black leader, breaking continuity, causing a pause in the narrative and a break in the viewer's expectations of uninterrupted story.

Which is, in effect, what the film as a whole does to Bertolucci's career. It is the strip of black leader, etched with a Godardian inscription, that interrupts the narrative of Bertolucci's cinematic development: a point of crisis and stasis between a beginning and a middle. The crisis is severe enough for the film-maker himself to seem

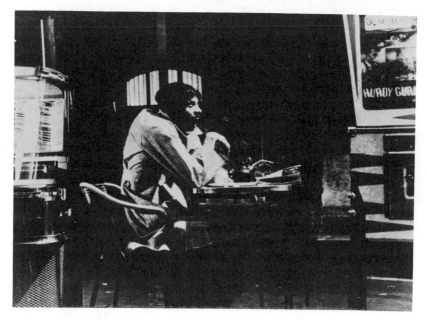

Doubles and allusions: Jacob II ...

unaware of precisely what he is doing. The black leader acts as his own
mask. Late in the film one of the Jacobs gives a speech to his theatre
troupe, who are seated amid some ruins. He lectures through a
megaphone as the camera makes a broad, double 360 degree pan of the
cityscape around them. 'Our subject is life,' he says. 'But if you find
that life lacks something, steal a camera and try to give style to life. Do
long panoramic shots of life. In colour and 'scope if your views are
broad.' This is a quintessential early-Godardian sentiment, in fact a
paraphrase of Godard, who had said about *Pierrot le fou*: 'Life is its
subject, with scope and colour as its attributes, for I have big ideas. ...
Life ... which I wanted to capture by way of panoramic shots of
nature, fixed shots of death, brief shots and long takes, sounds loud and
quiet.'[14] But Jacob continues as if Bertolucci were attempting to ignore
Godard's statement and the extent of his own imitation. 'Make fixed
angle shots of death. In black and white if you like Godard and if
Straub makes you cry.' The Godard Bertolucci's character talks about
within the film is not the Godard Bertolucci imitates *with* film. If he likes
Godard, why is he not making a film in black and white? It is almost as
if, on some level, Bertolucci were attempting to ignore or contradict the
very thing he is doing. In *Before the Revolution*, he had already worked
through the Godard who, in black and white, had intimately examined

28

individuals oppressed by their culture. The compulsion to imitate the Godard who used colour and 'scope seems to have created an amnesia about his past success and forced him into a project which his views were not broad enough nor his desire strong enough to manage. The result is a film which indeed contains shots of death – the momentary death of the imagination. (As far as Straub is concerned, it was to be another thirteen years, when Bertolucci made *Tragedy of a Ridiculous Man*, before the influence of this film-maker appeared.)

In *Before the Revolution*, Fabrizio's friend had said that a 360 degree shot is a moral fact. The double 360 degree pan in *Partner*, as Jacob makes his speech about Godard and Straub, seems to provide a moral and a caution for Bertolucci which he builds, almost unconsciously, into the form of the film. The shot encloses the characters, just as Jacob encloses his own creator with words that, on one level, deny what Bertolucci feels compelled to do with his film. Like the actors surrounded by the city and the camera's movement, Bertolucci is surrounded by his own imitation, even as he attempts to break out of it by having Jacob refer to the other Godard, the Godard of small black and white statements. Perhaps the moral is that, once they get started, doubles proliferate, surround and destroy each other. Bertolucci and Jacob, Jacob and Jacob, theatre and cinema, cinema and Godard, Godard and Godard, Bertolucci and Godard.

. . . and Jacob I in *Partner* (Pierre Clementi)

Perhaps this is the point. Perhaps, in order comfortably to enter a cinema dominated by Godard, Bertolucci had to deflect himself, first by digressions into theatre and finally by confronting, indeed effacing himself before Godard. In his introduction to the published script of *Before the Revolution*, Bertolucci wrote that 'You must rediscover each time that cinema starts from zero'. The statement is, of course, a basic premise of Godard's and an important one for Bertolucci to repeat, verbally and in his own cinema. *The Grim Reaper* was a start from Pasolini. *Before the Revolution* was the first start from zero. Although its form is greatly dependent upon New Wave methods, the film essentially comes from Bertolucci's own inquisition into what he could do as a new imagination entering the field of signifiers that makes up the cinematic tradition. *Partner* goes back to zero again, the zero level of the Godardian tradition, manifested in Bertolucci's refusal to carry on his own inquisition. The film is a halt called to his development as a film-maker, a moment of stasis and retreat, a gaze into the Godardian mirror through which – like Death in Cocteau's *Orphée* – Godard himself had already passed. In 1968, the year of *Partner*, Godard was already bidding farewell to commercial narrative cinema and many of the forms he had created for it.

Despite the fact that Godard had gone beyond where Bertolucci was, Bertolucci himself still needed to 'try out' Godard by direct imitation, to find the Godard inside himself; to stop his own development in order to absorb and expel the father of all contemporary cineastes. Here the Oedipal pattern that we shall see assert itself within Bertolucci's films seems to assert itself in the film-making act, as it had earlier in Bertolucci's relationship with Pasolini. That figure, incidentally, is also present in *Partner*. One of Jacob's students is Ninetto Davoli, a companion of Pasolini and one of his favourite actors. The actor appears under his own name and is, like all Jacob's students, recalcitrant. But his sweet rebellion signifies a freedom that seems to be opposed to the oppressive weight of Godard which rests upon the film. Pasolini – through his surrogate, Ninetto – is allowed to go his own way. Bertolucci and his double, Godard, like the two Jacobs, must confront each other until one or both are repressed in their turn. The father must be killed and the son must re-emerge changed and chastened.

There are explanations other than the psychological to account for the process of imitation and clarify the film as Bertolucci's attempt to position himself within contemporary cinema. *Partner* is Bertolucci's only film that deals directly with contemporary political events. *Before the Revolution* contemplates politics abstractly, subjectively, as part of the anxiety-ridden development of its central character. *The Spider's Stratagem, The Conformist* and *1900* deal with the politics of Italy's fascist past. *Last Tango in Paris* moves with the indirection of a Fassbinder film, encompassing larger political issues within the microcosm of the politics of the couple and the family. Even *Tragedy of a Ridiculous Man*, whose immediate topic is contemporary political terrorism, subdues its subject, makes it almost a hermeneutic beneath its narrative of father, son and the distortions of domesticity brought by property ownership.

Partner attempts to deal with the contemporary turmoil of the young during the late 1960s, a turmoil caused partly by American aggression against North Vietnam and which grew to encompass a massive, if not fully articulated, attack against the corruptions of western bourgeois society. The Vietnamese issue entered the Godardian text in 1965, in *Pierrot le fou*, and remained a part of the signifying structure of every film Godard made from then until the early 70s. The society that Godard perceived in the post-1965 films was always deformed in some way by the Vietnamese crisis, to the point that Vietnam enclosed the other issues, acts and events in his work. It is not surprising, then, that when Bertolucci decided to deal with Vietnam, which is a major concern in *Partner*, he should approach it through a Godardian frame.

Within that frame, Bertolucci attempts to express the conflicts over Vietnam through the conflicts of the two Jacobs, one the contemplative man, the other the man of anarchic action. Jacob is brought to greater political consciousness by his Other, who proves ultimately to be too anarchic, too murderous, too free a spirit for the controlled release of energy needed in the act of political protest. If, with the film, Bertolucci can subdue the spirit of Godard, within the film Jacob cannot subdue Jacob. Thought and action remain in an impasse. The theatre group rebels, perhaps out of timidity. The two mirror images are left alone with each other in a room with Vietnamese flags, in the midst of which stands a guillotine. Jacob II makes an anti-American, anti-imperialist speech, while the other – partially covering the double's words by wearing earplugs and speaking in voice-over – warns us of the threat of the anarchic force inside everyone. The double would kill Jacob in the guillotine (or vice-versa) along with the ambiguities of his consciousness. But all attempts to quell or control the spirit of revolt fail, and the film ends with the man and his image creeping out on to a window ledge, still searching for a bright idea with which to impress themselves on the world. A North Vietnamese flag is visible on a wall.

In the course of the general impasse many things are learned by the two parties, Jacob I and II and their mutual double, Bertolucci. In a virtuoso sequence one of the Jacobs sits among his books, staring at the camera. He repeatedly screams out the words, 'We must throw off our masks!' Jacob realizes that the oppressions of personae forced upon an individual must be forcibly removed, even if the removal results in the individual's destruction (a subject Bertolucci was to return to in *Last Tango in Paris*). Jacob's hysterical revelation reflects, perhaps, Bertolucci's own awareness that he cannot wear the mask of another cineaste.

Another mask falls: the mask of the theatre, the form in which Jacob attempts to work and which had attracted Bertolucci during this period. In a visually complex sequence Jacob and his double sit in two-shot, the double himself reflected in a mirror, the images fading in and out as they talk of the value of theatrical spectacle. 'Theatre,' they repeat again and again, 'theatre ... theatre', until all the images fade, the screen goes black, and another voice (Bertolucci's, I think) is suddenly heard whispering – 'cinema'. Early in the film, Jacob I sits in his room reading Artaud's *The Theatre and its Double* (a title whose ramifications double within the context of the film). Jacob quotes some lines from a statement Artaud makes about the cinema. *'To the crude visualization of what is, the theatre through poetry opposes images of what is not. However, from the point of view of action, one cannot compare a cinematic image which, however poetic it may be, is limited by the film, to a theatrical image which obeys all the exigencies of life'* (pp. 98-9, italics in text). In the 30s, and to a man attempting to revitalize the theatre, such an anti-cinematic statement may have had the force of necessity. In the late 60s Godard and others – including Bertolucci himself – had proved that film limits nothing, not poetry (a point Pasolini had made in his writings on cinema), not life, not the poetic expression of life. On the contrary, by the late 60s film was becoming the liberating form of expression, drawing sustenance, ironically, from the theories of another man of the theatre, Bertolt Brecht (a figure against whose ideas, as we shall see, Bertolucci fought).

In the end, *Partner* becomes an act of multiple, if incomplete, exorcism. It is a film which enables Bertolucci to lay the ghost of the theatre and (partly) come to terms with the spirit of Jean-Luc Godard. Theatre would never haunt him again and is absorbed into the powerful metaphor that structures his next film, *The Spider's Stratagem*. Godard would never disappear from his creative life, remaining to haunt it, reappearing from time to time, as one of the spirits behind the characters of Professor Quadri in *The Conformist* (who is given Godard's Paris address and telephone number) and Tom in *Last Tango*, and as an influence on the *mise en scène* of *Tragedy of a Ridiculous Man*. Nor would the Godardian obsession with the communal network of cinema ever leave Bertolucci, who continues, throughout his work, to allude to other films and other forms of art, convinced, like his mentor and tormentor, that cinema makes up a field of expression open to, indeed encompassing, all others.

32

Partner also seems to have clarified Bertolucci's ideas about the ways in which he could use film to structure his political perceptions. As I have indicated, he did not directly confront contemporary political issues in his films again. By imitating Godard, he comes to accept that this is not the form of expression with which he is most comfortable, something he knew even before he made *Partner*. In the *Cahiers du Cinéma* essay 'Versus Godard', Bertolucci expresses pleasure in the detailed observation of *Two or Three Things I Know About Her*, a film whose politics are exposed through an investigation of urban domestic life. He takes great displeasure in the political abstractions of *Made in USA*, which is, in fact, one of Godard's least felicitous works. This is a film in which – like Bertolucci in *Partner* – Godard seems to be going through Godardian gestures rather than making significant images. Bertolucci makes an important point:

> While *Two or Three Things* . . . originates in newspaper items, *Made in USA* is based upon a political assassination [the Ben Barka affair]. Let us call Roland Barthes to our aid so that we can clarify the difference between the two terms. Political assassination is, by definition, always partial information which necessarily refers to a situation that exists outside, before and around itself: that is, politics. The newspaper item, on the contrary, is total, or, more exactly, immanent information. Formally, it refers to nothing other than itself. But it is just here that Godard scandalously reverses this rule: *Made in USA* maintains a tragically closed structure, while the newspaper item of *Two or Three Things* . . ., which should have kept its beauty and meaning within itself . . . opens itself like one of those strange and ineffable flowers we see in dreams and hallucinations. . . . Now *Made in USA*, a political film, is the betrayer of its politics, paralysed in its great freedom by an ideological conformism, its colours fading because of the magnificence of their very brilliance. . . . Ultimately, of the two films, I like *Made in USA* less because it is too Godardian to be truly good Godard.

Clearly Bertolucci forgot what he had said about *Made in USA* when he made his own film. *Partner* is too Godardian to be truly good Godard, not to mention truly good Bertolucci imitating Godard. But with this film he was able to reaffirm the difficulties he experienced with Godard's political expression. Like *Made in USA*, *Partner* 'is the betrayer of its politics, paralysed . . . by an ideological conformism'. Bertolucci is ultimately too much of a theorist, and, more important, too caught up in the Marxist dilemma of thought versus action, to allow himself easily to plunge into a depiction of contemporary political

33

action. In his best work Bertolucci, like Godard, investigates the painful complexities of ideology – bourgeois and Marxist – rather than conform to them. When he does confront the subject of political assassination, in *The Spider's Stratagem* and *The Conformist*, he sets it in the past and takes pains to describe the psycho-political situation that 'exists outside, before and around' the acts. After *Partner*, Bertolucci is able to heed Godard's own comments about what Bertolucci is best able to do. At the end of Godard's *Le gai savoir*, the film's two participants discuss a kind of division of labour, indicating who among contemporary film-makers can best handle specific social-political problems. To Straub will go the task of addressing the politics of the family; to Glauber Rocha the politics of the Third World; to Bertolucci the task of dealing with Marx and Freud. During this period, Godard knew where Bertolucci's talents lay better than did Bertolucci himself.

In summary, *Partner* seems to be a film that Bertolucci *needed* to make in order to understand that it was the kind of film he could not make. He says about it, in retrospect, that it is 'my least natural film, because it came out of four years of empty, theoretical thoughts that were never tested in practice. . . . *Partner* is the film that has made me suffer the most'.[15] Out of that 'suffering' came positive results. Godard is subdued, reincorporated as one influence among many. Roberto Rossellini is rediscovered. Rossellini was himself an influence on Godard – it was a Rossellini story on which Godard based *Les Carabiniers*. Perhaps Bertolucci had to work through Godard to return to the figure he had already announced as a major influence. In *Before the Revolution*, Fabrizio's friend calls out to him: 'Remember, you cannot *live* without Rossellini.'

In his *Cahiers* essay, Bertolucci perceived the Rossellinian aspect of Godard in the latter's ability to capture the moment and to discover in it how observation of the everyday event enlightens and nurtures film-maker and viewer. Godard, Bertolucci writes,

interrogates and answers himself, protests, suggests, is ironic, explains to us that the shots, whether they are fixed, panoramic or travelling, are autonomous, with an autonomous resonance and an autonomous beauty, and that one must not worry too much about planning a montage, for in any case order is born automatically from the very moment at which we make one thing follow another. And that basically one shot has the same status as another (Rossellini knows this). If there is a poetic charge, a connection will be made whatever happens. . . . And when his extraordinary moral discourse takes on a slight tremor – and this happens often – it is as if it were confronting us with a forewarning of tragedy.

Early in his career, Bertolucci went through a crisis of sorts over the problem of editing, and I shall examine this problem, and its solution, later on. But as a practising film-maker, he had already proved his talent and judgment in executing, selecting and ordering his shots. *Before the Revolution* demonstrated that 'the possibility of tragedy' comes from a careful contemplation of shots and their arrangement in the film's montage (Rossellini knew this). Contemplating the loose and banal structure of *Partner* could only have reaffirmed what Bertolucci already knew.

More than Godard, in fact quite opposed to Godard's practice in his 60s films, Bertolucci's best image-making came to be grounded in the 'autonomous resonance and . . . beauty', the 'poetic charge' of the shot. After *Partner* he put into practice that quality of Rossellini he had already spoken of in 1966, the 'capacity of having things never too far away and never too close, the ideal distance that his camera has from things and from characters'. He needed to make *Partner* – a film with little resonance and less 'beauty', without a notion of 'distance', certainly a film without autonomy – in order to come to a better understanding of his particular ability to compose and edit. With *Partner* out of the way, he could rediscover his own cinematic imagination, and we can discover its origins and pursue its direction.

2 The Search for Form

> I wanted to tell a story in the present perfect tense, so that I
> could look at the present pretending to be already talking
> about the past ...[1]

Of course, it is easy for the critic to see patterns and progressions when
looking over a body of work in retrospect. The patterns are, in effect,
the critic's own discursive structures, for it is impossible, and probably
irrelevant, to reconstitute the film-maker's own intentions in his search
for form, or, in Bertolucci's case, the discovery of a comfortable form,
the abandoning of it, and the return to it with greater insight, felicity
and facility. Bertolucci had to work through the Godardian complex in
order to rediscover his own discourse; and so must the critic, almost as
an act of excavation. 'Agonia' and *Partner* have to be dug out of the
chronology of Bertolucci's work, separated and examined to see how
they fit into his development. Then, if not discarded, they must be
placed to one side, for in fact they constitute a detour from the course
that began to be plotted in *Before the Revolution*.

Before examining that film, it will be useful to define what I mean by
'form' and 'style', terms which are easily interchangeable, but which
should have some distinguishing significations. 'Form' is what the
artist produces and the critic discovers in the arrangement of all the
elements within a text, their relationship one to the other, the ways in
which they produce meaning and are given meaning through their
relationship. Form is the discoverable aspect of structure, the *name* of
structure given to all the aspects of the text, the total design that
includes *mise en scène* (composition, movement, use of colour, the
general articulation of space); montage; acting; narrative construction.* Form creates meaning or content, for without form there is
nothing: 'content', 'ideas', 'meanings' do not exist without a form to
generate them. Any utterance, from spontaneous conversation to a
carefully crafted film, is first and only a presentation of form, a
statement of something's existence. Interpretation – understanding – is

---

* This definition is close to Eco's description of the code (see *A Theory of
Semiotics*, pp. 48–150, and Metz, *Language and Cinema*).

36

itself a form-making process, the structure created in an attempt to understand another structure, like my reading of *Partner*, for example.

The artist's *expression* of form constitutes style. Reference to the linguistic model is useful here. 'Form' might be considered analogous to the concept of *langue* or language system (as, for example, the grammatic, phonemic and lexical structures of English or Italian are the determining forms of those languages). The comparison is very loose, because the system of a particular language is at the same time invisible in its totality yet 'known' by each of its speakers, whereas aesthetic form is visible in and as the text of the work. Unlike the language system, it is not shared outside of the specific aesthetic discipline; although certain formal structures, like perspective in painting, the chromatic scale in music, various prosodic forms in poetry, continuity editing in film, are known and can be called upon by practitioners within those disciplines. My point is simply that the formal codes of a specific art are not as global as the system of a given language. Like a language system, however, they must be learned, and once learned they may merely be repeated with minimal alteration (the so-called 'classical style' of American film is an example); or – like a poet who recodes the system of his or her particular language, or the film-maker who reworks the 'classical style' – they may be radically changed, expressed in ways that create new forms entirely or, more precisely, new expressions of the forms. It is in this sense that style is the expression of form and a rough equivalent to the linguistic concept of *parole* or utterance.

The various ways in which we express ourselves through speech constitute our individual use of, our calling upon and expressing of, the language system – the forms that control and enable our utterances. In any work of imaginative expression the artist speaks the basic formal properties of his or her particular discipline (novel, opera, painting, film), and expresses the particular structural alterations or recodings he or she has developed *from* the basic form of that discipline. The expression of the form is, as I say, the artist's style.

A major element of style – I am tempted to say a major *formal* element of style – is 'iterability'.[2] We can, of course, speak of the style of a particular work, as I have done in analysing the Godardian style that Bertolucci adopts in *Partner*. But we know a film-maker is developing, or has perfected, a style if we see it occur again and again in his or her work, creating an intertextuality between films and within the cinematic universe. The Hitchcock high-angle shot at a moment of narrative crisis, for example; the dance in a Ford Western (or a Bertolucci film); Welles's spatial distortions and use of low-angle shots – all are elements of style specific to these film-makers and occur in film after film. They are expressions both of the formal properties of the medium (camera angles, a theorist like Christian Metz would argue, are formal codes specific to cinema) and of the formal ground of the particular film-maker who uses them. They are expressions – articulations – of the ways in which these film-makers understand the world cinematically, which is to say, formally.

I would be optimistic if I were to promise not to elide or transfer the terms 'form' and 'style' in the course of this study. Discrimination is one thing in theory, another in the work of practical criticism. I will, however, attempt to use the word 'form' when referring to the textual whole of a Bertolucci film, as well as to the various cinematic and narrative codes he calls upon and modifies in the development of a particular text. 'Style' will refer to specific expressions of the form, its inflections, variations, iterations either within a particular film or from film to film in the course of the director's development. 'Development' does not imply uniformity, I must add. An attractive aspect of Bertolucci's work is his consistent experimentation, his eagerness to change formal and stylistic elements from film to film, even when the substance expressed remains similar – if indeed substance can remain similar within a differing form.

One further item should be noted concerning the matter of form and style: both are ideological statements (in *Before the Revolution* Bertolucci had said that they were moral facts, but 'ideological' has greater precision). Fredric Jameson states simply and eloquently that 'form is immanently and intrinsically an ideology in its own right'.[3]

The basic forms and expressions a society uses to present itself to itself, to its members, to others constitute its dominant ideology, the way its individual members collectively understand and articulate – or have articulated for them – their social and political relationships. Every individual of a given society invests in that ideology to some extent every time that individual speaks, or assents to an image or shares a gesture. At the same time, every individual also counters the ideology. Ideology is never a wholesale job lot, but rather a series of capital investments made by individuals, usually through certain brokers set up by the state – its political, legal, military, religious, media and educational systems, and the family.[4] For the individual within the society the ideology is purchased in quantities, rather like stocks or consumer goods, and held to see if the investment will grow or if, like a consumer good, it will be used and then discarded. The forms of this buying and selling are constituted by the ideology and constitute and express it in turn.

In a society, the artist is both consumer and producer of ideology. He or she may incorporate the dominant ideology wholesale, or question it, or counter it, creating in the work – *by means of the work* – alternatives to the dominant ideological discourse of the society. (This is a complex matter to which I shall return in my discussion of *1900*.) The form and its stylistic articulations make up the first level of an artist's ideological expression. Much has been written about the 'classic American' or 'zero degree' style in film, whose ideological presence is manifested by its attempt to efface itself, to disappear behind the content it produces so that an illusion of 'reality' is created, an illusion that states that what is being said in the film is 'real' because it exists unmitigated and unmediated. The modernist film-maker reverses the process, foregrounding form and thereby articulating the counter-argument that content is *made*, produced in certain ways, determined by the medium's particular means of production, and that the viewer must be aware of form as an ideological issue, as something he or she must deal with in order to get to content. The viewer has to understand that content is not 'there', but must be created. This was the project of Godard and the New Wave in the 60s, and it was picked up by Bertolucci in his second feature, completed in 1964.

The foregrounding of form is a political act, for it disrupts the manipulative power of the classical form and its 'invisible' structure, breaking its hold and, as I said, forcing the spectator to attend to the way meaning is made. When this process is used to express ideas counter to the dominant ideology, or to speak *about* ideology, then a complex text emerges in which form, style and substance interrogate each other, the viewer, the society at large, and the creator of the text itself. In this process the critic becomes both arbitrator of the interrogation and a co-creator, leaving traces of his or her own ideological determinations. Therefore, the 'search for form' that is the subject of this chapter is not only Bertolucci's, but the critic's as well; it is the critical determination of the 'Bertolucci' who emerges as the function of his films.

The 60s were Bertolucci's years of experimentation and of waiting. The young film-makers of France were establishing their own styles, expanding on their initial desire to counter the 'Tradition of Quality', seeking out what could be taken from Hollywood and transformed through their subjective intervention, creating narrative forms in which most of them (with the possible exception of Truffaut) would be free to move and alter as they went on. Meanwhile Bertolucci lurched about. Pasolini, Godard, Artaud, Rossellini imposed themselves on him, and with a certain passivity he permitted the imposition. He also suffered the vagaries of a production system which forced idleness upon him, in which he had to spend time making television documentaries between his fiction films. This may have frustrated his development for a while and caused him to accept the influence of Godard too late for that influence to be of any value except to show him that Godard was no longer an appropriate influence. In *Partner*, he fought Godard not by defying but by embracing his influence, thereby demonstrating both a willingness to try things out and perhaps a certain numbness, a momentary lack of imaginative drive.

The fact remains that in 1964 Bertolucci did make a film that gave the closest indication of what his cinematic development in the 70s would be, though he did not, or could not, follow it up for six more years. Whatever the reasons for the lag in development, the point is that *Before the Revolution* set the formal and thematic patterns to which he would ultimately return, with major changes and variations, in 1970. It was 'his' film, his first 'subjective' statement after the Pasolinian gambit of *The Grim Reaper*, and the first film that brought him international attention.

At first look, and based on an immediate impression of its visual form and narrative structure, *Before the Revolution* is simply a film of its time. The rapid, elliptical cutting, the playful elisions and disjunctions of time and space, the picturesque images of the Po in the sequence in which the film's central character, Fabrizio, confronts the impoverished landowner, Puck, are indicative of the work of a film-maker aware of early Godard and Truffaut, with a passing interest in the Antonioni of *Il grido* (in fact the film was shot by Aldo Scavarda, Antonioni's cinematographer for *L'avventura*). On closer examination there are major elements in the film that set it off from contemporary French and Italian influence. There is a depth of political enquiry, a complexity of intellectual struggle both within the major character of the film and within the film's formal apparatus that goes beyond the mere imitation of Bertolucci's cinematic contemporaries.

The French New Wave film-makers were attracted both to American genre films – the gangster film in particular – and to lesser contemporary American novelists, mainly writers of thrillers and detective stories. Their admiration of popular American film and literature was coupled with their hatred of what they saw as the pomposity and rigidity of the French cinematic tradition. They wished their films to manifest the innocent spontaneity of discovery – the often remarked 'return to zero' – an illusion of form just found, of narrative structured with a vitality unencumbered by convention. The spectator would participate in this vitality, the film text creating a space of creativity observed and joined.

Like the neo-realists, though without their interest in the problems of the working class, the New Wave film-makers would create films that appeared to be spontaneous observations of the world in its immediate particulars, of events captured without mediation. A contradiction arises here, particularly in the work of Godard, who at the same time as he was attempting to 'return to zero' was also obsessively, critically concerned with the *act* of mediation, with the structure of film itself and the questions about the way it reconstructed reality.

Into this contradiction stepped Bertolucci. First, he expressed no interest in the American gangster genre (even *The Grim Reaper* cannot properly be called a gangster or detective film, and it is too strongly founded in Pasolini to indicate much general American influence). And while, as part of their reaction against the 'Tradition of Quality' and its dependence upon scripts drawn from high literature, the New Wave either wrote original screenplays or adapted novelists like David Goodis and Lionel White, Bertolucci chose as the 'source' for *Before the Revolution* Stendhal's 1838 novel *The Charterhouse of Parma*. The result constitutes one of the more curious relationships between literary source and film in contemporary cinema history. Stendhal's work is a complex, somewhat ponderous, enquiry into the relationships of the lower nobility in northern Italy just after the Napoleonic wars. Its hero, Fabrizio, is part innocent, part romantic, part fool, who entangles himself in a series of romantic adventures, including a passionate attachment to his aunt, that lead to increasing disappointment, to his becoming – through an accident of romantic attachment – a preacher-hero of the masses, and, after the loss of his beloved, to a temporary withdrawal from the world.

Bertolucci's film seems to do little with its source but retain the names of the central characters: Fabrizio; Gina, his aunt and lover; Clelia, the woman he marries. Filmed in 1963–4, set in 1962, the year of Marilyn Monroe's death, the film deals with the middle class of Parma, Bertolucci's birthplace. Yet he himself refers to it as 'a historical film about ambiguity and uncertainty'.[5] Stendhal's novel is about the ambiguity and uncertainty of a doomed class in a country that was still without a national identity. Bertolucci's film is about the bourgeoisie, a persistent and at the same time persistently doomed class in an Italy that had long since gained a national identity, but which suffered, and suffers still, enormous splits between the groups and classes that make it up. *Before the Revolution* is indeed a 'historical' film, but not in the Hollywood sense. The history is contemporary, the emotional and intellectual struggles it presents are not shrouded in the ironies of court intrigue, but within the very contemporary concerns of the central characters. Where Stendhal speaks to the illusory status of ritualized behaviour and repressed passions, Bertolucci speaks to the fluid frustrations of political allegiances and ideals, the struggles of a young man attempting to come to terms with his own beliefs, his emotional

41

uncertainties and the intolerable stresses of competing ideologies.

Stendhal, as T. Jefferson Kline points out, is an 'absent presence' in *Before the Revolution.*[6] *The Charterhouse of Parma* does not so much inform the film as hover behind it in the far distance. Bertolucci does not 'film' the novel, use its structure, or even, to any important extent, draw upon its characters. He does, however, allow himself to play a subtle counterpoint with the work by rewriting it so entirely that the film casts a faint shadow of the novel that is never quite seen but sensed from time to time. Rather than the novel informing the film, *Before the Revolution* turns upon and informs *The Charterhouse of Parma*, contemporizing it (though not in the sense of 'bringing it up to date'). The two works remain discrete, enlightening each other by reference and inference, by dealing, in very different ways, with romance, class and ideology.

The visual and narrative structure that creates these elements is influenced to a degree by Godard and Truffaut. Even Pasolini is present, though only in passing and verbally, by means of a quotation from his poetry early in the film.* However, the rapid cutting, the loose framing, the ellipses and overlaps of time differ from the New Wave in an important respect. They are most often used to express a derangement of the senses and to force the spectator to see a world through the precarious and somewhat hysterical consciousness of Fabrizio and, by seeing through it, to see into it. This perceptual play was to become a major component of Bertolucci's cinema. In this film, and beginning again in *The Spider's Stratagem*, he demonstrates a much greater interest than Godard in exposing and relating the tensions and contradictions of the characters which his narratives create. Godard broke completely with the convention of psychological realism. Bertolucci attempts to recode it within a modernist frame.

The intricate process of character perception – the perception of the character by the film-maker and the viewer, and the character's perception of the world which is transmitted through the film-maker's gaze – is expressed in a variety of ways in the film, as if Bertolucci were creating a notebook of ideas, of possibilities of styles and approaches, some of which work, while others fail. An excellent example of an approach that does work involves the relationship, early in the film, between Fabrizio and his friend Agostino, a lost young man, mercurial and unreachable, who finally commits suicide, but whose presence colours everything that Fabrizio does and thinks throughout the narrative. Agostino is first seen in a far shot, at the door of a church. Fabrizio

---

* References and dialogue quoted from the film are based on the French text published in *L'Avant-scène*, the spoken dialogue and the English subtitles.

comes upon him after the film's opening sequence in which his own desperate character is quickly established through a series of shots of him running through the streets of Parma, intercut with aerial shots of the city and accompanied by his voice-over commentary. He is in frantic movement, anxious, searching for his intended, Clelia. He says that she is his destiny, and that she is the city – the Catholic middle class: omnipresent, predating his history and the city's, like the church she represents and which represents her.

Agostino has found her, with her mother, in church. And he ushers Fabrizio in, with a mock bow at the door like a servant, a gesture which indicates Fabrizio's future direction as well as Agostino's role in his life. At the end of the narrative Fabrizio re-enters the church to marry Clelia, and Agostino, particularly after his suicide, will be the servant of Fabrizio's guilt, guiding him through the labyrinths of bad conscience and bad faith. As Fabrizio enters the church, Bertolucci cuts instantly to three brief shots of statuary – the decorations of tombs – and to a fourth shot, a close-up profile of Clelia, wearing a shawl, staring away from the camera, off-centre in the frame. In the shots that follow we see Clelia with her mother, again intercut with statuary. Here the camera glides round the statues in an ironic allusion to Rossellini's lyrical tracks round the statues which the Ingrid Bergman character sees in a museum in *Voyage to Italy*. In that film the marble figures are given life by the camera's treatment of them, creating a contrast to the almost neurasthenic Bergman; here they are an immediate sign of the intellectual and ideological rigidity which the beautiful, cold Clelia represents for Fabrizio.*

Following this montage are three shots of Fabrizio gazing. In the first shot he is still looking at Clelia in the church. In the next two shots he is leaning against a tree, gazing off into the distance. Such fractures and distortions of space and time become an important element of the film's structure. The viewer's uncertainties as to the spatial and temporal location of Fabrizio's gaze, along with the uncertainties expressed by the gaze itself, emphasize the loss of emotional and perceptual equilibrium suffered by the character and communicated to the viewer through breaks in conventional continuity.

From the montage of stares, a cut is made to Fabrizio walking along the street with Agostino. Fabrizio asks the time of day; Agostino responds and smiles sweetly. Fabrizio suddenly turns to Agostino and tells him, with a mixture of urgency and despair, that he should join the

---

* There is yet another allusion to Rossellini later in the film when, as in Rossellini's film of Cocteau's *La Voix humaine*, Gina holds a long, agonizing telephone conversation with an old lover.

Communist Party. Poetry and politics give a sense to life, he tells him, and says (with some bad faith as it turns out) that he suffered anxiety and guilt before his contact with the party and with Cesare, his mentor and teacher. He has an appointment with Cesare and bids goodbye to Agostino, saying they will meet tomorrow. Fabrizio turns into Cesare's house (the action continuing in one long shot) and calls back to Agostino, telling him to go and see *Red River* (Howard Hawks's film about the relationship of an older and a younger man, echoed in *Before the Revolution* by the relationship of Fabrizio with the older Cesare and the younger Agostino). Fabrizio enters the house; Agostino gets on his bicycle and rides into close-up. A cut is made as he turns and cycles off into the distance.

At this point there are further breaks in the linear progression of the action. Bertolucci does not cut to Fabrizio and Cesare (whose presence is withheld until later), nor does he follow Agostino. Instead, he cuts from Agostino riding into the distance to a close-up of Fabrizio talking. As the camera pans with him to the object of his conversation, we discover that it is Agostino once again. As they walk together, in tight close-up, behind a chain-link fence, Fabrizio asks him why he is running away from home. Agostino is in emotional agony. He grabs the fence, refuses Fabrizio's invitation to join the Party, and denies that Fabrizio can possibly understand his situation at home and the awfulness of his parents. He walks off with his bicycle into the distance, leaving Fabrizio by the fence (the scene is played out in a neo-realist urban wasteland) and calling bitterly to him the very question that haunts Fabrizio himself – does he think the revolution will actually solve their problems?

The second sequence ends with Fabrizio holding on to the fence, frustrated with himself and his friend, and cuts back to the street by Cesare's house. There is a long shot of Fabrizio walking down the street towards the building, and a dissolve is made to a closer shot of him as he passes an open doorway by a wall. He turns and we hear a bicycle bell; the camera tracks towards the doorway; a drum-roll sounds and out rides Agostino. A circus music theme (perhaps in homage to Fellini and his composer Nino Rota) accompanies him as he circles round, bows to the camera, passes behind Fabrizio, and circles back. There follows a complicated montage of Agostino riding, doing tricks, circling and falling from his bike. Cuts are made quickly and arhythmically, with various shots of Agostino riding and falling which begin out of focus as the camera, mostly hand-held, attempts to follow this mad, self-destructive spectacle which Agostino performs for Fabrizio. He falls: 'That's for my father,' he yells. And falls again: 'That's for my mother.' He falls twice more until Fabrizio runs to help him: 'And

Aspects of one another: Agostino (Allen Midgette) and Fabrizio (Francesco Barilli) in *Before the Revolution*

that's for me,' he cries. Finally they both rest against the wall. Agostino admits to being drunk. Fabrizio asks him to see *Red River* with him, but Agostino pushes him off, insisting that Fabrizio keep his appointment with Cesare. Once again the spectator is repositioned, forced to question the temporal logic of the three sequences. Agostino walks forward, towards the camera, in despair, and the sequence fades to black. The following sequence introduces Gina – Fabrizio's aunt and soon-to-be lover – and his stiff, middle-class family.

The construction and placement of these sequences, the lack of clear transition or indication of chronology, the suggestion that they may not be chronologically separate but rather constitute versions of the same conversation, focus our attention on the struggle between the two friends. Fabrizio thinks he has solved his anxieties through his political affiliation and tutelage under Cesare. Agostino can find no such anchor or refuge, cannot escape his suffocation at home or the vagaries of his own personality. The two characters turn out, finally, to be aspects of one another, Fabrizio speaking a hope for ideological certainty, Agostino a despair of ever finding a secure belief or a dependable location of consciousness. Their interaction is therefore continuous and circular, caught between the memory of repetition and the despair of finding a conclusion. The two characters are caught within each other, and the lack of conventional chronology indicates the repetition of their uncertainty.

The final appearance of Agostino in the narrative is marked by his absence. Fabrizio discovers his friend's suicide. Again, Bertolucci reflects the character's response through his visual treatment of him. The sequence begins with a heap of clothes found on the river bank by a policeman. Agostino's bicycle is put into a police car. The camera gazes at Fabrizio and at the object of his gaze – the river and an enormous pylon that blocks the horizon (a composition in the manner of Antonioni). There is a far shot from behind Fabrizio, looking at him and some children swimming. Suddenly there is a dissolve, not to a different space or time, but to the very same shot, or nearly so, as the children come out of the river. Then a second dissolve occurs, again to the same shot, as Fabrizio questions them about his friend. This is followed by a jump cut to Fabrizio and one of the children, the huge pylon in the distance.

The dissolve is an old cinematic convention, and is always coded with the notion of temporal change. Here it is recoded and instantly given new significance, of disorientation, of a subjective, emotional time rather than an external chronology. Martin Scorsese makes excellent use of the effect in *Taxi Driver* (1976), in an early sequence where Travis Bickle leaves the cab garage. As he walks down a street,

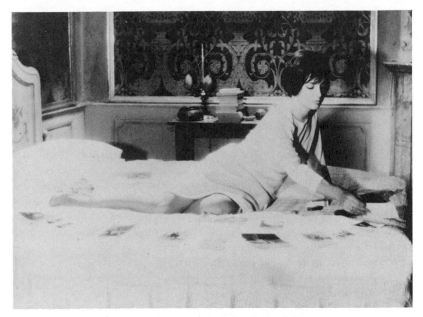

Homage to Resnais: Gina (Adriana Asti) in *Before the Revolution*

there is a dissolve which, as in *Before the Revolution*, changes neither time
nor place, but disrupts our linear, otherwise undisrupted point of view
of the major character. In Bertolucci's film the dissolves, along with the
shots of the pylon in the river, serve to shift and displace our access to
the character and express also the character's state of mind. Fabrizio
absorbs Agostino within himself, incorporates his friend's anxiety while
at the same time enlarging his own guilt. The sequence continues to
build the perceptual structure of this self-entanglement and
intellectual-emotional blockage.

Experimentation with temporal conventions generates textual
meaning and also generates Bertolucci's own position within the
development of 60s cinema. He joins the French (not only the New
Wave, but Alain Resnais as well, to whom an allusion is made in the
film when Gina sits on her bed with photographs spread out before her,
like the woman in *Last Year at Marienbad*) in reconsidering the conventions of the linear narrative and the unencumbered exposition of
character. Bertolucci carries this experimentation further, and with
greater facility, in *The Spider's Stratagem* and *The Conformist*. But here, in
all its raggedness, the young film-maker works out his own defiance of
cinematic 'rules' and, coincidentally, demonstrates in practice the
delight in cutting and the manipulation of the shot that he denounces

in the introduction to the film's screenplay ('One proposition: a law that forbids montage . . .').

As late as 1982, Bertolucci was still recalling the 60s Bazinian dream of abolishing the cut: 'I considered . . . [editing] to be a process of castration,' he says.[7] The statement echoes something Pasolini wrote in 1967: 'Montage thus accomplishes for the material of film (constituted of fragments, the longest or the shortest, of as many long takes as there are subjectivities) what death accomplishes for life.'[8] Theory and practice are, as so often, at great odds. *Partner* is the film in which Bertolucci tried to approach the ideal of the long take, of the un-castrated film. The result is a work without potency. In *Before the Revolution*, practice was permitted to get the better of theory. Like Godard, who similarly wrestled – in theory and in practice – with the problem of the shot and the cut, Bertolucci experiments with many variations on the two forms. He does not imitate Godardian experiments, but parallels them, seeking an articulate balance. He never again indulged in the kind of frantic cutting demonstrated here; with the help of Franco Arcalli, he developed the dialectic between shot and cut that gives his films their visual strength and narrative complexity.[9]

Bertolucci confronts another problem through the formal structure of these sequences. With the perceptual experiments, the building of a complex relationship between the characters and the viewer's relationship to them and to the narrative as a whole, he creates a reversal of the Brechtian premise that was, at the time, so powerful an influence on Godard and Straub, and later on Pasolini in *Teorema*, *Porcile* and *Salò*. The confusion of chronology, the complex cutting of the bicycle sequence, the unconventional use of the dissolve in the sequence by the river, 'distance' us from the action on the screen, make it strange, certainly cause discomfort for those who expect cinematic narrative events to follow the order determined by conventional film.

But at the same time Bertolucci allows proximity with his characters, precisely because the spectator is offered perceptions that parallel those of the characters – indicating their intellectual and emotional states – and because his characters act in a manner more expressive than Godard and Straub would ever permit. These film-makers want the viewer to experience the *ideas* of their texts, but not to achieve closeness to the characters which those texts generate.* They demand that the viewer draw relationships between the narrative events and his or her own social-political situation. Bertolucci wants the same thing, but also

---

* The concept of characters as function of a text or a narrative derives from the analyses of Vladimir Propp as developed by Fredric Jameson in *The Political Unconscious*.

48

has a more traditional desire of sharing with the viewer the emotions of the characters he creates, although he achieves this in a less than traditional manner. Constructing a complex perceptual and temporal matrix, he draws attention to character formation and presence. He creates emotional proximity by demonstrating the means by which it is achieved. Emotion is gained through an intellectual comprehension of the means of its production.

In the post-neo-realist, modernist tradition, Bertolucci lets the visual structure and the montage of the film communicate information which is often more essential than the dialogue. The form of the film, the ways in which character and environment are observed, creates a complex of images to be deciphered. Bertolucci lives up to the comment made in the film by Fabrizio's friend that style is a moral fact, that the articulation of cinematic structures does not merely 'show' the events of a narrative, but creates them as an act of commentary, judgment and statement. Style and its informing structure, Bertolucci recognizes, is an element of discourse; it 'speaks' to and of the events it records, communicates and creates, forming the text and acting as a perceptual addition to it.

Style is a moral fact and a political fact as well. At his best, Bertolucci never separates the two, aware – despite his differences with the Godardian interpretation of Brecht – that form is political and ideological by nature. Bertolucci manifests this awareness in a major sequence in *Before the Revolution* where Fabrizio and his mentor, Cesare, join a Communist Party workers' celebration. It is a climactic sequence in which Fabrizio's despair, his inability to embrace the ideology he knows to be correct, is made manifest. The surrounding events do not help him, but serve rather to isolate him in his moment of emotional and ideological crisis. He is not in touch with the people round him. Many of the workers, especially the women, seem more concerned with the just announced suicide of Marilyn Monroe than with the proceedings at hand. Fabrizio, walking back and forth with Cesare, complains that the proletariat are lacking in consciousness; no one fights for the just causes. He wanted to see the creation of the new communist man. 'I wanted a new man, a humanity of sons who could be fathers to their fathers' (a prophetic comment in the light of Bertolucci's later films). But Fabrizio fears that the workers are being given bourgeois ideals. Cesare counters that the workers do indeed want economic justice and equality, and his own calm demeanour implies an understanding of the gap between the left-wing bourgeois intellectual's ideal and the immediate desires and needs of working people.

Fabrizio walks on and sees the people working on the parade. There is a close-up of a young boy who asks an older man about the banners.

'They're next to Castro,' he says. The workers do in fact know something; their consciousness is forming, albeit without intellectual articulation and with a matter-of-factness that makes 'Castro' a presence even in poster form. But Fabrizio is impatient with what appears to him to be their indifference, their ability to be sidetracked by mundane affairs – like the death of Marilyn Monroe. Not only does he lack understanding and patience, but he is unaware of how easily he is himself sidetracked, by his love for Gina, by his impending marriage to Clelia.

In the course of events, Bertolucci returns to a close-up of Fabrizio. He asks Cesare what the Party did for Agostino, expressing his guilt and deflecting his own failure to reach his friend about a political movement which, in his anxiety and naiveté, he thought could solve all problems. When Fabrizio asks this question, Bertolucci cuts to Cesare moving to a park bench. He sits on the right, facing the camera, low in the frame, so that behind him trees can be seen, as well as the workers preparing their celebration. As he sits, he asks Fabrizio, 'What did you do for Agostino? You slept and his death woke you up. Why do you now demand the Party do what you did not?' At this point Fabrizio enters the frame from screen right, and as he sits on a bench opposite Cesare, Bertolucci executes a 180 degree cut so that Cesare is now on the left of the screen, his back toward the viewer, Fabrizio facing the camera on the right (no figures can be seen behind him). Both are still positioned low in the frame. Fabrizio answers Cesare weakly: 'Precisely because I did not do it.' Again there is a 180 degree cut, reversing the composition. Cesare, facing the camera, tells Fabrizio that the latter is now on the outside but believes himself to be more on the inside than the others. Two more 180 degree cuts follow. Cesare is seen once more on the right of the frame, facing the camera. He tells Fabrizio he has seen others in his situation. Yet another 180 degree cut: Fabrizio is now on screen right, facing the camera as Cesare asks him if he has the courage to talk about Gina.

At this point the camera begins a lateral track to the right, resting finally on Fabrizio, alone in the frame as he recalls a book Cesare once lent him (perhaps Marx's *The Eighteenth Brumaire*) that said men create their history in a conditioned environment. He gets up and moves toward Cesare's bench. He denies this basic Marxist premise, stating that men create their own history, despite the environment in which they live. As he sits on the opposite end of Cesare's bench, the camera begins a lateral track to the left, so that both are framed together, their backs to the camera, still low in the frame, the trees in front of them. Fabrizio complains that he is the example of the failure of that premise, unaware that his own traditional middle-class history is responsible for

Shifting perspective: Fabrizio and Cesare (Morando Morandini) in the park bench sequence of *Before the Revolution*

his current state of unrest. The camera tracks right as Fabrizio once again changes his seat, facing the camera, which holds on him as he talks about how Cesare wanted him to change. He is isolated in the shot as he says that, like a stone, he is unchangeable. He wanted to help Gina, to fill her with vitality, but managed only to fill her with anxiety. The camera begins tracking to the left, bringing both figures into the composition, as Fabrizio says that Gina suffered 'a fever of the nerves' (an incomplete observation on Fabrizio's part, for Gina's anxiety is more than matched by his own). After another track to the left, Bertolucci cuts away to a tracking shot of the workers preparing their banners. Fabrizio continues his speech off-screen, saying that he suffers another kind of fever – a nostalgia of the present, a sense of living far from the moments of his life. Bertolucci picks up other people, two women riding on bicycles, holding hands.

Fabrizio, still off-screen, says he does not want to change the present. There is another cut, the camera panning left past statues, as Fabrizio says his bourgeois future lies in his bourgeois past. He says that ideology has been a vacation for him, a trip to the country (the camera pans past a poster with the word 'Cuba' large upon it). The camera moves past a ducal palace. A cut is made to a shot of children carrying banners, starting as a left pan and then holding on them. 'I thought I was living in the years of the revolution,' Fabrizio says. 'But instead I lived in the years before the revolution. Because you always live before the revolution when you're like me.'

There is a cut to placards. A worker holds one of them up, marching and singing 'Bandiera rossa', an Italian Communist song that is heard many times in Bertolucci's films. Children march by holding banners. Fabrizio and Cesare appear, walking through the crowd and into the foreground, the camera panning left with them. Fabrizio is ahead of Cesare. He begins quoting from the *Communist Manifesto*: 'Communists don't lower themselves to hide their opinions and their intentions ...'. He begins to sob as he approaches the left side of the screen. 'They openly proclaim that their goals can only be achieved by the violent overthrow ...'. He cannot finish his sentence. Cesare moves behind him and to his left, finishing for him: ' ... by the violent overthrow of the whole traditional social order. The ruling classes tremble at the thought of a Communist revolution!' Fabrizio moves ahead, the camera tracking with him as he raises his head and concludes: 'The workers have nothing to lose but their chains. They have a world to gain. Workers of the world, unite!'

I have detailed this sequence for a number of reasons. Even though an ironic denouement of Fabrizio's affairs is yet to follow – his last meeting with Gina and his marriage to Clelia – the events described here constitute the climax of the film through a clear and moving expression of Fabrizio's anxieties and uncertainties, his conflicting desires and unresolved direction. The sequence states some of the central intellectual and political concerns of Bertolucci's work that will appear in many forms, reaching their most complex statement in *1900*. These concerns – the tensions between committed communist revolutionary activity and the attractions of bourgeois comforts and neuroses; the conflict between the working class and the intellectual, and between the intellectual, his own anxiety-ridden personality, and the felt need for collective action – are hardly new, certainly not invented by Bertolucci, but recapitulated by him again and again. They have been in the forefront of left-wing struggle and debate since perhaps the first bourgeois Marxist intellectual became aware of the anomaly of his or her situation.

Important here are the ways in which Bertolucci inscribes the conflicts, forms them for the first time in his work, with powerful cinematic, intellectual and emotional effect. The sequence takes place in an arena in which all the participants are somewhat out of place. The workers, celebrating their unity, seem divided in their loyalties, as interested in the death of Marilyn Monroe as in their political situation. But, as I have noted, they *are* involved in the events, engaged in preparing and carrying off their demonstration. Whether or not, as Fabrizio says, they have the proper 'consciousness' of their place in history, their solidarity is made clear by their presence together, by the references to Cuba, the singing of 'Bandiera rossa', their collective action. The two main characters are much more out of place. Cesare is the communist intellectual, the bourgeois leftist, comfortable in his knowledge and sentiments, yet apart from the people, separated by class and sensibility. Fabrizio, in his neat white suit, appears as an uncomfortable guest; Cesare, the people, the occasion, all conspire to act as his bad conscience.

Within this larger conflict is the intellectual and emotional conflict between the two men. Cesare is the first of the older father-teacher characters who appear in many of Bertolucci's films. He is the direct antecedent of Professor Quadri in *The Conformist*, the resistance fighter who lives in bourgeois comfort in Paris and is confronted by his former student and present would-be fascist assassin, Marcello Clerici. Cesare is also a distant relation of Joe's schoolteacher father in *La luna*. (There is another older figure in *Before the Revolution*, Gina's friend Puck, a former landowner, whose property is now mortgaged. He is roundly insulted by Fabrizio, but it is clear by the lyrical treatment given him and his surroundings by Bertolucci that there is sympathy offered to this aristocrat manqué, a Viscontian figure of the gentle and genteel man of property displaced by the modern age. A version of this figure reappears in old Alfredo – the Burt Lancaster character – in *1900*, and, in a very different guise, in the figure of Joe's stepfather in *La luna*.)

The confrontation of Cesare and Fabrizio on the park benches is the focal point of the sequence. Two purposes are served by it: one is straightforward cinematic bravura. The lateral tracks, suggested by Godard; the rapid 180 degree cuts, suggested by Bertolucci's own desire to break with cinematic convention, serve to break down those unwritten laws of classic American film-making whose major purpose is to protect the viewer from any recognition of artifice and the intrusion of cinematic reality. The conventional style rejects broad, seemingly unmotivated tracks and the 180 degree cut as intrusions by the cinematic apparatus upon the unmediated 'reality' of the narrative. These are devices whose primary significance is the attention drawn to them.

Bertolucci employs tracking shots throughout his work to express an energetic traversal of space, a *definition* of space which often counters the restricted perceptions of the characters who exist within the narrative and compositional frame. The 180 degree cut is a response to the spatial definition of the track; it has the effect of slicing the screen space and, as it were, flipping it round, creating a momentary disorientation (one of the reasons it is avoided in the classical style) and thereby relating certain states of perception and consciousness to the viewer. In *The Spider's Stratagem*, for example, there is a sequence in which Athos Magnani Jr walks through the night with his bicycle. The sequence is made up of two shots: in the first the foreground of the composition is filled with a close-up of two old men talking. Athos is seen in the background, in soft focus, slowly approaching the figures. As he comes up to them, Bertolucci cuts directly to the other side of the composition, the two old men, having moved aside to allow Athos to pass, now on opposite sides of the screen, as he continues to walk back into soft focus in the rear. The composition, the use of light and colour, and the 180 degree cut concentrate our attention, and, within the context of the narrative, serve to heighten a sense of strangeness and paranoia growing round the central character.

In *The Conformist*, stylistically Bertolucci's most delirious film, there is a sequence in which Marcello Clerici visits his mother, a dissolute drug addict who lives in a decaying mansion with her chauffeur. A lateral tracking shot follows his mother as she moves from the bedroom into her gleaming white bathroom. There, Bertolucci once again executes a 180 degree cut, so that the matching track which follows the mother out of the bathroom moves in the opposite direction, on the opposite side of the room, disturbing our orientation within the created space, echoing the disturbed orientation of the character in the space he has created for his life.

In both instances, the execution of the cut is more controlled, more precisely organized within the total construction of the respective sequences, than it is in *Before the Revolution*. But in all instances it has significance beyond mere self-indulgence (though undeniably Bertolucci enjoys indulging his considerable technical virtuosity). In this climactic confrontation between Cesare and Fabrizio, where the film's major thematic – the irreconcilable conflict between individual and collective needs – is worked out, Bertolucci creates a visual structure that forcefully directs his characters' perceptions to the viewer. His variations on stylistic conventions adequately register his intended meanings.

By setting the characters amid the crowd of demonstrators, off-screen, or low in the frame during the park bench sequence, he diminishes their stature to some extent. The main figures are, in a sense, 'cut down'; they remain central but their compositional placement is a reminder that their struggles are neither original nor unique and that they must be seen within a larger group. At the same time, within the fiction called *Before the Revolution*, the characters *are* unique, and so a complex of differences is set up visually between them and their surroundings, and between each of them as well. The Communist rally sets them apart. Fabrizio's personal agonies are contrasted to Cesare's more self-assured understanding of his pupil, himself, and his ideas. These breaks are communicated through the characters' significant positioning within the larger group of people and opposite each other on the park bench, an opposition emphasized by the 180 degree cuts (which force us to perceive their opposition), and through the lateral tracks across the benches that simultaneously connect and isolate the two.

Fabrizio is separated totally from the collectivity offered by Marxist ideology, which he looks upon as a 'vacation' from his psychological torments: a fact emphasized by the double 180 degree cut executed when Cesare tells him that Fabrizio thinks he is now 'inside' – in touch with himself (to use more recent jargon) – but, in fact, is more on the outside than he ever was. By rapidly fracturing the spatial continuity, Bertolucci emphasizes Fabrizio's mistaken perception and Cesare's insight. He places the viewer in a position of judgment, by not allowing the gaze to be comfortably situated. The lack of spatial continuity, elaborated by the camera movements that promise continuity and then deny it by refusing to incorporate both characters within the frame, emphasizes their emotional and ideological separation.

The disorienting shifts of perspective also echo Fabrizio's own recognition that he suffers a 'nostalgia of the present', that he cannot live in history or outside of it. His romanticism forces him to suffer the anxiety of a desire which can never be fulfilled, and it is contrasted to Cesare's knowledge that the individual is always at the mercy of history and at the same time required to join in a revolutionary struggle against history. Fabrizio is aware of the conflicts inherent in these propositions, though he attempts to evade or displace them. Bertolucci signifies the displacement both by the cuts and the tracks within the park bench sequence and by cutting away from the park benches, holding Fabrizio's lament on the soundtrack, while the camera wanders among the demonstrators who are able to manifest *both* individuality and collectivity: the girls on their bicycles holding hands in a simple image of connection; the children marching with their banners as Fabrizio pronounces the words that provide the film's title, his comment that he has always lived in the years before the revolution. The statement ironically echoes the epigraph from Talleyrand that begins the film: 'He who did not live in the years before the Revolution cannot understand what the sweetness of living is' – a lament of bad conscience, nostalgia, and the inability to reconcile personality to history.

The irony lies in the fact that Fabrizio has not experienced the

5

sweetness of living, but only the bitterness of middle-class self-indulgence, the loss through suicide of a friend he could not help, an agonized love affair with his aunt, and finally the engagement to a coldly beautiful, 'proper' middle-class woman. So when Fabrizio and Cesare finally emerge from the crowd of Communist celebrants, it is with sobs that Fabrizio recalls the strengths of Communist ideology and its insistence on collective action and revolutionary change. But by the time he finishes his quotation from Marx and Engels, he is once more alone, isolated from Cesare in the frame. This isolation is emphasized in the concluding sequences of the film.

When we first see Fabrizio in the film, he is racing through the streets of Parma looking for Clelia, his intended. At the end of the film he has found and marries her. The ironies and anxieties that separate the two events are consummated in the formal construction of the sequences that follow the Communist rally and precede the marriage. In the first of these we find the first of one of Bertolucci's obsessive allusions to a figure whose music and narratives haunt and inform much of his work – Giuseppe Verdi. 'Obsessive' is hardly too strong a word. Only *The Grim Reaper, Partner, The Conformist* and *Last Tango in Paris* contain no direct reference to the work of Verdi. In the other films, the composer's music is a demanding presence, often a formal imperative, sometimes the structuring ground that helps explain the film, that plays counterpoint with the dominant narrative or enlarges upon it. The Verdian substrate just begins to form in *Before the Revolution*, where the operatic allusion is used to extend the ironic circumstances in which the characters find themselves.

From the close-up of Fabrizio quoting (indeed, almost singing, as if in an aria) 'Workers of the world, unite!', with the sound of the music of the demonstration behind him, Bertolucci cuts to opening night of the Teatro Regio in Parma and a performance of Verdi's *Macbeth*. All the major characters of the film gather, the middle-class of Parma – as Bertolucci describes them[10] – there to be seen as newsreel cameramen photograph them. In the auditorium Clelia and her mother are in their box. Fabrizio joins them, shakes the mother's hand and sits down by Clelia. Through it all, on the soundtrack, the opening of the opera is heard: the witches' song, with its threats of violence. At the section where a drum sounds and the witches ask, 'Un tamburo! Che sarà?', 'A drum! What next?/Macbeth is coming. Behold, he is here!'* we see Cesare in a box with his friends. The irony is sweet. Clelia is the bewitching prophecy of Fabrizio's bourgeois future, and Cesare, though certainly no tyrannical killer like Macbeth, may have assumed

* The translation from the libretto by Piave and Maffei is by Glen Sauls.

the role of intellectual tyrant in Fabrizio's conscience, becoming, along with the dead Agostino, a source of guilt, the surrogate for Fabrizio's own inward gaze. The first thing Cesare does is to look through his binoculars at Fabrizio and Clelia, particularly at the latter, whose presence is emphasized by means of a dissolve to her from Cesare's point of view.

As the witches continue their chorus, we see more of the audience, including Fabrizio's mother and father – other silent prophesiers of doom – who also gaze up at their son and future daughter-in-law. The theatre lights go down. (In keeping with the structure of the film, Bertolucci does not follow a strict continuity of events. The opera may have started on the soundtrack, but not necessarily in the narrative space of the film. Bertolucci is not constrained by the continuity of the opera itself: he chooses from it what is important to his own narrative needs, a device he will use in all his Verdian allusions.) The next piece of music heard introduces Lady Macbeth's aria in Act I, scene 2. It is picked up at the passage beginning 'Vieni! t'affretta! accendere/Ti vo' quel freddo core! ...', 'Full of misdeeds is the path/to power, and woe to him who sets/his foot upon it doubtfully and then retreats!/Come, then! Hasten! That I may enflame/that cold heart of yours!/Boldness is needed to complete this task./I will give you courage'. As the music begins, we see in profile Fabrizio and Clelia in their box. Fabrizio turns to look at the auditorium and sees Gina enter, at which point the aria commences. Once again an ironic counterpoint of music and character occurs. In the course of their relationship, it was Fabrizio who thought he was giving strength to Gina. However, like Lady Macbeth, though without her evil intent, she proved the more powerful, the more neurotic figure. Like Fabrizio, she needed to discover the source and fulfilment of her own desires – even at Fabrizio's expense. Like Fabrizio, her quest proved sad and inconclusive. Neither attained power over their own personality or the other's. The only courage Gina gave to Fabrizio was the uncertain strength to repress his conscience.

Throughout much of this sequence Bertolucci's camera holds on Gina's face, darkened except for a strip of light across her eyes – perhaps an allusion to the lighting on Humphrey Bogart in Nicholas Ray's *In a Lonely Place*; most certainly a climactic emphasis on the fact that Gina's eyes and what they see provide a continual reference point in the film, looking at Fabrizio, judging, attempting to understand him. Fabrizio's mother, sitting off-screen next to Gina, talks to her about the ensuing wedding, wondering why Fabrizio and Clelia are marrying so quickly, worrying that Fabrizio should have taken his degree first.

Bertolucci cuts again into the libretto, leaping to the end of Act I and Macduff's cry at his discovery of Duncan's body: 'Orrore! ...', 'Oh,

Opera: Fabrizio and Clelia (Cristina Pariset) at *Macbeth* in *Before the Revolution*

horror! horror! horror!' With the opera providing the melodramatic grace notes to the character's unstated emotions, Gina looks up at Fabrizio and Clelia for the first time, as Macduff sings 'Contemplate voi stesso ...', '... See it for yourself'. She comments to Fabrizio's mother about Clelia's beauty, but says she cannot see Fabrizio, who is hidden behind Clelia. (Banquo is now singing 'Oh noi perduti! ...', 'Oh, we are lost!') Gina turns her face away, looks down sadly, then looks up. The murder of Duncan is announced and the chorus that ends Act I sings its call to God to avenge it. The lights go up and there are several shots of the audience, centring on a rapid zoom back from Fabrizio as he finally meets Gina's gaze.

As the trumpet call that begins Act II sounds, Fabrizio leaves his box to meet Gina outside the auditorium. Bertolucci moves rapidly in the score to Act II, scene 2, picking up Banquo's aria – which begins 'Studia il passo, o mio figlio! ...', 'Be careful of your steps, my son!' – at the point where he sings 'Come dal ciel precipita ...', 'See how the shades of night descend./The shadows grow deeper and darker.' The two former lovers follow each other through the winding passages of the opera house. As Gina bravely tells Fabrizio how everyone will envy him his fiancée, Banquo is singing 'Mille affannose immagini ...', 'Thousands of frightful spectre shapes/seem to predict disaster/and burden my soul with gloomy fears/of phantoms and unknown crimes'.

Fabrizio insists to Gina (and himself) that Clelia may not be very smart but is a good woman. The words of the opera contradict his attempts at self-assurance and speak to his bad conscience as well.

At this point in the libretto, Banquo and his son are being pursued by the murderers and the scene changes to the banquet at Macbeth's castle. Bertolucci follows the score closely here. The music is merry, Macbeth and his wife receive the praises of the court, and Lady Macbeth asks all to fill their goblets to the brim: 'Let pleasure be born,/let sorrows die.' In the opera it is, of course, a false merriment, for soon Macbeth will meet the murderers and see Banquo's ghost. Bertolucci leaves the opera before this grim section, depending on his audience to recall the disastrous conclusion to the forced happiness in the opera and to match it to the sadness connoted by his own narrative. For the irony doubles back upon the narrative events of the film. During the joyful music Gina and Fabrizio have their final conversation. They walk back through the corridors towards Clelia's box. Pausing, Fabrizio tells her that she understood him better than anyone; he walks towards her, admitting that he made her suffer. She only complains that she is cold, and Fabrizio walks to the rear, shutting a window, leaving Gina alone in the frame. On the soundtrack, Lady Macbeth is singing 'Si colmi il calice/Di vino eletto . . .', 'Fill the goblet to the brim . . ./Let pleasure be born,/let sorrows die./Have done with all hatred,/do away with all scorn./Let only love/and jollity reign here'. But here only sadness and separation reign. Fabrizio asks if Gina could fall in love with him again. There is a jump cut to Gina holding on to Fabrizio's arm as they walk to Clelia's box. He opens the door long enough to let us see Clelia inside and then closes it behind him. Bertolucci cuts on the music and the movement of the door to Cesare closing the gate of his house as he sets out to walk to his school.

I have been insistent in pointing out ironies that occur in the relationship between the music and the characters' activities. Obviously the characters and events of the film are neither Shakespearian nor Verdian, and the connections Bertolucci draws between them and Verdi's version of Shakespeare are more amusing in their glancing, suggestive connections and inversions than they are revealing. Cesare is no Macbeth; Gina no Lady Macbeth. Yet both are powerful characters who have a profound influence on Fabrizio. Each attempts to manipulate him, and though neither destroys him or acts the tyrant, they do affect and change his life – for the worse, as it turns out. The confusions they wreak upon him, along with his own inability to escape his class history, drive him into the arms of Clelia; and his marriage to her provides the final sequence of the film, in which Gina, distraught over the loss of her lover, goes slightly mad, covering Fabrizio's younger brother in embarrassingly passionate kissses. A fine, melo-dramatic Verdian touch.

Before the Revolution is no tragedy. But neither is Verdi's *Macbeth*. The opera, like all his work, is melodrama with – as is sometimes the case in his libretti – some political overtones (a tyrant is overthrown, oppression ended). Given its Shakespearian source, its narrative events are slightly less overblown than some of his other works, and Bertolucci does not choose it haphazardly. He is obviously delighted with the ironic associations between certain events in this Verdian narrative and in his own, finding irresistible, for example, the connection between Gina's discovery of Fabrizio and Clelia in their box and Macduff's cries of horror. But the Verdian connection goes much deeper than the ironies of association.

Gina makes it clear, in her conversation with Fabrizio in the halls of the opera house, that she hates Verdi and prefers Mozart. She remains the outsider and knows it, for she understands the fact that the people take his work quite seriously. 'They really believe it,' she says. And herein lies a first clue to Bertolucci's attraction to the composer and his work that continues throughout his films. The Italian love of opera is something of a cultural cliché, but one that contains some interesting realities. Verdi is, for one thing, an Italian cultural hero. His life spanned almost all of the 19th century, and his death in 1901 signalled the beginning of the 20th. As the new century begins in *1900*, we see a hump-backed figure dressed in the costume of a medieval court jester; he is a member of the peasant community and is named Rigoletto. Walking through the fields at night, he cries out, 'Verdi is dead!' The overture to *Rigoletto* is heard on the soundtrack.

Verdi did most of his composing during the period of the Risorgimento, and was deeply connected with the movement of Italian unification. People scrawled his name on walls as an abbreviation for the King under whom Italy would form itself as a nation: 'Vittorio Emanuele Re d'Italia'. There were, as I have said, political references or inferences in some of his work, but mainly he created spectacles for emotional abandon. His music was often brilliant. His narratives offered stories of overwhelming passion, bourgeois fantasies of love and sacrifice in safely distant worlds. (Verdi came from the middle class, 'and more specifically from the tradespeople of the middle class. And to these origins [he] remained totally faithful.'[11]) Here were operas in whose narratives a gypsy could throw her infant son into the fire because of mistaken identity, and vow eternal revenge; a daughter could defy her father by falling in love with his enemy and die when the assassin hired by her father inadvertently kills her after she has assumed her lover's identity to protect him. The broad gesture and melodramatic excess, the fantasies of stupefying passions and the ultimate resolution of the moral order, the obsession with sacrifice (particularly on the part of the female character), the intensification of emptiness – bloated signifiers often connoting only their own grandeur – are precursors of cinema itself, homologous with the Victorian theatre of the same era, the one leading to the cinema of D. W. Griffith, the other to Pastrone.

Verdi's operas are pre-cinematic cinema, and Bertolucci, so conscious of the history of cinema, could not help but realize a connection. Nor, obviously, could he ignore the national identity of Verdi and Italian culture: 'Verdi,' he says, 'corresponds for me . . . with a mythic dimension.'[12] Most important, he could not ignore the melodramatic excess of Verdi's operas and discovered a way to use it as counterpoint to the structure of his own films, sometimes going as far as to underpin them with the very structure of Verdian opera. In his major work – *The Spider's Stratagem, The Conformist, Last Tango in Paris* (the last two contain no overt reference to Verdi, but assume certain operatic forms and have verbal references to Puccini), *1900*, and of course *La luna*, whose subject is an opera singer who seems only to perform Verdi – the operatic work either forms a subtext or directly informs the narrative structure of the films. In other words, a Verdi aria may be used by Bertolucci as an ironic reference or as a means of expanding character or narrative connotation. An entire opera may provide the ground of a film, as does *Rigoletto* in *The Spider's Stratagem* or *Il trovatore* and *Un ballo in maschera* in *La luna*. In the case of *Last Tango in Paris* or *La luna* the film, as I say, can take on overtly operatic form and expression. However, unlike Visconti, Bertolucci never simply imitates operatic gesture but uses it as a structuring device, a text within, or a satellite of, the main text.

As a modernist, Bertolucci is concerned with the problem of melodrama and its ability to draw the spectator unquestioningly into the narrative structure. At the same time, he refuses many of the Brechtian codes of distancing that other cine-modernists were adopting during the early 60s. Verdi therefore becomes a replacement for Brecht in the formal structure of Bertolucci's films: out of the Verdian allusions he creates an alternative distancing device. Through the dialectic created by his acceptance of the Verdian extremes and his ironic-critical examination of them, his counterpointing of them with his own text, operatic melodrama is turned into a means for both the film-maker and the viewer more clearly to perceive narrative events without becoming engulfed by them. Opera and film narrative reflect on one another and create an awareness of the artifice of their conventions, warning the viewer against the potential melodramatic inflation of the film narrative itself.

Bertolucci does not go so far as to recode these conventions, in the way, for example, of a Brechtian like Rainer Werner Fassbinder. In other words, he does not flip melodramatic structures round to the point where they announce themselves as *meditations* upon the form, distancing the viewer so that the film acts as a lens through which melodrama may be examined, understood and then mined for whatever significance it may hold. At the same time, Bertolucci is conscious of the melodramatic elements which he constructs and tinkers with. Speaking of the use of opera in *Before the Revolution* and *La luna*, he says: 'Melodrama is inherent in the drama of characters, yet there comes a point when it overflows the stage and swallows them up, whether they are in a theatre box at the Regio or among the ruins of Caracalla [where the opera sequence which concludes *La luna* takes place].'[13] By countering the melodrama of the characters with the melodrama of Verdi, or absorbing those characters into operatic melodrama, Bertolucci allows them to re-emerge with their emotions perceived more clearly. The spectator is given some distance and the narrative enriched.*

As with many of the formal experiments in *Before the Revolution*, the references to Verdi are somewhat tentative. The use of *Macbeth* appears as another move in the quest for usable form. But already the operatic allusions are not restricted to the performance in the theatre; they work, more subtly, throughout the text. The film is, in fact, made up of set pieces, like scenes within an operatic act. There is the duet between Fabrizio and Agostino; the grand torments of Fabrizio's love affair with Gina; her 'aria' on the telephone; and of course the grand duet of Fabrizio and Cesare at the Communist rally. All this constitutes an attempt by a young modernist film-maker to refashion the sign system of his cinematic narrative. As a result, that narrative reflects its operatic origins, reflects the film-maker's obsession with opera, while simultaneously commenting on both the origins and the obsession. Bertolucci tries out the Verdian discourse within the cinematic, playing with both while in search of his own voice.

In this quest for a voice, Bertolucci discovers that film is indeed something like opera. It can be spectacular and melodramatic, its characters can express themselves with abandon – as long as the film's structure manifests the artifice of the expression and draws the relationships between intersecting forms. *Before the Revolution* shows clearly Bertolucci's awareness of these complexities; that he could, like his colleagues in France, tinker with old cinematic codes, loosen,

---

* Bertolucci's success with this method is not invariable. In *La luna*, character, film-maker and viewer are all consumed by melodrama.

transform, overturn and negate them. He could turn to operatic forms, without making an explicitly operatic film, and negate the closed, almost ritualized structures found in Verdi by restructuring them within the open, playful structure of his own narrative. Perhaps the final irony in the use of Verdi here lies in the fact that it is Verdi more than Stendhal who constitutes the formal base of *Before the Revolution*.

The association of cinematic and operatic forms, the restructuring of cinematic codes, the perceptual crises and resituations drive a narrative which in turn speaks of conflict, crisis and resituations. Fabrizio wants to satisfy conventional romantic yearnings while struggling with his need for collective political action. He would, finally, live the life of a romantic tenor, singing duets of love with Gina, indulging in the melancholy reveries of the bourgeoisie in a world that exists perpetually before the revolution. Like the characters in an opera, or in any melodrama, the figures in the film suffer and sacrifice. Gina is lost in her inability to find sexual and emotional satisfaction. Fabrizio sinks into a precarious, superficially safe bourgeois marriage (a ritual that will be re-enacted in *The Conformist*, where Marcello Clerici marries a middle-class woman to prove his normality). But surrounding these characters and their opera are the realities of history, the demonstration of the workers, the opposing figures of Puck and Cesare. Puck is himself an operatic character, who all but sings an aria about the loss of the countryside, which Bertolucci accompanies with painterly shots of the Po. Cesare does not sing arias. His is the voice of an impossible reason, the voice of the intellectual whose action is in his teaching. He does not attempt to indoctrinate Fabrizio, merely to show him a way. 'Maturity is all,' he tells his student, quoting from another Cesare, the novelist Pavese.* Without maturity, with only an intellect stifled by its own middle-class history, Fabrizio can understand Cesare's teachings but not act upon them. He must finally deny them.

We see the teacher twice at the end of the film. After the opera sequence he walks, alone, to his school where two small children follow him inside. Later, intercut with the sequence of Fabrizio's marriage to Clelia, a stifling bourgeois affair, we see Cesare reading to his class. The book is *Moby Dick*, perhaps the most 'operatic' of American novels (its Italian translation by Cesare Pavese[14]). Cesare reads Ahab's maddened call to his men to chase the White Whale. Appropriate in a way, for Cesare is something of a muted version of Ahab, and his own 'white whale', Fabrizio, is not caught but rather catches himself in the

---

* According to the screenplay, the quotation is from Pavese's last novel, *La luna e i falò (The Moon and the Bonfire)*. In his own maturity, Bertolucci was of course to make a film called *La luna*. The line itself originates in Shakespeare.

discreet ceremonies of his class. Of all the figures in the film – and quite unlike Ahab – Cesare remains the most composed: a still, assured centre *and* the active dialectic to all the characters around him. He holds together the diversity of the film's structure, and by creating him Bertolucci finds another way to control the operatic structure of the narrative. Cesare 'fathers' the narrative, as he attempts to father Fabrizio. Although unsuccessful in the latter attempt, he does provide the coherence for the former. He is one of the few 'fathers' in Bertolucci's work who is allowed to prevail without destroying. He may not triumph, but he provides the certitude of intellect and the calm presence which composes the frenzied activity that moves around and counter to him.

I must note briefly another formal element in *Before the Revolution* that looks forward to an important concern of Bertolucci's later work. I have mentioned that, in the Puck episode, Bertolucci indulges in some painterly compositions of the Po valley. In fact, one of the characters present in this episode is a painter, Goliardo Padova, sitting at his canvas on the bank of a river, painting and talking with the major figures. Just as opera provides a narrative base for many of the films, so painting provides an important element of their visual style. Bertolucci admits to the influence of Magritte on *The Spider's Stratagem*.[15] Two paintings by Francis Bacon provide background to the title sequence of *Last Tango in Paris*, and the colour scheme and some compositions in that film are directly influenced by Bacon's work. *1900* opens with a slow zoom out from Giuseppe Pellizza da Volpedo's enormous proto-social realist painting, *The Fourth Estate*, which depicts a large group of peasants. Paintings by the contemporary Italian primitive, Vittorio Ligabue, provide the background to the title sequence of *The Spider's Stratagem* and are referred to again in *Tragedy of a Ridiculous Man*.

This is all part of a complex event. Just as cinema has been compared to opera, it has also been compared to its ancestors, photography and painting. The three forms organize visual signifiers within a related composition determined by a frame. There have been attempts in film to imitate painting (Korda's film on Rembrandt is a major example), and film-makers have historically enjoyed the convention of using a painting as the background to a credit sequence and then making that painting 'come to life'. Jean-Luc Godard's *Passion* (1982) involves a film within a film which is made up of compositions imitative of classical paintings. A vaguely defined phenomenon of the 'painterly style' has appeared in some films of the last ten years, most notably Kubrick's *Barry Lyndon*, Terrence Malick's *Days of Heaven* and

Painting as style and content: the scene on the banks of the Po in *Before the Revolution*

Ridley Scott's *The Duellists*. In Kubrick's case, there is a purposeful attempt to create images analogous not to specific paintings, but to the compositional patterns of eighteenth-century art. In the Malick and Scott films, there is a manifest desire to create compositions that, in their stasis, their colour and their configuration of internal forms, suggest the conventions and signifying systems of representational art. The phenomenon works both ways, of course. Film has influenced painting, particularly in the 1910s and 20s. With the advent of photo-realism in the 70s, painting went back to the photograph and its filmic analogue for inspiration, reproducing in meticulous detail the visual structures of 'reality' that the invention of the photograph originally rendered unnecessary, even redundant, for the painter.

These interrelationships reflect the continuing modernist conscious-ness of form and convention, the understanding that 'reality' and its 'reproduction' are, in one sense, not separate events. 'Reality' is produced whenever it is rendered in a given form, and that form perceived in its turn. Only the conventions of form permit perceptual discrimination of 'realities', of the 'real world', of the photograph, painting, film. Filmic conventions developed out of an ideological need to create illusions of an unmediated 'realistic' world as it might be 'directly' perceived. Film's use of dramatic conventions and movement

65

within the frame, along with montage, separated it from the static contemplation of 'reality' inherent in nineteenth-century painting. But as has been pointed out by a number of critics, the articulation of space in classic narrative film, and the construction of the spectator's relationship to that space, follow the basic conventions of post-perspective, representational painting. That is, the viewer is given a privileged point of view in relation to that space, which is so created as to give the impression of belonging to the spectator. Film extends the privilege by effacing its structure of representation and, in a sense, inviting the spectator perceptually to enter its space, substituting it for the everyday 'reality' which is itself effaced in the silence and darkness of the cinema.

Those film-makers who make use of a 'painterly style' or, like Bertolucci, make a conscious effort to absorb the styles of specific painters within their own visual structures, call attention to these structures by, in effect, doubling them. Two visual styles – even if separately aimed at creating an illusion of 'reality' – when joined together create a dialectic of artifice. They negate each other's illusory space and foreground their existence as *made* images (photo-realism is an excellent example of this effect in painting itself). When the pictorial style is a modernist one – that is, when the painterly reference is used by a film-maker who is attempting to break down illusionist conventions – the effect of artifice, the foregrounding of formal construction, is heightened all the more.

There is also a connotative or diegetical effect. The visual presence of Magritte in *The Spider's Stratagem* or Bacon in *Last Tango* brings with it the signifieds of those artists' work. Magritte's tinkering with the reality of appearances and the appearances of reality, Bacon's desperate expressionist visions of the human form tormented and distorted, inform the films on a substantive level. Among many other things, the films engage themselves in the same concerns as the works of the painters who inform their visual style.

The references to painting in *Before the Revolution* are only apparent in the sequence with Puck, Fabrizio, Gina, Cesare and the painter Padova on the banks of the Po; but, like the Verdian allusions, they point to more complex relationships to come. Speaking of *1900*, Bertolucci said, 'like all of my films [it] makes use of all the materials not only of the cinema but of literature, painting, and music as well, of everything that's come before. Basically, cinema is really a kind of reservoir of the collective memory of this century.'[16] More appropriately, perhaps, of the collective aesthetic memory of the century, the memory of forms and expression. In the following chapters, I will examine how Bertolucci collected these memories and forged them into complex, vital statements, whose structures keep changing in response to an inquisitive cinematic intellect. *Before the Revolution* will return as the reference point, the seed bed of that intellect.

3 The Formalist's Strategies

> Every new film I make is affected by a sort of decree
> ordering me to change, by a fear of repetition that forces
> itself upon me to the point of preventing me from telling
> with words the same things I have shown in images.[1]

Before the Revolution establishes the basic formal patterns of Bertolucci's
work. The narrative development, the characters and conflicts which
will appear in various guises and situations throughout his major films,
the signifieds – denotations, connotations, thematic concerns – are all
present, in embryo or, in the case of the political conflicts, fully
realized. The influences and allusions – opera and painting, the work of
other film-makers – are present, in a rough and somewhat unintegrated
fashion. The act of integration occurs in the film Bertolucci made for
Italian television in 1970, *The Spider's Stratagem*, intellectually the most
complex of his films, politically the most intriguing.

In the two years following this film Bertolucci moved from strength
to strength, exploring the whole range of the modernist project. He
experimented, in *The Conformist* and in *Last Tango in Paris*, with different
possibilities of cinematic seeing, developing dialectical structures of
sexuality and politics in his narratives, intricate structures of
perception in his narrative form. With these two films he achieved the
status of international film-maker. Both films were distributed by
major American companies, Paramount and United Artists respec-
tively. The *succès de scandale* of *Last Tango*, the years-long censorship
battles that occurred from country to country, assured Bertolucci his
fame, even while eclipsing the importance of the film itself.

With this fame came the phantom of liberty, an opportunity to create
a film with an enormous budget, by European standards, and a
political content more direct and radical – in the root sense of the word
– than anything Bertolucci had yet attempted. The film is *1900*, and it
marks a major break in Bertolucci's career to date – a place of decision
and of a major alteration of form and style. It marks as well the place of
critical and commercial failure, of a major and losing confrontation
with the business enterprise that world cinema is, and a place from
which Bertolucci had, in a sense, to begin again.

Within his body of work, *1900* can be looked at in two ways: as an aberration, a miscalculated and misconceived endeavour that stands in the way of the 'major' films; or as a climactic point to which the other films lead and from which the succeeding films emerge. The first perspective wilfully ignores its importance as a text and as a phenomenon, the second implies a precarious teleology, as if *1900* were present in potential, waiting to be made and, once made, determining the director's future course. But the second perspective does have the greater validity. The film was conceived before *Last Tango*, and Bertolucci, his brother-colleague-co-writer and, one gathers, source of strong support, Giuseppe, along with his editor and co-writer of *Last Tango*, the late Franco Arcalli, worked on it for three years after *Last Tango*. After the debacle of its cutting, distribution and reception, Bertolucci, in effect, lurched about attempting to find a mode of expression that would counter, possibly even make up for, *1900*.

The film constitutes a 'break' in Bertolucci's film-making career, and I therefore want to break into the chronology of the films and discuss some aspects of *1900* before picking up that chronology with the films that precede it. Formally, *1900* embodies all the elements Bertolucci had been developing since 1964. But at the same time these elements are set out in a different manner from the preceding films; their 'utterance' or expression has other inflections, superficially more conventional, than those he had been developing earlier. The apparent shift away from modernist structures in *1900* will better enable us to understand those structures in the earlier works and the return to them in the succeeding films. In the breadth of *1900* every aspect of Bertolucci's political commitment and its inherent conflicts is made evident. The ideology of *1900* is more clearly articulated than in any of his other works. Even though I will discuss the political and ideological substance of the films in a separate chapter, it is important to repeat that 'content' is only created by a formal apparatus which is itself an expression of the ideological apparatus. Because the form and style of *1900* so well define the ideology, the film forms itself as the central text about which cluster all the others.

Finally, more than any of the other films, the form and substance of *1900* is determined – after its creation – by the confrontation of the film and its maker with an external ideology, that of the American motion picture industry, which caused its re-creation and contributed to its failure. This phenomenon, as much as the elements within the film itself, makes *1900* a focal text for comprehending the intricacies of production and reception, of 'subjective' film-making versus the commercial structures that make such film-making possible or impossible. *1900* was explicitly made for commercial distribution with the backing of American finance. In order to raise the initial $6,850,000 to start production in 1974 (the film was completed in 1976 and eventually cost over $8 million), Alberto Grimaldi (the producer of *1900* and *Last Tango*) sold distribution rights to three American companies. Paramount Pictures would have the American market; and, though perhaps Bertolucci was unaware of this (Grimaldi, at one point in the proceedings, claimed that he was), their contract called for a film that would run no longer than three and a quarter hours. 20th Century-Fox would distribute the film in Europe; United Artists throughout the rest of the world.*

Grimaldi procured American money; Bertolucci American stars (Burt Lancaster, Sterling Hayden, Robert De Niro, Donald Sutherland) as well as popular French players (Gérard Depardieu, Dominique Sanda). Equally important, within the context of the interplay between commercial and subjective forces, Bertolucci was able to experiment, for the first time in his career, with a 'commercial' style. In *1900* he employs the fundamental conventions of 'realist' cinema, including a basically linear construction (the film begins near the end of its narrative and then leaps to an earlier time to present the events that lead up to its starting point – a fairly conventional construction); and he uses characters who are developed and 'motivated' not only by political but by quite recognizable psychological mechanisms – love, friendship, jealousy, anger – a spectrum of convenient and manageable Hollywood conventions of human relationships. The film's images, while stately and painterly in their composition, signifying season and mood, are otherwise unobtrusive and undemanding in their straightforward development of narrative; they hide nothing nor do they demand from an audience a dedicated gaze, a search for subtleties of *mise en scène*. It is difficult to determine whether the choice of style was dictated by the commercial intent of the film, or whether Bertolucci was moving, independently of the film's production apparatus, away from modernist forms toward a more classical construction. Evidence indicates both motivations. What is important is that the style and the means of production intersected and collided simultaneously.

So begins the paradox and the destruction of *1900*. Despite all the commercial gestures, Bertolucci made his most defiantly non-commercial film. Its first cut ran six hours and fifteen minutes,[2] which Bertolucci immediately trimmed to five and a half hours. Its political

* The facts, figures and history of *1900*'s production and the subsequent battles over its length and distribution come mainly from dispatches and reports in *Variety* between 7 May 1975 and 23 November 1977.

content was collectivist – specifically communist, anti-fascist, and pro-worker ('worker' in this instance is the Italian peasantry) – going far beyond any of Bertolucci's Western European colleagues in its straightforward celebration of the socialist ideal. If the construction of its narrative elements attempted to recoup the linearity of conventional Hollywood practice, its running time was anything but conventional, linking it not to the Hollywood 'epic', but to the work of Jacques Rivette in France and Theo Angelopoulos in Greece as part of a project in the 60s and 70s that attempted to break the two-hour rule, test the conventions of duration, and develop a new kind of bond between audience and film, finally demanding that dedicated gaze the other aspects of its form attempted to diminish.* Bertolucci therefore subverted his own intent, making a film that would be all but impossible to distribute and would all but guarantee critical, as well as commercial, hostility. Even in Europe, where political content (and sometimes political form) is understood and accepted by most film critics and some filmgoers, the film's open celebration of communism and the peasantry caused much controversy. In America, the reaction of its distributor was outrage. When the enormous struggle that emerged from that outrage was settled and the film was put into limited release, the critical reaction was either one of hostility, bewilderment or – in a culture whose own ideology tends to reject political content in film (or any other art) as mere propaganda unworthy of serious attention – outright rejection.

Before detailing the struggle that ensued with Paramount when the film was completed – which will enable us to understand the conflicts within the film and between the film and the financial apparatus that made it possible – it will be helpful briefly to note a theoretical model that accounts for the complex interaction between the individual maker of a text and the social-economic-ideological forces that surround and determine both creator and creation. In his book *Criticism and Ideology*, Terry Eagleton breaks down this complex of forces into a number of interrelated components. These include the general mode of production, the economic-social structure of the society as a whole – capitalism, for example – and the literary (or, for our purposes, cinematic) mode of production, which functions either as part of the larger structure, as in American studio production, or counter to it, as in

---

* The long film is, of course, not strictly a modernist phenomenon. Hollywood has sometimes indulged films three hours or longer, and in Italy Visconti experimented with long films in the 60s and 70s – *The Leopard* and *Ludwig II* – which may have been an inspiration for Bertolucci. Like *1900*, both these films were cut by or for their American distributors.

government-subsidized production. Within these modes, or over-determining them, is the general ideology, the dominant discourse of a society that accounts for its mode of production by providing the rationales and the images that show that mode to be the best one possible. Embedded within the general ideology lies the aesthetic ideology, which always exists 'within a particular social formation which is in turn part of an "ideology of culture" included within the [general ideology]'.[3] As part of this enormous structure there exists the authorial ideology of the individual creator, who may accept or counter the general and aesthetic ideology, or develop some kind of conflicted combination of both. Finally, as a result of all of these forces working together or in tension with one another, there is the text, the work itself, which manifests the pressures and contradictions of all the other categories, while at the same time standing beyond them, both connected and disconnected.[4]

Bertolucci's authorial ideology shines clearly throughout the film, with all its ambiguities intact: his belief in communism and collective action; his hatred of fascism; his understanding of the delights of the bourgeoisie and the inherent conflict between that understanding and the dominant left ideology. All this is structured within a text that traces the rise of political consciousness of the peasantry in the province of Emilia through the first half of the 20th century, and follows the conflicts between the representatives of that class and those who oppose them. As a commercial entity, the film was made under the auspices of the general, dominant mode of cinematic production: the manufacture of a product that will make a profit for its backers. Money, as I said, came from large film corporations. (Paramount is actually a small component of an enormous capitalist enterprise, the Gulf and Western Corporation. In 1970, they distributed *The Conformist*, a more politically 'safe' film, and in 1981, from an entirely different source, *Reds*, which was a long film – though not five hours – celebrating the American left, but from a liberal perspective, with politics secured within the very conventional signifiers of a romantic melodrama.) The text, the aesthetic and personal ideology of its author, and the mode of production under which he worked could not survive the contradictions that resulted. In the end, the very force of these contradictions pulled everything apart *except* the dominant mode of production, which remained quite intact when *1900* passed into commercial oblivion.

Bertolucci, somewhat naively, expected that a work whose basic formal structure met the aesthetic expectations of the general ideology, that was produced under the auspices of the dominant cinematic modes of production, would receive, despite its length, the same distribution and attention as other important European political films. Perhaps more, given his reputation at the time. He must also have believed that he would be able to perform an act of subversion and use the dominant forms to create a text whose aesthetic ideology (realism) and authorial ideology (communism) would, finally, undo the dominant ideology. He hoped, in a dialectical stroke, to speak of the very things the dominant forms try to silence. The naiveté of all this is nowhere better expressed than in this comment he made in an interview after the film was screened in Cannes:

> Let's say that I wanted to make a popular film, that's the right word, I mean a film that could go even to the Midwest, the part of America most terrorized by the menace of communism, that barbaric destroyer of humankind, etc. I wanted to do that without being demagogic, but by talking on an elementary level about the struggle that people have carried on in order to overcome the exploitation of man by man, talking in a simple, direct way; emotional and involving, too, because if there's no involvement on the emotional level, I don't think you can get very far.[5]

The European communist film-maker speaks as if he were a liberal American director attempting to reach the hearts of the masses. To say that Bertolucci underestimated a number of elements, most importantly the ability of the dominant mode of cinematic production to keep itself and its ideology intact, would be an understatement. The result of such naive optimism was the near destruction of the film and of its creator as a 'viable commercial property'. While Fox distributed the film in Europe at almost its full length (Bertolucci trimmed twenty minutes before its European commercial release), exhibiting it in two parts that would be shown alternately, Paramount balked. Bertolucci claimed that his contract gave him the right of final cut; Paramount rested their claim on their contract for a three and a quarter hour film. At some point the producer, Grimaldi, without Bertolucci's knowledge, had a version prepared for them at that length, which by all accounts (including that of an Italian judge[6]), was so badly cut as to be indecipherable. Matters were exacerbated when Bertolucci, with Grimaldi's consent, refused to have any version of the film shown at the 1976 New York Film Festival because the English-language version was not ready. Paramount, meanwhile, tried to sell the film. From that point on incredible complications, legal entanglements and mutual bitterness arose among all parties. Events became so complex that at one point *Variety* had to follow up one of its reports on the matter with a clarification because telex messages had garbled information.

In September 1976, Fox made an offer to take over US distribution from Paramount, and exhibit a four hour and ten minute version made and approved by Bertolucci apparently under a judge's 'invitation'.[7] (Meanwhile, later in the month, Italian authorities briefly banned the first part of the long version which, when the ban was lifted shortly afterwards, made it one of the largest grossing films in the country for the period; unfortunately, Italian attendance later fell off by fifty per cent for the second part.) In November, when Grimaldi had not yet delivered Bertolucci's four hour cut, Fox withdrew their offer. In March 1977, there was a report that Grimaldi had locked Bertolucci out of the cutting room, claiming that he had refused to make the necessary cuts. But three distinct versions of *1900* apparently did exist at the time: Bertolucci's two-part five hour and ten minute 'original' cut; his approximately four hour and twenty-five minute version; and the infamous three hour and fifteen minute cut made by Grimaldi, who was also bringing suit against Bertolucci for going over budget and making an undistributable film. Bertolucci cancelled an arrangement he had with Grimaldi to make five films for him.

By April, Bertolucci seemed to be relenting, saying he was compelled to deliver a short version of the film to Paramount in order to fulfil his contract. Paramount and Grimaldi went to court over the distributor's attempt to block the letters of credit it owed the producer. The judge ruled for Grimaldi. There was a rumour that a small American distributor was offering to buy the original cut from Paramount – with financial assistance from the Columbia Broadcasting System!

Early in May the story made *Time* magazine, which reported that in New York a 'dapper Grimaldi' was calling Bertolucci 'an egomaniac, a very sick man', while the director was said to be 'biting his knuckles in his Rome apartment', charging Grimaldi with censorship and threatening to steal the negative of the four hour and twenty-five minute version (which Grimaldi was claiming had been destroyed). Barry Diller, chairman of Paramount, was quoted as saying: 'I don't like the three-hour version. I don't like the four-and-a-half-hour version and I don't like the five-hour version. Paramount will never distribute this film.'[8]

The melodrama reached its denouement between August and September. Paramount refused to allow the New York Film Festival to show the four hour and ten minute compromise cut that Bertolucci and Grimaldi had settled on for American release. The Festival left an open play date in its schedule; a settlement was reached in early September. The film played the Festival; Bertolucci was present, as he was at a later screening at the American Film Institute in Washington, D.C. The four hour and ten minute dubbed version was also screened at the

London Film Festival that November.* Bertolucci did not appear there as promised.

In the United States, Paramount sent the film out on limited release with little publicity. Diller all but got his wish that the film would not be seen. And somewhere along the line, Paramount cut another chunk out of 35mm prints (but not from the non-theatrical 16mm prints), including the opening Liberation Day sequence. Paramount therefore won its battle completely. The film was released in such a way (and with such negative reviews) that it was barely seen, and what was seen was something close to the three and a quarter hour version which the distributor originally wanted.

The consequences of all this were horrendous for Bertolucci and are troublesome for the critic. Obviously any director and student of film wants to have a work distributed in its original version (in fact, during the fracas a group of New York film critics signed a petition to that effect). The habit of deploring the crass meddling of producers and distributors has been deeply ingrained at least since the time of Erich von Stroheim's conflict with Irving Thalberg and will continue to be so as long as film remains a means for corporations to earn surplus value. But given this, and given Bertolucci's political acumen, one cannot help but wonder again what was on his mind when he made the film. In 1975, before the battle had begun, he was talking of 'the poetry and the prose, the dialectic between red flags and American dollars. I undermined this monument with such powerful explosives that it threatens to destroy everything around it. . . .'[9] Was Grimaldi correct in judging Bertolucci an egomaniac? Is it possible Bertolucci could not have foreseen the clash of ideologies and production modes which would result from his film, and that he would emerge the loser?

Equally serious questions arise for the critic interested in textual analysis. What *is* the text of *1900*? Bertolucci's first cut, which is impossible to see? His five hour and ten minute European cut? Or the four hour and ten minute dubbed American-British cut? (Grimaldi's truncated version and Paramount's reduced theatrical distribution print may be safely ignored.) From one perspective, the two latter versions cannot be looked at as unique works, representing the aspirations and articulations of one governing, directorial intelligence. Each is a version that resulted from some kind of external interference. But at the same time, they *do* exist. They are complete texts, given form by the director, albeit under duress. As such they await the response of audience and critic, a response dictated by a reading of them which assumes all the complexities that resulted in their existence.

* Sources vary by a few minutes on the length of the compromise version.

Must we, therefore, confront two *1900s*? The answer, regrettably, is both yes and no. I have been able to see, only once, and under a certain pressure of time, the undubbed, European version. I have seen the American version a great many times, but have not had the opportunity to compare them side by side. Therefore, discussion of the film's cutting pattern will of necessity be tentative, and I must agree with Bertolucci's own assessment, voiced both in public and to me on the telephone, that they are, essentially, different texts of the same film; that when he cut down the long version what he changed was its 'heartbeat', its 'rhythm' or 'music'. More precisely, in creating the shortened text of *1900*, he and Franco Arcalli worked one of the more masterful jobs of editing in the history of cinema.

The basic events constructed by the narrative are precisely the same in both films. They both begin on 25 April 1945, Liberation Day in Italy. The peasants hunt down the fascist Attila and his wife Regina. A young peasant, Leonida, holds a gun to the head of Alfredo, the *padrone* of the Berlinghieri farm, and brings him to the barn where the old *padrone* hanged himself, declaring that there are no more masters. The film then moves into 'flashback', to 1901, the overture to *Rigoletto* heard on the soundtrack; a peasant dressed as Rigoletto announces the death of Verdi. On that day two children are born: the young Alfredo, whom we have already seen in the framing narrative, and the bastard child Olmo, who will become the revolutionary leader of the peasants. Both films trace the intricate and intertwined histories of owners and peasants, and both focus upon the relationship of Alfredo and Olmo, with the fascist, Attila, acting as the club, the *santa manganello* that breaks them apart.

Both versions concentrate on the rise of socialist consciousness among the peasantry, the varying fortunes of Alfredo and Olmo, the terrors visited upon the country in general, and this farm community in particular, by the rule of the fascists; both end with the triumph and celebration of the peasants at the end of the Second World War, and their defeat by the partisans who, acting as the unification committee for the post-war government, take away their arms. Both films indulge in variations of a coda in which Alfredo and Olmo struggle alone into the future of history, owner and worker, *padrone* and peasant, becoming symbols of continuing class warfare.

In short, Bertolucci cut no major events from the film, with a few exceptions, such as a sequence in which Alfredo, returned from home duty during World War I, indulges in some crude sexual play with his niece Regina, who will become Attila's wife (he masturbates her with his rifle), and a sequence in which Olmo exhorts the peasants, in despair over their oppression by the fascists, with a rousing revolution-

76

ary speech. But, as I say, nothing is removed that changes *1900*'s narrative thrust or direction. The structural changes made to reduce the film's length by one hour essentially involve the removal of certain shots and scenes from *within* sequences which are otherwise left to stand within the narrative, and a kind of trimming of certain shots – removing, for example, the end of a camera movement that settles on an object, or cutting short the movement of figures in a landscape.

The original *1900* is a film of leisure, detail and social-political passion. Though not of intensity. It bears no relationship to the slow, purposive building of political allegory found in Angelopoulos' four-hour *O Megalexandros*. With the exception of the final sequence, Bertolucci is not concerned with the allegorical abstractions, the political movements removed from time that concern the Greek director. The original *1900* instead builds its narrative structure on a straight-forward sequence of events, which create the illusion of being historically determined. The characters and their conflicts, though politically motivated, are developed within the codes of psychological realism familiar to any filmgoer. The American version of the film foreshortens all this. Its narrative is more direct, less concerned with detail, and poorer in *mise en scène* and the carefully articulated rhythm of the European version. But I must repeat that both versions work from the formal codes of realism to an extent greater than any of Bertolucci's previous films. Those conventions are what I wish to concentrate upon now. Of necessity, I will depend upon the American and British texts, referring to the European version when possible.*

In order to understand the generation of these conventions, I want to return to the painterly aspect of Bertolucci's style which I referred to at the end of the last chapter. The work of René Magritte informs much of the visual structure of *The Spider's Stratagem*; *Last Tango in Paris* uses the tormented figures of a man and a woman in two paintings by Francis Bacon during its credit sequence. The credits for *1900* are placed over a painting as well. There is a slow zoom back from the figures that make up a gigantic canvas by the late nineteenth-century Italian post-Impressionist, Giuseppe Pellizza da Volpedo. While Pellizza had been a major Italian exponent of the 'divisionist' style, in the manner of Seurat, the canvas revealed at the beginning of the film is a markedly 'realistic' work, depicting a group of peasants marching forward. In the foreground are two men looking straight ahead, jackets over their shoulders. One holds an arm across his stomach; the other has the thumb of his left hand hooked under his vest. On their left, looking at

---

* In early 1985 the American distributor, Films Incorporated, announced that the full-length, subtitled Italian version would finally be available in the U.S.

77

Pellizza da Volpedo's 'Il Quarto Stato' (The Fourth Estate), which appears in the credit sequence of *1900*

them, is a woman with a child in one arm, the other arm outstretched, almost in an imploring gesture. Behind them are three long rows of people, looking in various directions, some with their arms and hands held forward, as if talking, gesticulating – indicating by the gesture the desperation that has led to their march. The general movement signified in the composition is that of purposive, collective action. Behind the figures is a vaguely defined landscape. Before them an open space, the spectators' space, which the marchers appear ready to enter. The colours are predominantly brown and green, as they are in *1900*.

The title of the painting, completed in 1902, is *The Fourth Estate (Il Quarto Stato)*. Earlier versions of the canvas (which were done in a more recognizably Impressionist, divisionist style) were titled *The Ambassadors of Hunger*, *The Living Torrent*, and *The Worker's Progress*.[10] Pellizza had undertaken the progressive canvases that lead to *The Fourth Estate* under the impetus of his own socialist inclinations. He wrote in 1895 that he was making 'an attempt ... to raise myself above the vulgarity of subjects which do not conform to a strong idea. I am attempting Social painting ... a crowd of people, workers of the soil, who are intelligent, strong, robust, united, advance like a torrent, overthrowing every obstacle in its path, thirsty for justice.'[11] This comment could have been used by Bertolucci as an epigraph for his film (and in fact is used, by virtue of his 'quoting' the painting).* So closely does the style and content of the painting generate the style and content of the film that one might transfer Pellizza's description of his work as 'Social painting' to the film, and look at it as an example of 'social', 'socialist' or, perhaps, socialist realist cinema.

Unfortunately 'socialist realist' carries with it a great deal of ideological and historical baggage. Memories are called up of an ideal, imposed by the state, of monumental figures of workers in static poses, of an impoverished, oppressive realism that permits no stylistic variation, no entrance into the work of an individual authorial aesthetic or ideology. But despite its often unpleasant history, one finds that 'socialist realism' embraces a variety of artistic forms and articulations.

* And, like Pellizza's work, Bertolucci's suffered a similar critical fate. One of Pellizza's critics said (in a statement prophetic of *1900*'s reception and effect) that the figures in the painting 'leave the spectator cold, as they will leave the capitalist or the authority towards whom this collective demonstration is directed, indifferent.' Other critics of the time, 'used to gruesomely realistic or pathetically sentimental depictions of the working classes, found this idealized version hard to accept.' There was one major difference between the reception of *The Fourth Estate* and *1900*. In the case of the former, 'only socialist critics ... appreciated its message'. In the case of the latter, even left-wing critics found much to dislike in the film.

In cinema, the term can be applied to the political film of late Weimar Germany, to Italian neo-realism, to the Brechtian-Sirkian modulations of Rainer Werner Fassbinder (particularly in *Berlin Alexanderplatz*), to any film that, working within the broad limits of cinematic realism, defines the struggle of working people against oppression. In his book *Soviet Socialist Realism* C. Vaughan James writes: 'Socialist-realist art must portray reality objectively and assist the masses to understand historical processes and their own role in them'[12] – a statement that puts Bertolucci's remark about making a film which talks 'in a simple, direct way' about 'the struggle people have carried on in order to overcome the exploitation of man by man' in a somewhat less naive light.

To examine *1900* under the socialist realist rubric helps us understand its form, the problems created by that form, as well as the film's place in Bertolucci's career. The experimental, modernist structures of his work up to *1900* were part of the general attack on cinematic realism being carried on during the 60s. By the mid-70s, he had decided to return to more conventional forms with which he would express a clear socialist commentary on class struggle. In retrospect we can see that *1900* belongs to a general movement, on the part of many European film-makers, back to older realist conventions. But at the time of its inception and execution, I think Bertolucci was not so much aware of a change occurring in cinema history as attempting to perform another dialectical manoeuvre, part of which involves, yet again, a reaction to Godard and that film-maker's own reaction to the events of May 1968.

Bertolucci seems to have viewed Godard's withdrawal from commercial narrative film-making and the formation of the agit-prop Dziga Vertov group with both aesthetic and ideological disdain. This reaction seems evident both in the films Bertolucci made in the early 70s – culminating in *1900* – and in some comments made in defence of his own rapidly changing aesthetic. Regarding the ability of art, and film in particular, to change anything in the dominant ideology of a given culture, he is quite pragmatic and anti-Brechtian: 'in the sense of having any political impact, being truly effective, no. What you change with films is ... nothing.'[13] As if in direct response to Godard's cine-activism of the late 60s and early 70s is Bertolucci's comment (repeated in various interviews) that 'I definitely do not think, as many believed in 1968, that the camera can be a machine-gun'.[14] The statement reveals an overreaction to, indeed some anxiety about, the direction some film and much film criticism took in the years after 1968. In their article 'Towards a Third Cinema', Fernando Solanas and Octavio Getino wrote: 'The camera is the inexhaustible *expropriator of image weapons*; the projector, *a gun that can shoot 24 frames per second.*'[15]

But most radical film-makers simply hoped that cinema could be a means of political enquiry and revelation. Godard was foremost among them, calling not for the making of political films, but for the making of films politically. He would rework the entire structure of image building and image reception. He would restructure the means of production and distribution (as his colleagues in Latin America and other developing countries were attempting to do at the same time).

Bertolucci moves in the opposite direction (though simultaneously in the same direction as many of his colleagues in Europe), embracing traditional cinematic forms and – to his ultimate dismay – conventional means of distribution. The 'realist' models he adopted guaranteed that *1900* would not have the effect of a 'machine-gun', for in their formal construction they tend to comfort the audience rather than attack them. Yet at the same time he did hope that his film would have a didactic effect. By expressing a socialist ideology through its realist form, Bertolucci believed the film could reach a large audience who would otherwise be put off by modernist structures or the agit-prop hectorings of some of the Dziga Vertov films (recall again his statement about the film touching the hearts of an anti-communist mid-western audience).

The contradictions and self-deceptions pile up. While Godard moved in a straight trajectory, from the experiments with conventional narrative forms in the early 60s through the complete rejection of those forms in the late 60s and throughout the 70s (until he attempted a return to commercial cinema in the early 80s), Bertolucci begins his career by questioning the conventions and then attempts to embrace them by making something akin to a political *Gone With the Wind*. However, if we look at this process more closely, in dialectical fashion, other curious complications appear. From the very beginning of his career Bertolucci, like Godard – like all cine-modernists – had an enormous affection for American cinema while at the same time wanting to counter its conventions, knowing they were both deceptive and exhausted. Like Godard, he was scornful *and* envious of American film's ability to hide its form and thereby make the means of its production invisible. He knew, to the contrary, that, as Terry Lovell states, 'images are ideological because they hide their own processes of construction'.[16] He wished therefore to foreground ideology by foregrounding form, placing the spectator in an active role within the process of the production of meaning. By means of that activity, the viewer would not be manipulated by an illusory appearance of reality created by images and narratives that denied their own existence.

Therefore, it is possible to conclude that, contrary to its immediate effect and Bertolucci's own intentions, *1900* is *not* a realist film. Despite its ostensible use of the classical codes of continuity, character development and motivation, despite (or, as we shall see in a moment, because of) a camera style that embraces character and environment in the familiar 'epic' movements of a large-scale American (or British, or Viscontian) historical film, it in fact subverts all of these. Part of that subversion exists, of course, in the film's political discourse: as I have noted, the *socialist* aspect of its realism reacts with its formal apparatus to create a tension between the saying and the said, between form and the content generated by the form. Another aspect of the subversion exists precisely in the history of Bertolucci's preceding films and those of his modernist contemporaries.

What separates *1900* from the conventional realist mode is (to borrow a deconstructionist notion) the phenomenon of 'difference' – with the double meaning given to that term by Jacques Derrida of 'differ' and 'defer'. While Bertolucci defers to Hollywood realism, the film is *different* from Hollywood realism because too much has come between *1900* and the forms of the classical style that precedes it. And what has come between is precisely the work of such as Rossellini, Pasolini, Godard, Straub and Bertolucci and their rethinking and reworking of the conventional forms. James Monaco has said that 'after 1960, every film made, whether its director intended it or not, had to be seen with this dual vision: it was at once a story and comment on storytelling'.[17] Consciously or not, all films since *Breathless* differ from the old realist forms because those forms have already been exposed and may no longer be used in a state of innocence. Any attempt to return to the classic forms (and this is true even in the work of the most unselfconscious contemporary American hack) only exists within a state of *difference* between those forms and what has been done to them by film-makers in the 60s and early 70s. The classical form *only* exists on the other side of the space created by the examination and exposure of that form by modernist film-makers. Bertolucci could return to 'realism' only because he knew that illusory realism no longer existed and could not be recreated without automatically reflecting upon its own existence as a conventional form. A trace of the modernist project falls upon every film made after the early 60s.

1900 is therefore seen twice (or, given its two texts, four times), once as a lyrical-melodramatic (indeed somewhat Verdian) celebration of the rise of socialism, the fight against fascism and the struggle of classes and generations in a northern Italian peasant community from the turn of the century to 1945, and again as a reflection or rumination upon the means of formally creating such a narrative. We move therefore from a concept of 'socialist realism' to 'meta-realism': a realism conscious of itself and its history.

One manifestation of this is evident in the film's montage structure and the theory supporting it (bearing in mind that we are dealing with the montage of a work which exists in two different cuts). Approaching the film by means of this particular structural element links it with the earlier discussion of Bertolucci's ideas about cutting, and also places it in the context of a major theoretical concern of neo-realist and modernist film-makers. In the 60s Bertolucci despised montage – in theory, at least. He looked upon cutting as a form of castration, of 'imperialism'. His thinking paralleled the ideas of André Bazin, whose theories formed the basis of New Wave practice and drew inspiration from a positive attraction to neo-realism and a negative reaction to the practice of classical American cinema. The neo-realists called for a long, unmediated gaze of the camera eye on the given world. American film construction depended upon shots of short duration and rapid alternation, building a narrative out of bits and pieces in such a manner as to create the illusion of continuity. Bazin called this method of construction into question. Believing he was theorizing an aesthetic of realism, he called for the use of the long take, in deep focus when possible, that would permit the spectator an uninterrupted gaze into a cinematic space analogous to the perceptions one has of the existing 'real' world. Now Bazin was aware that this analogy is based on artifice, that seeing cinema and seeing 'reality' are not the same thing. What he never quite thought through, however, was that the long take, by breaking with Hollywood conventions, would draw attention both to those conventions and to the *un*reality of the film image. The longer we are permitted to gaze at a shot, the more we tend to become aware of its existence as a shot; that is, as an event specific to cinema.

The modernist film-makers who followed Bazin's theoretical lead wrestled with the problem. Godard attempted to deal with it both in his 50s theoretical writings and in his 60s films, in which he often alternated shots of long duration with jump-cut sequences that defied spatial and temporal continuity. The Hungarian film-maker Miklós Jancsó tried literally to reduce the cuts in his films to a bare minimum; his 1971 film about peasant socialism at the turn of the century, *Red Psalm*, contains only twenty-seven shots. Bertolucci, in his preface to the screenplay of *Before the Revolution*, had asked for a film that contained, at the most, only twenty shots (Jancsó later bested that desire in a film, *Electra*, that contained only four cuts, one for each change of the film magazine in the camera).

As late as 1971, Bertolucci was still attracted to the theory of the long take, despite the fact that he had begun working with his editor, Franco Arcalli, in perfecting a fine sense of editing structures. 'I move the camera as if I was gesturing with it,' he says. 'But imperialism is an enemy of these "gestures", of the assembling of the daily rushes into an ensemble of gestures. The moment of imperialism is the editing of the film. This is when one cuts out all that was direct and "gesticular" in the rushes; this is the moment when the producer takes over. He takes the electrocardiogram of the film and cuts out all the high points, in order to create a flat line.' Bertolucci praises the editing of Griffith and Eisenstein, but goes on to say: 'I said earlier that editing was a beautiful invention, an expressive device; just like the trade unions were great at one time; but in the next moment, capital stepped in and interfered in the unions, like in America. . . .'[18]

Even though Bertolucci did come to peace with and find facility in the editing process, it is clear that he was still seeking the modernist's ideal of an unedited film. In *1900*, cutting practice more successfully matches his earlier theories than do the previous films (again I speak rather tentatively about a film that was, in fact, edited three times and under duress). With the exception of *Partner*, and in a manner completely different from that film, *1900* depends somewhat less on cutting and montage than the earlier work. The shots are not particularly long, although longer in the original than in the British-American version. The linkages between shots are employed to move the narrative from place to place, or to create parallel actions, or to enter small but important details into a sequence as if in support of the characters and events. In the film's prologue, for example, the young peasant, Leonida, enters the *padrone*'s house to bring him to trial at gunpoint. As he goes in, Bertolucci cuts to a shot of the child wiping his feet on the doormat, a ritual gesture of respect offered at the very moment when the old rituals and orders of respect are meant to be destroyed. Leonida leads Alfredo through the barn, and there is a sudden cut to a high-angle shot, bearing down on the *padrone*. The cut and the camera's gaze look forward (or, more accurately, backward) to the sequence in which the old Alfredo hangs himself in the same barn. This is one of the few expressive cuts in a film where most narrative information is revealed within shots rather than through their association (quite the opposite practice to that of *Before the Revolution* and the films between). But despite – perhaps in the face of – the film's linear style and apparently conventional *découpage*, there emerges a response to that style: a concentration on the shot rather than on the cut.

Speaking of his camera practice in *1900*, Bertolucci said: 'The camera has a dialectical relationship to the actors and is not merely recording the event, but is an invisible participant with its own soul. Sometimes the camera even enters into competition with the actor – while the actor moves, the camera moves independently. I think that in *1900* this invisible character, the camera, has found its own maturity and has become more natural than in my previous movies.'[19]

'More natural'! Once again we are faced with the notion of *1900* being a more realistic work than Bertolucci's previous films. However, despite the fact that the camera no more has 'its own soul' or acts 'more naturally' here than elsewhere, there is a certain truth in what Bertolucci says. The camera in *1900* is a quieter, slightly more withdrawn instrument of observation, although it does engage in stately crane shots and sweeping movements typical of Bertolucci's and Storaro's style – sometimes rising above a scene into the trees and pushing the branches away with its physical presence. Mostly, however, it tends to embrace action rather than intrude into it. In this film the camera style comes closest to the Rossellinian ideal of observing figures in a significant environment, finding the perfect distance, and framing, embracing and absorbing the action that is set up for the camera rather than creating and manipulating it (as it does, for example, in the almost expressionist style of *Last Tango*). Instead of gesturing independently of the characters, perceiving more than they do, the camera here accepts the process of the characters' political movement, envelops and, in effect, assents to it. In its camera style and its reliance on the shot, *1900* moves through neo-realism and modernism, recapitulating and counterpointing those forms, using them as a base on which is built the superstructure of a more recognizable and conventional cinematic realism.

I admit to the possibility of creating an over-ingenious argument. The cutting pattern of *1900*, even while alluding to the long take, is essentially quite conventional. Shots are matched, sequences are built by means of the classical codes of shot/reaction shot, and the spectator is securely situated within spaces that are defined by the interchange of gazes. But in the *difference* created between the conventional and the neo-realist and modernist structures and in the tensions that exist between form and content, *1900* defines its success and its imperfections. The dialectic of its form is, finally, insufficiently worked out; the conflicts between the ideology under which it was made, the ideology it speaks, its immediate form and the formal history of contemporary cinema that it seems simultaneously to deny and to embrace, almost guarantee an imperfect text. A work doomed by the conflicts within it and which surrounded it.

At the same time, because it embraces so much, and because it represents Bertolucci's major effort at reaching a large audience with a difficult political discourse, *1900* will act as a critical touchstone in the discussion that follows. I will be returning to it at various points, using it as a means of moving backward and forward in the examination of Bertolucci's career. With a notion of his variations on the modernist project, we are in a better position now to examine closely the three films of the early 70s with which he established his style and his reputation, films filled with intellectual and rhetorical flourish, articulating a form that generates meaning through a complex interaction of shot and cut, of allusion, gesture and perceptual subtlety.

In *The Spider's Stratagem*, *The Conformist* and *Last Tango in Paris*, Bertolucci examines and develops a number of the formal strategies nascent in *Before the Revolution* and suppressed in *Partner*. He experiments with temporal structures by means of editing and through the expressive possibilities of spatial organization within the shot, especially as these are articulated by camera movement. He perfects an intricate relationship between the perceptions of the character within the fiction and the perceptions of the viewer observing the fiction. In speaking about *Before the Revolution*, I noted that from time to time in that film Bertolucci attempts what might be termed a cross-match of perceptions, manipulating the viewer's situation inside and outside the narrative, within and without its characters' own point of view. He allows the viewer to share a character's perspective and at the same time creates a separation from it to allow a larger perception that generates understanding beyond what the characters see and feel. The perceiving eye is a constant point of reference in this film. The viewer outside the narrative, like Gina within it, looks at Fabrizio, concentrating the gaze. In a playful sequence of jump cuts, Gina comes into the frame again and again wearing, each time, a different pair of spectacles. In another sequence she views Fabrizio through a camera obscura which, in this black and white film, reflects to her a colour image of Fabrizio as he cavorts outside.

Constructing the perceptual act as a major signifier of a film is by no means a strategy unique to Bertolucci. The forming of the spectator's subjectivity in relation to the fiction created by the film is fundamental to the classical Hollywood style. Critical reflection upon this formation is a major element of Hitchcock's variations on that style, and a matter of investigation by such modernist film-makers as Antonioni, Godard and Fassbinder. Bertolucci takes the enquiry further and makes perceptual interplay a major element of both the form and the subject of his major work. In so doing, he creates a counterpoint of melodrama and distanciation – of the placement of the viewer within the narrative and at a speculative distance from it – in a manner quite different from Hitchcock, Fassbinder and, especially, Godard.

And, of course, Brecht. In my discussion of *Before the Revolution* I pointed out Bertolucci's unhappiness with the Godardian interpretation of Brechtian theory. As interpreted by Godard, Brechtian theory insists that the spectator remain always distant from the events occurring in the spectacle being viewed. The essential structure of the Brechtian model places the spectator in a contemplative stance, refusing identification, refusing to allow the film to become a 'mirror' (in the sense in which Jacques Lacan uses the metaphor) within which the spectator sees an illusory image of self, with only a hint of difference and 'otherness'.[20] Brecht wants difference and otherness to be clearly enunciated by the text. He insists (again to revert to Lacan) that the spectator is an adult, existing in the symbolic realm of language, who must always know that he or she is not contained in the spectacle or even reflected in it or by it. Through the separation, the spectator is permitted at all times to be aware of the text, to see, to listen, to comprehend, and finally to learn the text's ideological lessons.

Bertolucci, on the contrary, is profoundly concerned with the 'mirror stage', with that moment of imaginary identification of the child with its self and its mother. This concern, with all its attendant Oedipal apparatus, becomes a major subject of Bertolucci's films and a major aspect of their form. He wishes to move the viewer through something analogous to the processes of identification and separation which Lacan discusses, probing the cinematic analogue of the mirror stage, the relationship of observer and screen image, and the recognition of otherness that must attend it. He attempts to manipulate the function of the screen as both mirror and Other, creating upon it images which reflect the spectator, engulf him or her, and – often at the same time – indicate the difference between the spectator and the image, the self and that which is not self. The narratives that result from this complex process are themselves *about* perception, identification, separation and loss, the way characters see themselves and others and are confused by both.

The Conformist most profoundly demonstrates these processes, for its subject is the way a particular individual perceives himself and the world, himself *in* the world, and the way the spectator both participates in the character's perceptions and sees what the character cannot see. One of the film's structuring principles is hallucination, the creation of events within a *mise en scène* which refuses a clear separation of what is and is not seen and known, understood or remembered. From this structure emerges a dominant metaphor of blindness and sight. The central narrative takes place in the 1930s and concerns an individual, Marcello Clerici, who, because he thinks he was involved in a homosexual incident as a child, during which he killed his seducer, lunges towards normality by marrying an 'ordinary girl' from the middle class and becoming a Fascist agent. In this role he is sent to locate and help in the assassination of his former professor, Luca Quadri, an Italian resistance fighter who lives with his wife, Anna, in Paris. The 'story', from a novel by Alberto Moravia, is continually threatened by the cliché that attempts to explain fascism as a displaced manifestation of sexual abnormality. Fortunately, Bertolucci manages to transcend the cliché by structuring his film in such a way that its form and style place the sexual concerns of its character within more profound aberrations. The film articulates the contradictions that mark the fascist mind in ways more instructive, satisfying and provocative than repressed homosexuality.

Hallucination, blindness, the distortion of vision inform the structure of every shot, every cut in the film. Even its temporal structure is formed to manifest the fragmentation of perception suffered by a man of bad memory, bad conscience and bad faith. Bertolucci takes Moravia's plodding, linear narrative and breaks it into pieces of mis-recollection and bad intent. The film begins close to its moment of climax, with Clerici sitting in a Paris hotel room, just before dawn, awaiting the call from his fascist colleague which will initiate his mission, the assassination of Professor Quadri. The hotel room is alternately lightened and darkened by the flashing of a red neon sign outside, creating an intensity of light and dark that recalls all those hotel rooms and their adjacent neon signs in so many 30s and 40s movies. (The effect of the light on Clerici's face, and the way Bertolucci cuts to the close-ups of that face, influences another admirer of 30s and 40s American cinema, and of Bertolucci as well: it is the inspiration for the opening sequence of Martin Scorsese's *Taxi Driver*, in which Travis Bickle's face reflects the red lights of the streets surrounding his cab.)

Clerici gets his call and is troubled by the knowledge that the professor's wife will be accompanying her husband. He priggishly covers his own wife's naked backside, walks out past the arcades of the old Hotel d'Orsay, and is picked up by his henchman, the strong man provided to him by the fascists, Manganiello (named Angelo in the novel; Bertolucci changes it into an allusion to the *santo manganello*, the nickname of the club used by the fascist *squadristi* to beat up their opponents). The two drive through Paris and into a misty, wintry landscape towards their victims. As they drive, as Bertolucci examines their faces, or observes Clerici leaving the car and walking beside it, the 'past' intrudes upon the 'present' and the narrative is created through a series of flashbacks, some of which are out of sequence. Time and events slip through Clerici's grasp and, when caught, take the appearance of things partly seen, wrongly perceived, or perceived with such distortion as to signify to the viewer the lack of clarity within Clerici's memory and his perception of the events at the very time in the fiction they were meant to occur. The viewer is, in turn, required to perceive and understand the misperceptions and to respond to the considerable energy and visual acumen that Bertolucci demonstrates in creating them.

Here is one example. Clerici recalls his first meeting with the fascist official who gave him his job. As he is driving with Manganiello, the camera isolates him in a close-up. The music of an Italian popular song of the 30s fades in on the soundtrack, and there is a cut to a shot of a radio studio, the camera dollying in on Clerici from behind as he looks through the studio glass at three women singing, in the manner of the Andrews Sisters. A piano is to their left, the orchestra on the right. The background is white, with a black Art Deco design painted on it. With the studio window bordered in black at top and bottom, there is an impression that Clerici is looking at a movie screen. A voice is heard talking to him about his forthcoming marriage, and Bertolucci cuts to a 180 degree reverse shot which reveals a figure seated at a desk behind Clerici. (This is not a reverse in the conventional sense, for Clerici is not looking at the person speaking, and the space behind him is unknown to the viewer until the reverse shot is made; the effect produced is of a disorienting arrangement of space.) The figure revealed, we will learn, is Italo, Clerici's friend and a Party propagandist, who is about to give a radio talk on the spiritual alliance between Italy and Germany. He is blind.

There is a reverse shot back again to Clerici, who turns round, explaining to Italo that what he wants from marriage is the appearance of normality. There is a third reverse, back to Italo, and the two banter about Clerici's fiancée and his sexual activities with her. The reverses end with a sudden close-up of the Italian Andrews Sisters, happily singing their song, 'Who is Happier Than I', followed by a cut back to Clerici in the car, deep in thought, wrapped tightly in his hat and coat, the windscreen wiper, in soft focus before him, diagonally cutting across the left side of his face, which is slightly in shadow. The scene cuts back to the singers and then to Clerici, this time from an angle that has shifted some 45 degrees from the previous shot of him in the studio. He is in profile; in the rear a door can be seen opening; a figure looks in announcing that Italo has two minutes until his broadcast. Clerici asks Italo if he is certain the Party Secretary will arrive. The camera tracks to the right, to Italo, who assures Clerici that the Secretary is interested in him and will come. In all the shots of Italo throughout this part of the sequence, the main source of light is the lamp on his desk. The resulting chiaroscuro creates an extreme contrast between the bright white of the studio and the cavernous darkness of the space occupied by Clerici and Italo on the other side of the glass.

As Italo comments that while everyone in the world wants to be different, Clerici wants to be the same as everyone else, Bertolucci returns to the shot of Clerici against the window, the white studio and the singers behind him. He begins pacing back and forth – the camera tracking with him – moving from the white of the studio to the dark of the adjacent wall, talking of his father (who, we learn later, is confined in a lunatic asylum), who was once a fascist, who once met Hitler. Clerici turns and again faces the studio as the singers finish and run off. A woman announcer is heard summing up the programme. Clerici turns and the shot changes to Italo surrounded by the dark; he walks round the room's blackness, startled by Clerici's information about his father, the camera following him until he moves across to Clerici's right by the studio window and blindly looks off in the opposite direction.

Italo's blind gaze, his wanderings in the dark, the movement of the camera and the cutting create, as I said, a spatial disorientation within the area the two men inhabit, which is exaggerated by the contrasts of light and dark – the film's major visual signifier. The spatial dislocation is echoed on the soundtrack as suddenly a strange whistling, a kind of imitation bird call, is heard on the soundtrack (it is in fact the old RAI signature for the news, and may not be so strange to a native Italian viewer). Bertolucci cuts to a medium close-up of a fat man making this noise into a microphone. But the figure is not in central frame. He is to the left, against the white background of the studio; more than half of the right side of the screen is black. The anomaly of this sound and figure, particularly as it is inflected by the framing, following abruptly on the strange story we have just heard, continues the disruptive effect of the sequence. The spectator wishes to learn more about Clerici, but composition, camera movement, cutting all intrude upon our desire for plot; they are unwelcome and at the same time seductive, for they too provide us with information, more sensuous, mysterious and incomplete than that offered by the dialogue.

The disruptions continue. The camera tracks left past the whistling man and moves to a position behind Clerici, who is still looking through the window into the studio in which Italo has suddenly appeared. On the soundtrack, the announcer introduces Italo and he begins his speech, his fingers flying over his braille script. As the camera tracks from the whistling man to Clerici, the focus changes from the background (Italo seated in the studio) to the foreground (the back of Clerici's head). As Italo begins his talk about Germany and Italy the studio lights go down, Italo is highlighted against a dark background, while, simultaneously, Bertolucci changes focus again, so that Italo is clearly seen in the background, Clerici in soft focus in the foreground. He then cuts to a 180 degree reverse, but this time from the opposite side of the studio glass, so that we see Clerici peering out, the reflection of Italo superimposed upon him. Clerici begins to move towards his chair, and the object of his gaze is now reflected above him (and since the shot is made from the other side of the glass, other objects are reflected on his face); he then turns and sits, chin in hand, waiting. The following cut is directly to Italo, talking of the 'Prussian image' of Mussolini and the 'Latin image' of Hitler. He is involved in his speech, composed slightly off-centre, to the left of the frame.

A cut is made back to the previous shot of Clerici, still from the other side of the glass, but closer to him than previously. The reflection of Italo is in soft focus, the image of the ideologue impressed upon his pupil. The darkness of the space occupied by Clerici is highlighted by the table lamp in the background of the composition. There is another reverse shot to Italo, speaking now about the grand fascist anti-democratic, anti-parliamentarian revolutions, and then a cut to an oblique angle of Clerici, this time taken from within the dark room next to the studio. The camera is at a distance from him (he is still resting his head in his hands) and the border of the window, distorted by the angle of the shot and the camera lens, is brightly lit. The points of attention in this shot are carefully controlled: the spectator is first aware of a new and disorienting angle and looks for a familiar object. Clerici, in the position in which we have previously seen him, draws the attention of the gaze, which is still troubled by the distorted border of light created by the studio window, and by another figure in the room. Not until Clerici himself starts and looks up, and this other figure moves his hand, does the spectator clearly make out the positions of two men in the dark. No indication is given as to how this other figure arrived at his place, and his presence surprises Clerici, who appears to have been sleeping.* The viewer is permitted to see more than Clerici has, and at the same time only permitted to see *when* and *as* Clerici sees. Once again the viewer is placed outside and inside the hallucinatory realm of Clerici's memory.

The two men begin talking, Clerici anxious to know if he has been accepted into the Party apparatus. Bertolucci executes something like a conventional reverse shot, from behind Clerici, looking at the Party Secretary. The room remains dark; on the left, a desk with the lamp on it unbalances the frame. The Secretary recalls for Clerici how the latter first came to his office with proposals, and Bertolucci cuts to a flashback within the flashback, to a high-angle shot of an enormous space, the interior ground floor of a building, with a lone desk in the

---

* The oneiric aspects of Clerici's perceptions are discussed by T. Jefferson Kline in his essay 'The Unconformist'.

centre. Clerici enters and demands to see the Secretary. There is a cut to a lower angle of Clerici, the camera suddenly booming up as he walks off into the vastness of the room. (The influence of Welles' *The Trial*, with its enormous spaces and active camera, is marked here, and will reappear often in the course of the film.) Over the visuals we hear the Party Secretary in the radio studio talking to Clerici about why people want to join the fascists – some out of fear, most for the money. As he talks of this, Bertolucci returns to the radio studio and indulges in what are for this sequence some fairly standard over-the-shoulder shots of Clerici and the Secretary, who says that Clerici does not seem to have any of these usual motives. Clerici asks how soon he can expect an answer. 'Soon,' he is told, and the shot changes back to the *other* side of the studio glass, so that we now see but do not hear Clerici and the Secretary talking. The reflection of Italo hangs between them, his speech (which can be dimly heard behind their entire conversation) momentarily becoming prominent on the soundtrack. Bertolucci returns to a shot over the Secretary's shoulder, looking at Clerici, who will not answer the questions about his reasons for wanting to work for the Party and only reasserts his willingness to take part in a mission. The Secretary tells him he will introduce him to the Minister, and puts on his hat.

A cut is then made to a point presumably after this interview. Clerici is seen once again in the enormous spaces of the Fascist office building, walking down a corridor whose windows cast alternating shadow and light, then up a flight of stairs, the camera situated underneath so that only Clerici's shadow is seen. Before he enters the room there is an inserted shot of a woman's legs dangling, then a shot of Clerici looking through a curtain, followed by a point-of-view shot to the woman herself (a woman who will appear twice again in the course of the film). She and Clerici exchange glances. She sits on the Minister's desk. He invites her to lie back on it; she lies across the desk, following the movement of his hand, yielding to his embraces. The camera zooms back to reveal that Clerici has in fact been observing this strange ritual from the far reaches of another enormous hall. Once again our perceptions have been skewed. It is not particularly clear at what chronological point Clerici has seen this, for after this scene he is back in the corridors of the Ministry. Men go by, their heads hidden by statues they are carrying. Clerici is called back to the Minister's office (or perhaps this is his second visit, the sequence with the woman on the desk having occurred when he first visited the office). The toadies accompanying him express their pleasure at his willingness to volunteer for an assignment against an anti-fascist. At this point, Bertolucci returns to Clerici in the car.

Distorted perceptions: the Minister's office in *The Conformist*

This entire sequence (which in actual running time is relatively brief) serves as an example of the style of the film as a whole. Almost expressionist in its exaggeration of space, hallucinatory in its displacements and distortions of what the character perceives, playing continually with what is seen, not seen, thought to be seen both by Clerici and the viewer who observes him and shares his observations, it sets up the structure of an unstable and oppressive world in which the character wanders. Clerici wants to believe he is in control of this world – gaining control is the driving force of his life. But the way this world is created by Bertolucci indicates that it in fact controls both the character and our perception of him. An interesting phenomenon occurs in the process. Moravia's novel (at least its English version) creates a banal character in the most banal prose. Moravia's Clerici is a spiritually dead man in a deadening bourgeois environment (the Fascist substrate of this environment is only alluded to in the novel), who attempts to embrace that environment and is destroyed in the process. The verbal and narrative structure of the book monotonously iterates the character's quest for normality – an irony quickly used up, dissolved in its own obviousness.

Bertolucci's film, on the contrary, is almost explosive in its energy. Rather than attempt to reproduce the banality of Clerici's personality, the film generates a passionate excitement about that personality by signifying, through the way he is observed, the chaos, the grotesque distortions, the hysteria of the personality and its political confusions. This could have been a dangerous gambit were it not for Bertolucci's control over the film's structure. He could, like the Italian futurists, have fallen into the trap of celebrating fascism by adumbrating the signifiers of energy and destruction that mark its ideology.

Obviously Bertolucci does not celebrate fascism, but attempts instead to capture a sense of the hysteria, indeed the schizophrenia, of the fascist's (or at least this one fictional fascist's) view of himself and the world. Entering Clerici's perceptions, he takes enormous pleasure in recreating a kind of nightmare vision of Rome and Paris in the 30s, which is constituted not so much out of history as out of the history of cinema ('my memory was ... of movies, pictures of this moment,' he says[21]). For example, in another flashback sequence Clerici visits his fiancée, Giulia. In classical *film noir* style, the room they are in is marked by the shadows cast by Venetian blinds. But Bertolucci goes beyond classicism, beyond the inhibitions of an American director in the 30s or 40s. He exaggerates the *noir* style, and his exaggeration not only excites the eye but further informs the structure of the film. Giulia wears a striped black and white dress whose pattern echoes the room's shadows and, as she and Clerici talk, as they momentarily get caught up in a sexual passion (cut short by the appearance of Giulia's mother), the shadows of the room literally roll across them – an artifice of lighting unmotivated by any actual event within the sequence, yet a significant part of the general lighting pattern of the film. Later, in a flashback sequence that makes up the narrative of Clerici's stay in Paris with Professor Quadri, the two men meet with their wives for dinner in a Chinese restaurant. Manganiello calls Clerici away, the

Exaggerating the *film noir* style: Stefania Sandrelli and Jean-Louis Trintignant in *The Conformist*

clear-eyed fascist murderer warning Clerici not to betray the cause. As they talk, huddled in a dark corner, the bright restaurant kitchen in deep focus to their left, Manganiello makes a light bulb above them swing back and forth, casting them both in a violent alternation of light and shadow (an image that comes to the film not only from 40s *noir* but from Hitchcock's *Psycho*, via Clouzot's *Le Corbeau*, Welles' *The Trial* and Godard's *Alphaville*, films that also deal with the matter of perception, misperception, and, in the latter two cases, with an ideologically controlled cultural blindness).

Other apparently unmotivated stylistic 'excesses' occur throughout the flashback sequences which pursue the enquiry about the uncertainty of perception. On their honeymoon trip to Paris (which Clerici uses as a cover for his job of locating his former professor) Clerici and Giulia are observed in their train compartment. She tells him of her seduction, as a child, by a lecherous family friend. Outside, landscapes flash by which are clearly back-screen projections. As with the shadows in Giulia's flat, there is no attempt to make these images appear 'real'. Objects and colours outside the window change rapidly, illogically, as if they were a dreamscape.

In an earlier flashback sequence, Clerici visits his slovenly, drug-addicted mother in her decaying mansion. The would-be ordinary man is appalled by the spectacle, all the more so as he is being followed by Manganiello and wishes to impress him with his own disgust at the woman, her house, and her chauffeur lover (whom Manganiello dutifully beats up). The sequence is formed in typical bravura fashion: the camera tracks Clerici on his way to the house from a low angle, moving through billowing autumn leaves on the street (an image suggested by the novel, though it occurs there in a different context); there is an exaggerated Dutch tilt (an extreme angle tilted off the horizontal line of the frame), which – contrary to all conventional, classic film practice – is then *un*tilted to a horizontal level during the shot. In other words, we see the tilt (a conventional signifier of a distorted or threatened point of view) and we see the results of the camera straightening itself out of this position, a gesture which reflects upon cinematic camera angles as well as the states of mind those angles may signify. Inside the house, Bertolucci continues to exploit the cinematic flourishes at his disposal, using the 180 degree reverse shot as Clerici's mother moves from the dark bedroom to the glowing white bathroom, the shot cutting to the opposite side of the room, and tracking with her as she walks back out.

These exaggerated lighting effects, camera movements and reflexive gestures indicate, indeed create, the excesses of Clerici's character, who in his attempt to be normal only reveals his own madness and that of the ideology surrounding him which he wishes to embrace. Bertolucci invites the viewer to partake of the film's visual energy and at the same time come to understand its function in creating character and narrative meaning. Again a dialectical principle is active in the film's structure. The vitality of style is negated by the devitalized emotions and intellect of its central character. But the viewer is simultaneously revitalized by the energy of the film's images, forced by them to be alert, to see, to understand the very things the character is blind to.

The dialectics of perception that make up the form and substance of *The Conformist* are controlled by a consistent literary/philosophical referent that structures the entire work, a metaphor that holds all the 'stylemes' – the individual stylistic inflections that together make up the film – in order, giving them a syntagmatic consistency. That metaphor is Plato's myth of the cave from the *Republic*, the archetypal discourse of blindness and control, featured in the story of prisoners, chained in a cave, facing a wall. Behind them their captors hold figures before a fire so that these images are reflected on the wall (as the movie image upon a screen – a constituent of the metaphor Bertolucci was quite conscious of [22]). The only thing the prisoners can see before them are the shadowed reflections of the 'reality' behind them.

This metaphor is fully articulated in the film's central set piece. Once revealed, it radiates back and forth through the narrative, enlightening and giving meaning to all its parts. When they meet in Paris, Professor Quadri reminds his pupil that the myth of the cave was the subject of Clerici's unfinished doctoral thesis. The two discuss the myth while Bertolucci recreates it in his construction of the sequence. They talk in the professor's study. On either side of the room is a large window. Clerici gets up from the desk he is sitting at and reminds Quadri that when the professor entered the classroom, the windows were always closed because he disliked sunlight and noise. Taking Quadri's role for the moment, he repeats this gesture, closing the window on the left, throwing the professor into silhouette and putting himself into complete shadow. From the other window light streams into the room. Quadri moves behind the shaft of light, so that both their figures are barely visible.

Clerici begins to recite the myth, describing the tunnel-like cave, and Quadri moves towards the open window which illuminates him from behind. Clerici continues the story: 'Inside are men who have been living there since childhood.' Quadri moves in front of the window; its shaft of light illumines cigarette smoke on the left side of the composition. 'Chained together, they are forced to face the interior of the cave. Light glows from a bonfire some distance behind them. Between the fire and the prisoners, imagine a low wall, similar to the stage on which a puppeteer moves his puppets.' As he talks, and just before Quadri changes his own position, Clerici moves out of the shadow into the shaft of light and the foreground so that his figure is half illuminated. The two figures now confront each other, though the camera is at a low level so that Clerici's figure dominates. Clerici recalls that the lecture was given in 1928. 'I remember,' says the professor, his back against the open window, light streaming over him. Clerici faces him, still in half light, and continues the story. He moves his right arm across his face as he speaks: 'And now, try to imagine other men who pass behind that wall, carrying different statues of wood and stone' (at this point, an alert viewer might recall the earlier sequence in the government offices in which men moved through a corridor carrying busts and other statuary in front of their faces). As he speaks, the camera cranes up slightly and Clerici moves his hand across the shaft of light from the window, causing a shadow to move over his own face. He snaps his right arm upright, as if giving a fascist salute, and continues: 'The statues rise above the wall'.

Bertolucci cuts to a shot of the professor by the window, still in partial silhouette. He says that Clerici could not bring him a better gift from Rome than these memories. Bertolucci then cuts back to Clerici, against the opposite wall, his right arm still upraised, his shadow on the wall behind him. He lowers his arm in a characteristically self-conscious gesture and there is a cut back to Quadri by the window, identifying the quotation from Plato, and then a cut to another shot of Clerici, closer to him this time, his figure framed to the right, his shadow still prominent behind him. 'How much we resemble them [the prisoners],' Clerici says, in an uncharacteristic moment of insight. Quadri asks, 'What do they see?' Clerici repeats the question, and as Quadri says, 'You have just come from Italy. You should know', Clerici turns round and faces his own shadow on the wall. The camera stays on Clerici's back as he says, 'They see only the shadows projected on the back of the cave', and gestures with his hand towards his own shadow.

There is a cut to a close-up of Quadri, in complete silhouette. 'Shadows! The reflections of things!' he emphasizes. A cut is made to Clerici as he turns round, his face illumined by the light coming from behind Quadri, as the latter continues drawing the analogy: 'That's what is happening today in Italy'. 'If those prisoners could speak,' says Clerici, and there is a brief cut to Quadri, still silhouetted against the window, as Clerici continues, 'they might call' – cut back to Clerici – 'those shadows real.' Another cut to Quadri, still in silhouette, this time a long shot, almost from Clerici's point of view. He agrees with his former pupil, saying the Italians confuse the ' "reality" of the shadows for true reality'. Bertolucci returns for a brief close-up of Clerici, his face partly hidden by shadow.

There is a return to the earlier two-shot of Clerici and the professor, from a low angle, Clerici in the foreground, in half light, the professor against the window in silhouette, and they discuss how the myth of the cave was to have been Clerici's thesis. Quadri moves towards Clerici, and both move to the left of the frame as Quadri expresses his disappointment in his pupil and in Italy. In the rear of the room, Clerici, partly illumined from the front, Quadri's back to the light, exchanges quiet recriminations with the professor.

At this point Bertolucci breaks into the sequence with an insert of Anna and Giulia at the professor's mimeograph machine. Anna shows Giulia how to work it, making it go faster, calling out 'faster, faster' in mock sexual frenzy.

On the return to the study, Clerici moves to the right, in front of the desk, as Quadri says that he himself had only one choice, to leave Italy and let the country know the significance of his flight. As he says this, he moves into shadow as Clerici moves to the window, taking up the professor's position, in silhouette. 'You left and I became a fascist,' Clerici says. Quadri responds by saying that a real fascist doesn't talk the way Clerici does. While saying this, Quadri moves towards and opens the left window, which brightens the room; Clerici turns round

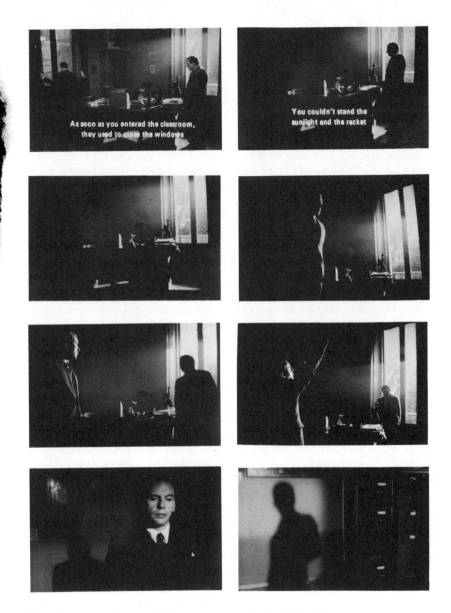

Lives in shadow: the myth of the cave sequence in *The Conformist*

in the light from the right window as his face becomes illuminated by the light from the left one. As this occurs, Bertolucci cuts to a shot of Clerici's shadow on the opposing wall which briefly appears as he moves into the light emanating from the right window and then immediately disappears as Quadri finishes opening the other window.

The force of this sequence lies both in its virtuoso display of lighting and camera placement (its stylistic rendering) and the subtle way in which it illuminates the Platonic allegory, the place of the allegory in the film and the way two men function as components of the allegory. This is a film about lives lived in the shadows, about shadows that seek other shadows: a malformed personality entrapped by unclear memories who seeks to clarify himself by embracing an ideology constructed with lies, based upon promises of strength and domination offered to the weak and repressed. But if Clerici is the most unseeing character in this fiction, the one most given to hiding in the dark of his bad conscience, none of the other characters is permitted full entry into the light. Quadri would seem to be Clerici's opposite, the man of the left, of conscience, fighting for the anti-fascist cause. But his comfort in Paris is at the expense of comrades imprisoned in Italy.

Both men move right and left, shifting positions and allegiances. Quadri is seen in an ambiguous light – literally, since he is in silhouette throughout much of the sequence. But Clerici is presented clearly as the man wrestling with the darkness, unable to come openly into the light, trapped by the shadows, even if, in the final image of the sequence, his shadow does disappear (an indication that the prisoners – though not this prisoner – can escape the chains). At the same time Clerici is in a position of strength, signified by the foregrounding of his figure which slightly dwarfs his mentor, and which points forward to the narrative fact that he will be responsible for Quadri's and Anna's murder. Yet his is a temporary strength born of blindness, by an inability to discriminate between his own personal weakness and the ideology he enters in order to provide an illusory compensation for it. The sequence represents a struggle, an attempt, against his will and knowledge, for Clerici's perception to emerge from the darkness. He knows Plato's allegory (and the professor knows that a man who speaks as Clerici does cannot be a true fascist), and yet he cannot accept its relevance to himself. When his shadow disappears at the end of the sequence he is alone, without even an illusory self for protection, an image that foreshadows the end of the film.

The myth of the cave, as I said, is the controlling metaphor of *The Conformist*. Extremes of light and shadow dominate the film's visual structure. Blindness and the confusion of the imagined and the possible, the world as defined by the self – as opposed to the self defined by the world, the Other – dominate Clerici's movements, decisions and indecisions. At every instance what he sees and what his memory recalls are equally untrustworthy. This is especially evident during those sequences in which Bertolucci constructs the homosexual incident Clerici recalls having as a child and uses as an excuse for his actions as an adult. The incident is related in two separate flashbacks during Clerici's ride with Manganiello to assassinate Quadri. The first is told in achronological order. It begins as Clerici gets out of Manganiello's car and walks in front of it. His movements and gestures are matched with shots of Clerici as a child, stopping a limousine driven by a man named Lino. As the chronology of the various shots that make up this particular moment is sorted out – intercut with shots of Clerici back in the car with Manganiello – it becomes apparent that young Clerici had been sexually molested in some way (the images leave it unclear) by his classmates. The limousine he stops may be his family's, or just a passing car. He is taken to an old house, and the rest of the incident is related in a flashback within a flashback. Clerici is in church, making confession at the insistence of his fiancée (he does not believe in God or church). The confession he offers is constructed into the concluding narrative of his childhood memory.

The images of this memory are as hallucinatory as the others. The young Clerici is pursued through an old building by Lino, the camera tracking through sheets blowing on a clothes line, into an empty room with a bed and a crucifix. Lino removes his chauffeur's cap to reveal long flowing hair; he refers to himself as 'Madame Butterfly', and offers both an embrace and a gun to the young Clerici, who chooses the latter and fires it round the room, the camera madly panning the walls as the bullets fly. Lino, according to Clerici's memory, is shot, and we see the child sit huddled by the chauffeur's body before he leaves through an open window.

These images are intercut with those in the confessional, the ghostly figure of the priest barely visible through the grating. The priest demonstrates an interest in the events that amazes Clerici himself: 'Did you kiss? Did you touch each other? Are you telling the truth?' he asks. 'Yes,' answers Clerici, but with a slight, disconcerting smile. He is absolved, finally, but not so much for past deeds as for present politics. 'I'm confessing today for the sin I'll commit tomorrow. Blood washes away blood. Whatever price society demands from me I will pay.' The priest asks if he is a member of a secret or subversive group. 'No, no. I'm a member of the organization which hunts down subversives,' he answers. 'Then you are absolved of all your sins!' In a curious, almost disbelieving gesture, Clerici pokes his head towards the confessional screen and puts his hands to his eyes in an attempt to see this politically

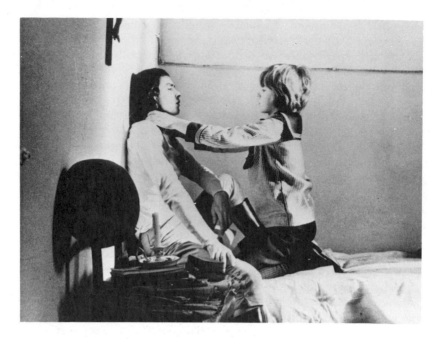

Confessional memory: the young Clerici with the chauffeur Lino (Pierre Clementi)

astute father confessor.

Indeed, Clerici himself cannot always believe what he sees and hears. In his existence in the half light, he cowers and cringes, peers into the dark and the light, confused by both, caught up in his own hallucinations, which are sometimes passed on directly to the spectator with no clarifying mediation. I have referred to the fact that two women (played by Dominique Sanda, who also plays the role of Quadri's wife, Anna) appear before Anna herself is ever seen. Each of these figures is a prostitute. The first is the woman spread across the desk of the fascist minister, a figure the viewer sees in close-up, until a rapid zoom back indicates that Clerici himself is seeing her from a great distance. Her second appearance is as a prostitute in the brothel where Clerici stops for his orders on his way to Paris. She embraces Clerici, declaring herself mad.*

---

* Bertolucci gets this idea from Moravia, who suggests that the woman in the brothel and Anna (named Lina in the novel – to link her with Lino, the chauffeur) look alike. By using the same actress, and tripling rather than doubling her appearance, the film-maker goes the novelist one better in developing possibilities of perceptual dislocation.

Anna herself is an ambiguously sexual figure who attempts to seduce both Clerici and Giulia. The text offers no explicit reason for this triple incarnation, other than implying that it is one more manifestation of Clerici's miscognition of reality, suggesting as well that he perceives all sexually desirable women as whores. Anna becomes for him the ultimate whore and seductress. The irony is that, of all the characters in the film, Anna is the most clear-sighted, the one who understands the reality that Clerici represents but cannot himself see. He is the bringer of death, the grim reaper, and Anna's comprehension of this, her attempts to ward off Clerici's mission by offering herself first to his wife and then to him, results only in her own destruction. (I will examine Anna's character in more detail in the final chapter when I discuss the role of women in Bertolucci's films.)

The flashback sequences of the film end as Clerici and Manganiello reach the snowy forest where Quadri and Anna are ambushed. Quadri is stabbed by Manganiello's men in a scene choreographed to recall Julius Cæsar stabbed in the forum (more accurately, film versions of Cæsar stabbed in the forum[23]). Anna pleads for Clerici's help. He remains hunched in the corner of the car, paralysed by fear and cowardice. He refuses her cries, closes the car window; Manganiello's men pursue her and shoot her down.

The narrative leaps to July 1943 and the fall of Mussolini. Clerici is now living with Giulia and their young daughter in a flat that recalls the tenements in neo-realist films of the late 40s, yet is still inflected with the surreal quality that marks the style of the film. An old man is sitting in a corner, stroking a chicken; the daughter's room has wallpaper with a pattern of sky and blue clouds, like a vision out of Magritte. Clerici takes to the streets, 'to see a dictatorship fall', and the streets are filled with flashing lights and obscuring shadows. Crowds go by, people drag a bust of Mussolini along the ground – the prisoners are freed from their chains.

Clerici meets the blind Italo, points to his fascist badge, saying 'Something has stuck to you'. In a dark corner of a Roman street he discovers Lino, the chauffeur whose presumed death started Clerici on his blind lunge towards normality. The sequence is filmed in extreme chiaroscuro. Lino sits with another gay man by a fire they have made for warmth. The revelation of Lino's existence ruptures Clerici's tenuous perceptions, removing the overwhelming shadow upon which he has based his life. The discovery that his would-be seducer and victim is still alive puts the final lie to every act Clerici has subsequently committed. As a result he attempts to blind himself to his past actions by extrapolating guilt and casting his mind's shadows on to other people. He denounces Italo to the passing crowd, who sweep

Clerici and his daughter towards the end of *The Conformist*

him away. He yells hysterically that it was Lino who murdered Luca and Anna Quadri (not far from the truth for a man who has lived in the mistaken memory of what another man did to him and he to the other man). Finally, with the crowd gone, with Lino fleeing in terror, Clerici is left alone and in a position that again recalls the prisoners in Plato's cave. He sits by an iron gate, across from where the gay man to whom Lino was talking is preparing for bed. By Clerici's side is a fire which illuminates his face. Bertolucci cuts momentarily to the gay man, who is winding up an old record player (on the soundtrack we hear the Italian Andrews Sisters seen earlier in the radio station), and then back to Clerici, who turns his head towards the gateposts and the spectator. He moves into threequarter profile, illumined by the fire, and stares. The film ends.

Marcello Clerici becomes what he always has been, a trapped figure, living in the illusory half light of bad memories and false perceptions; and the gaze he offers at the end promises no real comprehension, only the possible dawning of some shadowy recognition. But it is a look offered more for the audience than for the character, the viewer rather than the viewed. It constitutes a closure which is really an opening in the text, providing the audience with room to look, just before the shaft of light from the rear of their cave – the film projector – is about to go out.

If *The Conformist* is a film about a character's perception, about the ways things are seen and not seen, with a formal structure that deliberates and ruminates on that problem throughout, *The Spider's Stratagem* is a film about *being* perceived, a somewhat different problem, treated by Bertolucci in a very different manner. In *The Conformist*, the central character is trapped in the illusions of his own paranoid gaze. *The Spider's Stratagem* is also concerned with illusions and paranoia, but creates them externally; they are generated *for* the central character and the viewer. The film is about history as hallucination, as a palpable material to be manipulated, produced (even in the sense that a film is produced), a spectacle in which everyone becomes a player.

The film was made just prior to *The Conformist*, and was one of the first theatrical features to be financed by RAI, Italian state television. 'I remember,' says Bertolucci, 'never wanting to concede anything to the television format, and I was actually, almost as a revenge, filming it *against* television. ... *The Spider's Stratagem* is a film made entirely of wide-angle and long shots. That's why it works on a cinema screen, but loses its intensity on television.'[24] In fact the film works well in both media, and perhaps sets the form for subsequent European television films which ignore the self-imposed conventions of American television and its insistence on a predominance of medium and close shots.

But it is not merely television conventions that are attacked in *The Spider's Stratagem*. This is the film in which Bertolucci finds his own voice, the voice that is first noticed in *Before the Revolution* and is buried under the Godardian discourse of *Partner*. With the help of Vittorio Storaro (in the first of their five film collaborations), he manifests the elements of visual style, including the long, luxurious tracking shots, the rich colouring, the ability to register and make significant the textures of walls and buildings – the articulate environments which define the characters of the narrative – that mark his films of the 1970s. He also brings to fruition the synthesizing sense that first became evident in *Before the Revolution*, that ability to bring to bear on the form and content of his work influences from a variety of sources, creating a text of complexity and reverberation.

Of all Bertolucci's films, *The Spider's Stratagem* is the most modernist in its structure, actively and consciously foregrounding its attack on the conventions of classical cinema. Where *Before the Revolution* pulled, in eclectic fashion, on some of the early structural elements of the French New Wave and *Partner* imitated the forms of mid-6os Godard, here Bertolucci demonstrates that he has absorbed the influences of 6os cinema, understands them, is fully aware of the dialectical play of forms that makes the modernist work above all a reflection upon its own existence, and can go on to enrich the dialectic. The design of *The*

Spider's Stratagem is made up of various pieces, of influences and suggestions, drawn from cinema, opera, painting and literature, which are pulled into a discourse that at the same time effaces those influences. It feeds upon them, synthesizes them while requiring that they be recognized and their significance understood. As a modernist work the film both is and is not a complete text, and its various elements, once known, become something more than structure: they form a context out of which the text itself emerges.

The text in turn controls the various elements that feed it, and the film becomes a contrapuntal play of influence and construct, which finally is one of the things the film is *about*: the interplay of influences, constructions, formal devices erected by characters out of a desire to alter history, a desire that leads to their and history's destruction. As in *The Conformist*, form and substance inform one another. Although the film speaks of characters who attempt to alter the structure of history and turn it into an operatic spectacle, an opera that may, finally, last for eternity, the film's own discourse organizes its elements with a certainty and control that is never in danger of destroying itself. Rather it creates from and for the self-destructive actions of its characters an affirming structure that reveals their actions, separates the viewer from them and provides a vitality of insight into a moment of history in which vitality was negated.

Like *The Conformist*, *The Spider's Stratagem* concerns the fascist period in Italy. But, unlike the later film, it is not a luxurious re-creation of the 30s. Rather, set in an ephemeral present, it concerns the encroachment of the past and the re-creation of the present into the past. A young man, Athos Magnani Jr, returns to his home town (to which Bertolucci gives the name of 'Tara', the plantation in *Gone With the Wind*, that great Hollywood fantasy of passion and history frozen on a back lot). He comes to seek the truth about the murder of his father, a great anti-fascist hero, idolized by the town. The truth he discovers is a lie. His father betrayed his cause, and to cover the betrayal had himself killed by his comrades in an elaborate plot so contrived as to make his death a spectacle that turns himself and the town into a legend.

I say that, in *The Spider's Stratagem*, the past encroaches upon the present. More precisely, the diegesis of the film – the fictional world signified by its narrative – takes place in two times, the past and the present, which overlap and destroy each other. Once Athos Jr steps off the train, at the beginning of the film, he enters the history of the 30s, in a town where time has stopped, and where the 'present' time of his investigations and the 'flashbacks' that elaborate the story of his father as it is told to him intertwine until they become part of an elaborate structure which finally entraps young Athos himself.

This brief description may suggest that, in its play with time, the film has certain aspects of the science fiction/time travel genre about it. The fact is that Bertolucci had been planning a science fiction project in the 60s called *Infinito futuro* ('Endless Future').[25] *The Spider's Stratagem* could be considered the reverse of that idea and be called 'Endless Past', except that it has nothing of the science fiction genre about it. The basic cinematic source for the film is neo-realism. Not the neo-realism of working-class characters trying to find a living among the shattered remains of post-war Italy, but the *idea* of neo-realism that builds its texts out of precise and detailed observations of character in a land-scape, the idea to which Bertolucci would return again in *1900*. Here he establishes a sense of place, a 'there-ness' of the town of Tara (the actual town of Sabbioneta, in the area of Verdi's birthplace and near Bertolucci's birthplace, Parma) whose streets, walls, buildings, fields and outlying villas provide not merely a background, but the environ-ment and definition for the narrative's events and characters.[26] Bertolucci integrates character and place so that they co-determine each other. But the balance here is different than it is in, for example, *Rome, Open City* or *Bicycle Thieves*. In the classic neo-realist structure, character and place define each other. In *The Spider's Stratagem* the town and its deformed history *determine* the characters. They have become the place, which in turn controls them.

To repeat, this is by no means classic neo-realism, nor the imitation of neo-realism Bertolucci indulges in *The Grim Reaper*, nor the socialist realism variant of *1900*. In *The Spider's Stratagem*, Bertolucci realizes the modernist potential in neo-realism. Rather than build upon it ex-plicitly, as he does in *1900*, with the implication of difference that the history of modernism demands we recognize, he overlays the neo-realist structure with other elements which at the same time negate and foreground it. The result is that neo-realism is turned into a self-conscious form, forced to struggle dialectically against those elements that insist it give up its self-effacing structure of direct observation. Two of these elements come from outside cinema. One constitutes a major source for the visual construction of the film, a source to which Bertolucci has referred in many interviews – the paintings of René Magritte. He has pointed out that the night sequences of the film, with their stark dark blue coloration, punctuated by sharp, hard light (for example, in a sequence in which Athos Jr lights a match to see in the dark, Bertolucci hides a small spot in the actor's hand so that the match will emit a cold, clear luminescence), are suggested by Magritte's various canvases under the title *The Empire of Light*. What he does not say is that many of the daytime sequences are also influenced by Magritte, as well as by the Italian surrealist De

Chirico – especially those shots in which Athos Jr is tracked by the camera down streets surrounded on each side by the archways and colonnades of buildings. What he only infers, and what becomes clear upon close reading of the film, is that it is not so much an individual canvas and not only the signifiers of Magritte that influence the film, but the *idea* of a Magritte painting, the signifieds of such works as *The Promenades of Euclid, The Fair Captive II, The Human Condition I and II*, or *The Youth of Icarus* – those works in which a landscape is partly covered by a canvas standing on an easel, which is not really a canvas but a sheet of glass through which a section of the same landscape is seen.* Indirectly, but more pertinently, the film is analogous to the work of Magritte which is the very exemplum of modernist art and deconstructionist criticism: the paintings of a pipe, each of which contains the inscription: '*Ceci n'est pas une pipe*'.

Magritte was the portrait-maker of artifice; not the surrealist he is usually called but a meta-realist, a critic of realism whose essays are paintings rather than words. He made paintings *about* painting, about the way in which the world is perceived through the conventions of representation. His works speak to the central modernist notion that the primary signified of imaginative expression (painting, novel, poem, music, film) is the signifier – the work itself and its formal reality.[27] In applying this notion to film, Bertolucci extends it, working Magritte's insights into a form that is both visual and narrative. The 'reality' of the film, the details of place and character and event, is not 'real', but an artifice of convention, and doubly so. Realism – neo-realism or otherwise – is created by the forms and apparatus of cinema; and within that artifice, within the realm of the cinema-created fiction, the reality perceived is not real, for it has been created by the characters who were in turn created by the fiction. The realm of *The Spider's Stratagem*, like a Magritte painting of a landscape within a landscape that is and is not a painting within the painting, is a fiction that is and is not a fiction within the fiction.

The town Athos Jr sees is not the town he sees; the present he believes he inhabits is not the present, not the past but a locked intersection of the two. The father he searches for is not his father but a

---

* T. Jefferson Kline points out the influence of other Magritte paintings, in particular *Man Reading Newspaper, In Praise of Dialectic, Golconda* and *Not to be Reproduced*. The latter work is a particular influence. It shows a man looking into a mirror. We see his head from the back; the mirror reflects not his face, but the back of his head (see 'Father as Mirror', *Psychocultural Review*, 1979, pp. 94–7). Other Magritte influences are *Nostalgia* and *Memory of a Voyage III*, which contain the figure of a lion.

fiction created by the father and his friends *and* the film which we come to, as Athos comes to the town, with our coded expectations of realism, linear progression of time, and clear closure of event and character. But *'ceci n'est pas la réalité'*. No film is, of course; films are coded ruminations upon reality. *The Spider's Stratagem* merely takes this phenomenon a step further by using the expectations of reality created by film as one of its subjects, turning upon those expectations, resituating the perceptions of the viewer and of the character viewed.

Magritte supplies the visual referent for this foregrounding of artifice and the questioning of the relationship between subject and object perceived. But *The Spider's Stratagem* is a narrative, not a painting, and Bertolucci is able to join a literary influence to the painterly. In this instance it is Jorge Luis Borges' short fiction *Theme of the Traitor and Hero*. The literary sources of Bertolucci's other films – Stendhal's *The Charterhouse of Parma*, Dostoevsky's *The Double*, Moravia's *The Conformist* – are something like prods, their narratives providing Bertolucci with stimuli, with ideas for characters and events which he then changes and expands upon, reworking them into his own cinematic fictions. The relationship between the Borges fiction and *The Spider's Stratagem* operates in an entirely different manner. Bertolucci not only borrows and then changes the events of the fiction ('events' is no more accurate a word than 'plot' to describe Borges' fictions, which are about the making of fiction and the phenomenon of 'plot'), but, as in the case of Magritte, he uses the concepts that Borges' narrative suggest.

In many respects, Borges' fiction and Magritte's paintings share a common ground, a common idea about the artifice of language and its codes (of written language in the first instance, visual in the second); both are concerned with the epistemology and cognition of their different means of expression. Magritte's paintings speak to us about the way we know, or think we know, or do not know the world through painting; Borges speaks of the way worlds can be created and· uncreated, known and misrecognized through written language. His fictions are about the making of imaginary worlds which come to have a distinct reality because language makes them, and ,anything that is created is 'real' within the context and conventions of its means of creation. Such is the case with *Theme of the Traitor and Hero*. The voice who speaks the fiction admits to imagining it – 'I have imagined the following argument ...' he says. The 'argument' involves, he decides, the hero of a betrayed Irish rebellion who was killed under mysterious and theatrically dramatic circumstances, in a theatre, with elements of *Macbeth* and *Julius Cæsar* elaborating his murder. The investigator of the events and narrator of the fiction – who is himself invented by the voice who creates the fiction (who is in turn a creation of Borges) – is the hero's great-grandson, Ryan. Ryan discovers that the hero was in fact the betrayer, who organized his own death with the aid of his friend Nolan in order to save the fatherland and the reputation of its betrayer. The entire city of Dublin becomes part of a preordained ritual, which is taken by history as truth, absorbed by history to such an extent that all investigations of the event become re-created in its fictive image. Ryan is himself caught by the fiction, predicted, indeed created by it: 'He understands that he, too, forms part of Nolan's plan. . . . At the end of some tenacious cavilling, he resolves to keep silent his discovery. He publishes a book dedicated to the glory of the hero; this, too, no doubt was foreseen.'

Clearly Bertolucci follows the 'events' of this six-page fiction rather closely (more closely than his other literary sources, even Moravia's *The Conformist*), significantly changing the relationship between the hero-traitor and the person who investigates his death to one of father and son, and also changing the time, placing it in a very concrete, too 'real' historical setting, Italy's fascist period. More important, he follows Borges' concept very closely, examining the 'labyrinths even more inextricable and heterogeneous' that form about the act and the attempt to unravel it. As with Magritte, both form and idea infiltrate the cinematic text, nourishing it, opening out its modernist potential.

Out of a neo-realist base, Bertolucci creates a film that manifests the details of an existing place and its inhabitants, while at the same time negating that illusion through a narrative whose subject and form is illusion: the illusion of cinematic reality as well as the illusion created by a narrative in which time and history are deformed by betrayal, its discovery, and the absorption of the discovery into the spectacle that produced the original deformation. The viewer must therefore observe the film from a number of perspectives simultaneously. He or she accepts the 'exotic but apparently 'real' location of the film and its characters; then must deal with the unusual behaviour of the characters within this location; and finally work out, with the film-maker, the elision, perhaps even collision, of the various perspectives of reality-illusion. The film becomes (and here is where the influence of Godard remains present and in control) a commentary not only upon its own internal events, but upon the way cinematic events are made for and perceived by an audience.

Let me offer one example to begin with. Athos Jr visits one of his father's friends, Gaibazzi, the salami curer, who takes him into his 'uranium chamber', the storeroom where the meats are hung. They move about the hanging salami, Gaibazzi piercing them with a pick to smell their ripeness while talking to Athos about Athos's father and the friendship of years ago. He speaks of their rather naive notion of fascism at the time, the way they considered themselves more like actors in an opera than resistance fighters (a reference that will grow in importance as the film progresses). In constructing such a sequence, a film-maker would ordinarily have two or three choices: it could be filmed in one take, the camera either remaining still, observing the conversation or, more in keeping with the camera style of this film, tracking the characters amid the salami; it could be cut in the classical style, by means of a series of over-the-shoulder shots of the two participants; or a Godardian choice might be made, forming the sequence by means of jump cuts, creating ellipses in the conversation, removing transitional passages. Bertolucci chooses a variation of the latter approach, executing the sequence by means of a form selected from the grammar of classical construction which few film-makers would ordinarily employ for a sequence meant to take place within one time and place. He interrupts the dialogue and the movement of the characters with fades to black. When he cuts back into the sequence after any one of the fades, the two participants are still talking, with no overt indication that much time has elapsed.

In classical cinema the fade to black *always* signifies a moment of closure, the end of a sequence, often denoting a dramatic pause, with the promise that at the other end of the fade the action will continue at a different time and/or place. But nothing of the kind happens here. The fades occur, triggering the viewer's coded response, which is then frustrated when the sequence resumes close to the point where it was before the fade.

This tampering with a major cinematic code, frustrating and confusing the viewer's conventional response, is part of the process of creating multiple perspectives which I spoke of earlier.* Athos Jr (and the viewer) have experienced many inexplicable events before this point in the narrative. He has met Draifa, his father's mistress – named after Dreyfus, she tells him (a character with this name is referred to in the script of *Before the Revolution*, though not in the finished film) – who presents herself to him like a figure in an opera, walking in a stately manner through the lush colonnades of her villa, the camera tracking her with an equally measured stateliness, covering almost 360 degrees of space. During their first conversation, when Athos threatens to leave, she indulges in a dramatic fainting spell. He has arrived in the afternoon; when he does leave, only a small period of time seeming to have passed, it is night. Later, Athos is mysteriously locked in a barn.

---

*And which I noted in *Before the Revolution* where, instead of the fade, Bertolucci uses dissolves which do not change time or space. He uses that device once in *The Spider's Stratagem*.

In his hotel room, he is greeted early in the morning by a man who knocks him unconscious (someone has written on the door, 'It is only a beginning'). He attempts to visit, and is thrown out by, Beccaccia, who was (and apparently still is) the chief fascist landowner of the town and his father's sworn enemy. Hanging over all these events is the mystery of who Athos Sr was and why his son is now being treated so oddly. The style of the film, through the sequences we are discussing, has a marked ceremonial and surreal quality, the camera moving carefully amid walls and lights, dwelling on figures in the landscape, magnifying the darkness, observing, with Athos Jr, mysteries that seem to have no answers.

The anomalous fades to black during the conversation with Gaibazzi begin to define both the mysteries and the form of their creation. Within the denotative logic of the sequence the fades have no place, at least no coded place, for they do not create a recognizable process of stimulus and response in the viewer (presence of fade producing the expectation that one spatial-temporal unit is ending and another about to begin). But at the same time they do function in their conventional syntactic roles when they are perceived as formal devices that inform the viewer about the 'reality' of events in Tara and the way in which Athos Jr is becoming caught up in them. Instead of signifying changes of time and place and the closure of a sequence, the fades express the slippages in time that occur in Athos Jr's, Gaibazzi's and the spectator's perceptions of time and place within the fiction. From the moment he enters Tara, Athos fades out of time and into the web spun by his father and his colleagues who, in 1936, to hide his betrayal of their plan to blow up Mussolini during a performance of *Rigoletto*, elaborated Athos Sr's own assassination in a grand masquerade that turned the entire town into a theatre in which the performance continues as if time had not moved on. So it is Athos Jr who is unconsciously fading in and out of the conversation with Gaibazzi, as well as Gaibazzi himself, who lives in a time that is the present stuck in, or always reverting to, the past. The fact that, after each fade, the characters are seen in the same place and time (or apparently so) is part of the film's grand illusion. For no one within the fiction is ever exactly in the place and time they think they are in. The fades become then a visual sign of time lost and history at a standstill. They figure as perceptual lapses during which nothing, and a great deal, takes place.

At the end of this sequence Gaibazzi and Athos Jr have lunch. As they leave the salami room, the camera observes them from a great distance. During their lunch Bertolucci suddenly places his camera in yet another room, looking up at the two characters seated at the table from a low angle, at the distance of a small flight of stairs. The two men are composed in the upper left-hand corner of the frame, and the effect is of their being observed by someone else, spied upon, distanced from their own moment. Which is exactly what is happening. The authorizing point of view of this shot is partly that of the viewer, who is forced again to assume the ambiguous perspective of a lost and distant time which is at the same time the present, the un-history of Tara observing two of its figures caught in its web.

Earlier, Athos Jr has again visited Draifa to ask her more about his father. He was very funny, she tells him, and Bertolucci introduces the first of the film's 'flashbacks'. It is night, and Athos Sr, walking with his three friends, contradicts the time. 'This is daylight,' he says, and crows like a cock. Athos walks and the camera pans with him 360 degrees around the field. The cocks begin to crow. Time is denied, but not only in the game of making the cocks crow. When Athos first visited Draifa, she showed him a picture of his father, commenting on how alike they look. All the town's people he meets comment on the resemblance. When the father finally appears in 'flashback', we discover that not only do they look alike, they *are* alike. The same actor plays both characters; the only difference in their appearance is that the father's hair is combed differently, and he always wears a tan safari jacket and a red scarf. The identification is pointed up later in an extraordinary shot of Athos Jr staring at the statue of his father in the town square. It is a hallucinatory moment: the statue is painted, its eyes white, the scarf a bright red (the painting of the statue is reminiscent of the Odysseus sequence in Godard's 1963 film *Contempt*, where statues of the ancient Greeks have bright paint applied to their eyes). As Athos stares, the statue moves, the shots intercut as if father and son were staring at each other. But the strangeness of the cross-cutting is exaggerated by the fact that the statue has been attached to the camera; and as the camera turns, so does the statue, the walls behind it seeming to drift past as if they were a back-screen projection,[*] the connection between the two emphasized by this strange, dream-like point of view. (More than a connection. In an earlier sequence in which Athos first looks at the statue, he walks past and behind it so that the statue eclipses him completely.)

Other odd temporal overlaps occur. The friends look the same in the 'past' as they do in the 'present'. There is no sign of change in their age or temperament. The salami curer, the schoolteacher Rasori (who locks behind doors the old women in his house when Athos Jr pays his

---

[*] I have noted previously the relationship of this effect to a similar one in Leone's *Once Upon a Time in the West*, for which Bertolucci wrote the original screenplay.

The Spider's Stratagem: time past (Athos the father) ...

visit), the outdoor cinema owner Costa (who is showing Robert Aldrich's 1961 Western *The Last Sunset*, a film about generational conflict) have not moved through time; like everyone else in Tara they are locked into the moment of Athos Sr's death, caught in his web, which, finally, is more analogous to a kind of Klein Bottle of time.*

One major sequence demonstrates the phenomenon with such dexterity and élan that it stands as the formal centre of the film. In the midst of that strange point of view shot in which Athos Jr sees the statue of his father moving as if suspended in space and time, Draifa walks into the background, in soft focus, moving in the same direction as the statue turns. She is dressed in white, holding a white parasol over her head against the summer sun. Bertolucci cuts to a closer shot of her, smiling, walking against a deeply coloured blue wall. She stops

---

* At the end of the sequence with Costa, Athos Jr helps him pull up the screen of his outdoor cinema. Bertolucci's description of the event refers to the influence of Magritte: 'In *The Spider's Stratagem* ... the big screen of the open-air movie house ... reveals the countryside hidden behind it when it is lifted. So many banalities could be said about a screen, which, when it is lifted, shows the same reality as the one the camera had projected and imprinted on it until then.'[28]

114

by a wooden door; a blue building can be seen through the entrance. She turns and Athos comes to her, taking her arm and walking. The door swings open as they leave the frame; the camera holds and then tracks along the blue wall – an object blocking our view in a space undefined by the human figure.

Following a cut we once again see Draifa and Athos walking away from the town. He wonders if his father's friends are conspiring against him, remarking that all his actions and decisions seem to be foreseen. As they continue their walk, the camera observes them surrounded by the town's buildings. They move to the top of a hill. Flies buzz around them. (Reference to creatures abound in the film, beginning with the paintings of domestic and predatory beasts by Vittorio Ligabue that appear beneath the opening credits.) Athos, standing at a distance from Draifa, turns to her and asks how his father was 'intimately'. Draifa herself turns and faces the camera, at which point the narrative then cuts to the 'past', to a sequence in which Draifa, like a spider turning a web, wraps a bandage round Athos Sr's back (it is only later that we learn why he has a back injury: when he told his comrades that he had betrayed their cause, they attacked and beat him). The camera drifts between the two characters as Athos Sr turns and moves to receive the bandage. Draifa slaps him when he refuses to tell her who is

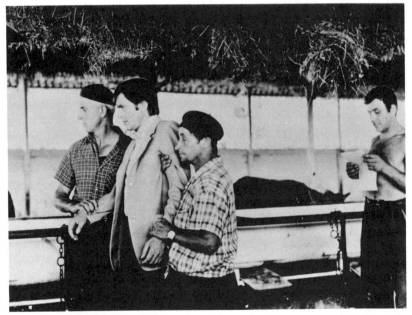

... time present (Athos the son)

better, she or his wife, and she moves away, to a mirror that reflects both her and Athos.

The sequence cuts briefly back to Athos Jr and Draifa walking among some trees – where presumably she is relating this story – and then returns to the flashback, in which Draifa and Athos Sr continue to talk about their relationship. She calls him a coward. As she walks about the room, his mirrored reflection is seen in soft focus. The camera then pans round the walls of the room, passing the mirror which now reflects no one, as we hear on the soundtrack the voices of people speaking German. Draifa moves into the frame and walks to a window that looks out on a long corridor with rows of columns on each side (the same corridor appears in a photograph of Athos Sr that hangs on Draifa's wall). Through the window we see a woman running to pick up a child. Draifa calls for Athos, and the scene cuts back to the 'present' as Draifa sits down in a field and indulges in another melodramatic faint, falling straight back into the cornstalks.

The sequence returns to the 'past', to Athos Sr looking out of the window with sounds of a snarling lion on the soundtrack. In a trick montage that might have delighted Bazin, Athos Sr and the face of a snarling lion are intercut as if they were looking at each other. Down the long corridor outside the window come a group of men and a woman in uniforms with whips and nets to capture the animal – an event we never actually see, for Bertolucci suggests the capture rather than shows it. Obviously, this saves the expense and danger of having a lion on the set. More important, the anomaly of the event, the slow, almost dream-like movement of the circus people outside the window, the suggestion of the beast's presence, create an enigma, an aura of meaning as yet undefined.

Not until later in the narrative do we learn what the lion was about. Gaibazzi, Costa and Rasori are invited by Draifa to spend an evening at her villa with the old fascist Beccaccia (who called himself the bull, they say – and sounds of a bull are heard at points of the narrative in which Athos Sr's betrayal is discussed). Athos Jr, dozing in a chair, overhears them tell a story about a lion that escaped from a German circus and, when caught, sickened and died. As the story is related, there is another flashback in which Athos Sr's friends bring him the head of the lion, decorated with an apple in its mouth, on a platter. Gaibazzi leads them, singing the Monks' chorus from the fourth act of *Il trovatore*: 'Miserere d'un' alma già vicina ...', 'Have mercy upon a spirit approaching/The departure that has no return;/Have mercy on him, the divine goodness;/Keep him from being the prey of hell.'[29] On the soundtrack Bertolucci cuts to a recording from the same section of the opera, Leonora singing 'Sull'orrida torre ...', 'Over the horrid tower,/Ah, death seems/With wings of darkness/To be poised . . .'

The appearance of the lion seems to turn upon a double allegory. In its association with the German circus the lion refers to the German presence in Italy, which will ultimately sicken and die. The songs of death and mourning from Verdi ironically extend this (the 'horrid tower', for example, refers to Beccaccia, whom the friends refer to as a fascist tower); but they also point to another death. In the opera they are sung for Manrico, Leonora's lover, imprisoned and soon to be murdered by his rival, the Count di Luna. At the end of the opera, Manrico is revealed to be Luna's brother, stolen as a child by a gypsy who murdered her own son and brought up Manrico in his place. The opera has a fantastically complicated story, to which we will return in the discussion of *La luna*. By making reference to it at this point in the narrative of *The Spider's Stratagem*, Bertolucci extends the allegory of the lion so that it refers not only to Germany, but to Athos Magnani, father and son, as well. Athos Sr is the would-be hero – a lion and a tamer of the fascist beast, a status which he betrays. He has himself murdered by his comrades to cover his crime and passes the curse of his actions down to his son. The idea of the betrayal of child by parent is suggested by *Il trovatore* and is extended by Bertolucci through the major operatic reference in the film, *Rigoletto*, which I shall discuss presently.

The sequence of Draifa's story in which the lion makes its initial appearance concludes as Athos Sr watches its capture through the window. The camera, positioned behind him, pulls back to reveal Draifa, who is looking slightly to her right, *narrating the events as if she were talking to Athos Jr in front of her, in the present*. She then turns back to Athos Sr, who can be seen throughout this shot still staring out of the window. The camera tracks back to him, and the scene cuts once more to Draifa lying in the field in the 'present', asking Athos Jr to help her up.

The elisions of time, the exaggerated gestures, the mysterious signifiers of the German circus and an escaped lion, the glance and address sent across temporal spaces, all encapsulate the movement of *The Spider's Stratagem* towards a breaking down of narrative and perceptual certainty. This structure, played out in its fullest articulation within this sequence, reappears in variations throughout the film in small movements and large gestures, in little ambiguities which crop up, disappear, and then reappear later on. I have noted a number of them, such as the fact that no one seems to age with time. Others involve Athos Jr's complaint that there are only old people in the town, while in his hotel he is looked after by a very young, poetry-quoting, cigarette-smoking boy. Near the end of the film Athos Jr makes a rambling speech in the town square – part direct discourse, part voice-over expressions of his own confusions, with flashbacks to various episodes that have occurred. He makes reference to fascism, and as he does so a young boy in a red shirt walks forward and Bertolucci briefly, and from an angle in which it is difficult for the viewer to discern precisely what is seen, picks up a group of young boys running by, wearing red bandanas. They are young images of Athos's father, or the continuing promise of a left-wing battle against the right, and the continuing threat of its failure.

Ambiguities about youth and age, about politics, are intertwined with confusions about sex. The young boy at Athos's hotel holds up a rabbit, asking Athos its sex. 'Male,' Athos says. 'No, female,' the boy insists. Draifa has a serving boy who, late in the film, Athos discovers painting his toenails. 'What kind of boy are you'? he asks. The servant responds by removing her hat and letting her hair flow down.

Sexual confusion, political confusion, the confusion of identities, father and friends, father and town, father and son locked in an illusory and unalterable web, a masquerade created to save the ego of a coward. Bertolucci signifies the entrapment of father and son, son and father in this temporal grid by means of a montage sequence. Athos Jr runs through the woods from his father's friends. The shot is intercut with another of Athos Sr, running from the same friends through the same place at some time in the past. We see the legs of one figure intercut with the upper body of the other (who is not Other, but the same – both characters played by the same actor, both characters aspects of a single persona, extending the theme of doubles in *Partner*), alternating repeatedly until the two figures become fused, just as their separate times become confused as one. The fusion is so complete that Athos Jr cannot in the end break free. At one point he is attacked in the town square by fascist hoodlums, for whom he remains the Resistance fighter his father once was; at another, he tries to efface his father, almost literally, by defacing his grave. He tries, finally, to leave Tara and escape his father completely. At the station his train to Parma is delayed. 'Sometimes they forget we exist,' the station master tells him. In a final hallucinatory image, three old men in a work car roll by on the tracks, pushing themselves along with poles. Athos looks out along the tracks and sees the weeds growing between the rails. They become more luxuriant as the camera tracks up the tracks. There is a shot of Tara, set forever amid the corn fields. A return to the railroad tracks shows them overgrown with weeds: no train has passed by in many years.

Athos Sr has ensnared reality, his son, his friends, his mistress, the town of Tara. He has woven together a great spectacle, an opera made up of bits and pieces of other spectacles, just as his creator, Bertolucci, has woven together a film made up of allusions to other works. Within the fiction these bits and pieces were brought together during the night of the father's death. They include prophetic warnings from *Julius Cæsar* and *Macbeth*, a letter from a gypsy warning him not to go into the opera house, a man in black on a motorcycle carrying more letters of warning. Athos Jr is told that that the motorcyclist was actually a cousin from Cremona playing a role. Film history tells us that the black-clad motorcyclist is Death's bodyguard from Cocteau's *Orpheus*, a film in which history becomes an eternal return. *Macbeth* is a Shakespeare play and a Verdi opera. The gypsy comes from another Verdi opera, *Il trovatore*, to which Bertolucci has already alluded in the music played over the ceremony of the lion. These references are part of a complex of operatic allusions. During the gathering of the friends at Draifa's house, Gaibazzi sings part of an aria from *Un ballo in maschera*, aptly directed at both the fascist Beccaccia and at Athos Sr: 'Eri tu . . .', 'It was you who besmirched that soul,/The delight of my soul . . ./You who trust me and suddenly loathsome/Poison the universe for me . . .' As a fascist, Beccaccia besmirches all; as a betrayer, Athos in effect joins the fascists, and by raising the fascist concept of spectacle to a universal proposition he 'poisons the universe' for everyone. But the reference to *Ballo* goes beyond its narrative: the opera is based upon a play about Gustave III of Sweden, who was assassinated in a theatre, just as *The Spider's Stratagem* is about a 'hero', assassinated in a theatre.*

These small operatic allusions are only satellites of the major allusive structure of the film, one that absorbs the others, including Magritte and Borges, and creates a never seen spectacle which supports that other spectacle created by Athos Sr at the moment of his death. The father's original plot to murder Mussolini hinges on his idea to have a bomb go off in the middle of a performance of *Rigoletto* which Il Duce will be attending. The explosion would occur at the end of Act I, when Rigoletto's daughter, who is taken by his enemies to be his mistress, is carried away by courtiers. Rigoletto, the hunchback fool, recalling the curse put on his own head by an offended Count, cries out: 'Ah la maledizione!', 'Ah! the curse!' At which point the bomb would go off.

---

* Italian censors, sensitive about the political implications, caused Verdi's librettist to change the location of the opera. It is set in Boston. There is an earlier reference to *Ballo* in the film. During the dialogue between Athos Jr and Gaibazzi, the latter says that the anti-fascism of the four friends was of a conspiratorial nature, like Samuel and Tom, who conspire against Riccardo in *Un ballo in maschera*. I am grateful to Martin Mangold for helping me identify the passages and pointing out the relevance of the opera's history to the film.

Athos betrays his own plot, informs the Carabinieri so that Mussolini will not appear at the performance. When Athos Jr finally discovers all the pieces of the puzzle, it is again at the opera house (he has been there already, for a meeting with the fascist Beccaccia, who informed him that as much as he hated his father he was not responsible for his death). Once again *Rigoletto* is being performed; history returns in cyclic patterns. This climactic sequence of revelation begins with Athos Jr at the railway station at night, hoping he will be able to leave Tara. Visually – as happens so often during the film – Bertolucci entraps the figure, here by photographing him through the windows and within the walls of the station (which is lit like Magritte's *The Empire of Light*). On the soundtrack, the overture to *Rigoletto* is heard. Shots of the town, its street lights and the empty railroad tracks are intercut with those of Athos. The music reaches a crescendo. The sailor who got off the train with Athos at the beginning now runs to catch his train out. He is the only character allowed to leave the town. Bertolucci tracks his camera beneath the trees and hanging street lamps, past the loudspeakers broadcasting the opera to the peasants outside the hall. Athos is drawn by the music and leaves the station for the opera house.

As he walks, Bertolucci cuts on the soundtrack from the opera's overture to its first major aria, the Duke's lively song about his love for all women: 'Questa o quella', 'For me, this woman or that is the same/As the many others I see around me ...' Two old men stand on chairs, ears pressed to the loudspeakers as if hypnotized by the music. Athos walks round the streets, passing by the elderly opera lovers frozen in their places, until he approaches the front of the house, guarded by police on either side, as if it were many years ago and Mussolini was indeed in attendance. At this point, Bertolucci jumps forward in the opera (just as in *Before the Revolution*, we see no performance and the music on the soundtrack is cut to counterpoint the events). Rigoletto has just met Sparafucile, the killer for hire, whom he will ultimately ask to murder the Duke, who is in love with his precious daughter, Gilda. The curse given Rigoletto by Monterone, the old Count whose own daughter had been seduced by the Duke and who was mocked by Rigoletto at court, still wrings his heart: 'Tal pensiero perché conturba ognor ...', 'Why does such a thought keep troubling/My mind? .../Will misfortune strike me?/Ah no! That is folly!' But no, this is not folly. The thoughts of his father obsess Athos and misfortune will indeed strike as the truth is revealed. By the time Rigoletto is singing 'Ah no! è follia!', Athos has reached an ox-cart, held by a little girl and containing a group of old women listening to the opera. They tell him about the night of his father's death, about the gypsies with their warnings and the man in black on the motorcycle. In

Revisiting the past: the three friends at *Rigoletto*

the opera, Gilda is asking her father, 'What worries you so?/Tell your poor daughter./If there's some mystery . . . reveal it to her . . ./Let her know about her family.' These are, of course, the very questions Athos is trying to put to his own father.

As soon as Athos enters the theatre, a leap in the libretto is made. What we see is an establishing shot of the auditorium, then the three friends in their box. Athos sits in his father's old box which is on the opposite side of the auditorium. When he and the three old men make eye contact, there is a series of intricate movements: the camera pulls back from the box where the three friends sit to Athos, changing focus each time and cutting at the end of the movement. At each cut one less friend is seen in the opposite box, until Athos finally turns and sees all three of them entering his own. The visuals here are complex; the match with the opera more complex still. In the opera, the Duke and Gilda are in love with each other, though she does not know what a heartless cad he is. The courtiers do not know that Rigoletto has a daughter and think Gilda is his mistress. They kidnap her in order to get back at Rigoletto, the sharp-tongued court jester. It is the end of the first act, and in the narrative of the film history is about to return in another cycle.

When we first see the three friends, Gaibazzi is in raptures over the music and has to be brought to attention by the other two. They point out Athos, and exactly upon the reverse shot – from the point of view of the friends to Athos alone in his box – Gilda, in the opera, is being carried off by the courtiers. She cries to Rigoletto, 'Soccorso, padre mio!', 'Help, father!' On the cut back to the friends, the courtiers cry 'Victory!' 'Help,' Gilda cries as the camera pulls back to Athos. These matches of image to libretto are both extraordinary and hilarious, for indeed Athos has figuratively called on his father for help all through the film, to succour his son, to clarify memory so that both may be released from the trap that, until this moment, the son did not know his father had created. And the more he sought his father, the more Athos discovered the labyrinths of lies and betrayals his father left behind him. At this moment, he is about to find out directly the details of these lies. His father and the co-conspirators are about to have their victory. In the opera, poor Rigoletto has been blindfolded and rendered help-less – as, less literally, has Athos. As the camera begins its series of movements and changes in focus from the friends to Athos, the trapped Rigoletto is singing, 'Non han finito ancor! ... qual derisione!', 'They still haven't finished! ... What a joke!'

In the narrative of the film they have, in fact, not yet begun. On the soundtrack, as one friend after the other leaves the box to come to Athos – the action at one point interrupted by a nighttime version of the frequently recurring shot of the town and its surrounding corn-fields, the moon hanging in the sky – Rigoletto is crying plaintively after his daughter. As the friends arrive at Athos's box, he gets up, and as he does he catches sight first of Costa, then of his own reflection in the mirror facing his seat. At the precise moment when he and the viewer sees his reflection, Rigoletto cries out, 'Ah! la maledizione!' The curse has returned. It is the very point at which Athos Sr was going to set off the bomb to kill Il Duce, and where he was killed in his place. Athos Jr, seeing himself/his father and the friends reflected back to him, realizes, finally, that his father was murdered by them. They now proceed to relate the details of Athos's story to his son, completing the circle of the web.*

I suggested that Bertolucci's use of Verdi subsumes Magritte and Borges in the allusive structure of *The Spider's Stratagem*. It would be more appropriate to say that *Rigoletto* provides the connections between

---

* Immediately after his revelation, Athos turns sideways in his opera box, the angle of his head and its reflection in the mirror approaching that of Magritte's painting *Not to be Reproduced*. In fact, father and son have been reproduced as the same figure.

them. For one thing, the profound artifice of opera is made more evident when placed in the context of a modernist film; and the artifice of film, already brought to the fore by its modernist structure, is further exposed when counterpointed to the opera. The opera's melodrama is cooled in its contact with the film narrative, and, simultaneously, the film narrative reveals its suppressed melodrama through contact with the opera. *Rigoletto* is melodramatic spectacle; *The Spider's Stratagem* is about the political effects of spectacle, in particular the fascist penchant for rhetorical action that snuffs out signification beneath the burden of bloated signifiers. By alluding to the operatic spectacle without actually showing it, Bertolucci permits the viewer to comprehend, without participating in, the spectacle that Athos Sr created to hide his treachery. This is not to suggest that there is anything of fascist spectacle within *Rigoletto* itself, but that in the relationship of opera and film narrative Bertolucci is able to inscribe a notion of a father's act, the psychological and political enormity of which can only be expressed through the indirection of allusion.

Finally, *Rigoletto* informs the film every bit as much as does Borges' *Theme of the Traitor and Hero*. *Rigoletto* is about a fool whose blindness leads to the betrayal of his only love, his daughter Gilda. He hires a killer to murder the Duke with whom his daughter is madly in love. Gilda, dressed as a man, discovers the plan and substitutes herself for her lover. She is stabbed and stuffed in a sack, which Rigoletto pulls along to dump in the river. He hears his daughter's last sighs and discovers to his horror what has happened. Like *Rigoletto, The Spider's Stratagem* concerns a father who betrays his offspring and, in a reverse of the events of the opera, a son who mistakes the identity of his father. The betrayal and the mistaken identities are not expressed melo-dramatically, but are the results of melodrama and of a curse, here the one Athos Sr put on the town when he betrayed it and betrayed his betrayal by turning it into a spectacle to perpetuate the illusion of his own heroism. Athos Sr, like Verdi himself, wishes to make melodrama. In a flashback sequence that occurs after the three friends enter Athos Jr's box – a flashback that pieces together the story of the father's actions – Athos Sr is seen with his comrades on a rooftop overlooking the town. He embraces the town with his arms, promising to make all Tara a theatre, and its history a theatre, with himself as the leading actor. As he announces his plans, the overture to *Rigoletto* is heard once again. Athos believes all this will expunge his own act and help continue the fight against fascism. The result is that, as with Rigoletto and his daughter, Athos destroys what he should save – first the town and then his son. He reproduces fascism with his gesture.

Athos would have killed Mussolini during an opera. Instead he makes an opera out of history in which everyone acts a role and sings the same arias again and again. He has himself killed, and in turn kills his son, not literally (as I say, Bertolucci represses the melodrama) but by preventing him from acting on any other stage but that of the narrative created by the father, woven by him into the web that entangles all the other participants in the spectacle. Athos Sr would have rewritten *Rigoletto* with himself as the central character. He is both cursed and puts a curse on his own son, who, finally, becomes his father.

The narrative of *The Spider's Stratagem* is no less fantastic than the narrative of *Rigoletto*. Yet the intense reflexivity of its form, the way it deliberates over its own melodramatic potential, and the insistent ideological analogy it draws between the spectacle of fascism and the spectacle of Athos's production of history give the fantastic the force of intellectual enquiry. Like Verdi, Bertolucci can use style to generate the fantastic in a way that mitigates its absurdities. Verdi overrode his absurd libretti with musical structures that absorbed them. Bertolucci creates events with a visual style, with colour, movement and cutting that become, in effect, his own musical structure, as attractive as the composer's and more eloquent. More than opera, the style has meaning and moral force.

Obviously, Bertolucci's medium of expression, his authorial and aesthetic ideologies, and the political dimensions of his work, are rather different from Verdi's. Yet one has to account for the almost obsessive concern on the film-maker's part to find a dialectical structure that might draw the relationships between them, both honouring and negating the nineteenth-century composer by absorbing his work and restructuring it within a modern, cinematic context. As long as Bertolucci keeps in mind that the relationship is a dialectical one, the effect can be astounding, as it is in *The Spider's Stratagem*, or in *1900*, which attempts to use certain elements of nineteenth-century melodramatic realism. When he approaches Verdian excess with an uncritical eye, as in *La luna*, the reinscription process breaks down. When he drops all overt allusion to Verdi, which in the period we are discussing occurs only in *The Conformist* and *Last Tango in Paris*, one of two things happens. He either maintains a rigorous modernist structure that controls the nascent melodrama of the work, as in *The Conformist*; or he begins to replace the reflexive elements, the jarring spatial, temporal and perceptual dislocations, with a more conventional chronological structure and attention to character that tends to elicit a conventional emotional response.

A definite pattern can be seen emerging in the progress of Bertolucci's post-*Partner* films. *The Spider's Stratagem* draws on a number of modernist influences, plays them off the Verdian base, creating a kind of echo effect between nineteenth and twentieth-century modes of expression. The allusions to Verdi then stop for two films, the first of which maintains its modernist allegiances, while the second shows some initial signs of shedding them. The narrative proper of *1900* begins with the tearful announcement that Verdi is dead and then goes on to recoup that loss by returning to some of the familiar structures of nineteenth-century melodrama, maintaining modernism as a hermeneutic, accessible only through dialectical analysis. After the disastrous experience of *1900*, Bertolucci attempts a resurrection of Verdi in *La luna*, but by this time the reference points have become reversed: the modernist structure lies outside the film and the operatic becomes the driving force. Finally, in *Tragedy of a Ridiculous Man*, which contains only one reference to the composer, Bertolucci restructures the formal premises of his work, maintaining a realist narrative, at least in so far as chronological development is concerned, but suppressing melodrama and emotional response more than he had since *Partner*.

The pattern of development will become clearer with a discussion of *Last Tango*, a film that can be examined from three different perspectives: as a *succès de scandale*, Bertolucci's most popular film, gaining its fame – or notoriety – from the many censorship battles fought over its exhibition; as a 'revolutionary' expression of sexuality; as an intricate formal construct that climaxes the various experiments in cinematic narrative formation that began in *The Spider's Stratagem* and begins to move them in other directions. The first problem is now a dead issue. Censorship battles are usually temporary and ultimately not as important as problems with distribution. Censorship articulates the fear still felt in some quarters of the emotive force of cinema, and in Italy reflects the existence of Catholic authority and old fascist legal codes. In the long run, censorship helps a film's commercial viability by stimulating interest. A producer's refusal to distribute a film or, as in the case of *1900*, distributing it poorly after enforcing cuts on it, destroys a film textually and commercially. The sexual content of *Last Tango* was always overvalued and often misunderstood. Its images of simulated fornication may have helped publicize the film, but it is not reducible to those images. In the last analysis the film is not about sexuality but about the perception of sexual relationships, the structuring of emotion, and the ideology of romance, the self and the family. *Last Tango* is a political film that does not speak explicitly of politics; a modernist film whose reflexivity is deflected through an intense emotional aura.

Last Tango in Paris is Bertolucci's first full-length film after *Partner* to be set in the present (*The Spider's Stratagem* is set in a present whose presence is deconstructed as a knowable and secure position). Repressing the explicit political explorations of the preceding films, it concentrates instead on the subjective, sexual elements that were only one part of their structure. 'Represses' is the operative word. *Last Tango* discusses politics from the inside out, from a social-psychological perspective, demonstrating the individual, emotional aspect of the political rather than the politicization of the psychological – the process that characterizes *The Spider's Stratagem* and *The Conformist*.

This act of repression can also be detected in the organization of the narrative. *Last Tango* manifests a change in the exuberant temporal play of the two preceding films, marking a definitive alteration in Bertolucci's style and echoing a change that was occurring in cinema worldwide – a movement back to straightforward chronology, to the classical narrative structure of 'logical' progression from one point to the next, complete with cause, effect, motivation and closure. In this respect, *Last Tango* is among the first films of the 70s by a modernist director to announce the end of modernism.

The causes of this end are a matter of speculation, some of it rather banal. Cine-modernism had simply run its course; the first generation of modernist film-makers had played out their imaginative energy; film criticism was, by this time, absorbing that energy and, within its own discourse, enlarging upon the critical enquiry that had once been conducted in the films themselves. In the particular instance of Bertolucci's development, the problem is both more complex and more definable. It is unlikely that Bertolucci would consciously follow the changes that were occurring in modernist cinema, for these became clear only in retrospect. In the early 70s, when *Last Tango* was made, one still looked with hope at the work of Coppola, Altman and Scorsese in America, and at the early experiments of the new German cinema. Although Godard was about to withdraw from commercial cinema, his influence was still present. However, one can speculate that Bertolucci was concerned with creating a more popular work than he had done to this point, that his choice of subject-matter and star had great commercial possibilities. He may well have felt that these possibilities could best be realized within something approaching a conventional narrative structure, in which temporal organization would not create a barrier for an audience and in which the security of emotional response would replace the threat of a political discourse.

I am not ascribing a cynical calculation of effects on Bertolucci's part. What I am suggesting is a search for accessibility, which was successful in *Last Tango* and which failed in *1900*, where politics re-entered as an explicit narrative function and collided with the expectations set up by a narrative structure more conventional than its predecessor. Nor am I suggesting that in *Last Tango* Bertolucci set out to create a simple film. It may be his most emotionally rich work, but the emotion is not generated at the expense of a thoughtful, intricate form and a complex, expressive style. Despite its chronological linearity, the narrative is intricately structured. The characters – particularly Marlon Brando's Paul – dominate the narrative more than they do in the earlier films, focusing the gaze on figures who fit more comfortably within the codes of emotional expression than do Marcello Clerici or Athos Magnani. At the same time the characters are inscribed into a *mise en scène* whose light and shadow, colour and movement dominate them, comment upon their activities and, like the preceding films, initiate a perceptual investigation that moves beyond the characters and their fictional locality.

Many of the formal elements I have traced in Bertolucci's films remain and are refined in *Last Tango*, and some new ones are developed. I noted that the film is without overt reference to Verdi, and that this partly accounts for the change in the film's narrative structure. Yet even without explicit reference, the film is in many respects the most operatic in Bertolucci's canon up to this point. For one thing, Gato Barbieri's music provides an emotional foundation to the narrative so powerfully insistent that, as in opera, the narrative often turns into a function of the music, which becomes its driving force. What is more, the film is filled with sequences analogous to operatic duets: the dialogues between Paul and Jeanne, Paul and his mother-in-law, Paul and Marcel (his wife's lover), for example. Paul's extraordinary monologue over his wife's body is one of the great arias in contemporary film. One might stretch a point and suggest that the film is, in fact, Bertolucci's version of *La traviata*, itself set in Paris. The role of Violetta, the suffering romantic courtesan, shifts between Jeanne and Paul. At the same time, Paul also takes on aspects of Violetta's unhappy suitor Alfredo, as well as Alfredo's father Germont. That stern, patriarchal figure first appears as an absent presence in Jeanne's dead father, and is then assumed by Paul. The repressive influence of this figure provides, as we shall see, much of the film's implicit political substance.

The painterly influence on *Last Tango* is more immediately apparent than the operatic, and functions more directly than in *The Spider's Stratagem*. The film's credits appear over two portraits by Francis Bacon, one of a man in white underclothes, lying on a red divan against a yellow wall and green floor (it is the left panel of *Double Portrait of Lucien Freud and Frank Auerbach*, 1964); the other is of a woman in white jacket and brown skirt, seated, arms and legs folded, on a wooden chair in a room with black walls and purple floors, with the silhouette of a rat in the lower foreground *(Study for Portrait (Isabel Rawsthörne),* 1964). During the credits, the portraits are shown one after the other, then placed side by side – as they are in a catalogue for a Bacon exhibition that took place in Paris just prior to the making of the film and which Bertolucci visited with Vittorio Storaro and Marlon Brando.[30]

The portraits foreshadow the film's two major characters, Paul and Jeanne, and prefigure both its visual style and its psychological perspective. Bacon's influence on the film is so intensive that at many points Bertolucci imitates Baconian composition. After the sequence in which Paul sodomizes Jeanne, for example, there is a montage of Paul lying on the floor in various positions (the montage is punctuated by shots of the metro roaring overhead). In the first shot, the camera gazes through a doorway at Paul lying on the floor on his side, his right arm extended. Behind him is another archway and behind that another room. In the rear is the mysterious white draped object that dominates many of the shots in the apartment. The second shot of the series is closer to the figure, who is now on his back, legs crossed, the infamous butter lying nearby to his left. The final shot is a closer version of the first, Paul lying on his side. The position of the figure and the enclosure of the room are analogous to the Baconian style. As is the lighting: each of these shots is bathed in the yellow-orange light that pervades most of the interior shots of Paul and Jeanne's apartment, and can be seen in windows and through doorways in many exterior shots. The light acts as the cinematic equivalent to the yellow-orange colour that Bacon uses as background to the figures in many of his paintings.

With full understanding of the difference between painting and cinema, Bertolucci gets as close as he can to the re-creation of a Bacon canvas – through composition, through the use of colour, through the positioning of his characters' bodies within the frame. By using mirrors and glass he attempts to suggest the distortions of Bacon's figures, the impression of the human body dissolving into a painful, featureless mass. In short, he goes as far as he can in creating cinematic equivalents to the form and meaning of Bacon's work: the psycho-sexual pain of existence within the enclosures of the contemporary world; the expression of immanent dissolution under the pressure of that pain. This is, minus the implicit political interpretation that Bertolucci adds to his narrative, essentially what *Last Tango in Paris* is 'about'. That Bertolucci can merge the formal presentation of that content with the work of a major contemporary painter is a sign not only of his own continuing interest in painting but of his insistence upon carrying out the modernist project of allusion: the recognition of the formal and contextual relationship of different works and different modes of expression, the comprehension of the enormous text, the chain of

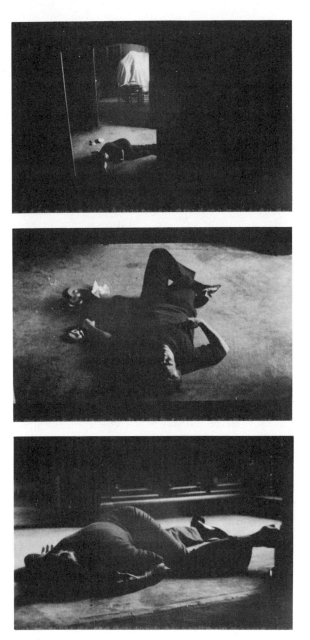

The Baconian style in *Last Tango in Paris*: the montage of Paul

signifiers produced by the imagination linked together, refracting, fragmenting, relocating the experiences to which they give form.

Bacon himself takes part in this phenomenon, and his work is influenced by photography and the cinema. He was, for example, taken with the image from *Battleship Potemkin* of the woman with pince-nez and bloodied eye, and in 1957 made a canvas entitled *Study for the Nurse in the Film 'Battleship Potemkin'*. A movie camera makes up an incongruous presence in his 1970 *Triptych: Studies from the Human Body*. In the middle panel two bodies on a green table melt into each other in the act of love-making. In the right panel a male figure, trapped within a closet frame, works a camera which is pointed at the figures in the middle. In each of the panels the figures are surrounded by the yellow-orange colour which Bertolucci translates into the light that bathes the room in *Last Tango*. Bacon's paintings are a static cinema of agonies within rooms, of figures seen as if reflected in horribly distorting mirrors or as if they were bodies which had been dissected. In his use of allusion, in his painterly form, in his content, Bacon summarizes major modernist impulses. 'What painting had never shown before,' writes John Russell, 'is the disintegration of the social being which takes place when one is alone in a room which has no looking-glass. We may well feel at such times that the accepted hierarchy of our features is collapsing. ... The view out front ceases to be the only one, and our person is suddenly adrift, fragmented, and subject to strange mutation.'[31]

Last Tango places its central character in a Baconian room of yellow light, a character who refuses the looking-glass of the external world to the extent that he attempts to deny the identity of names. But rather than collapse, this drifting, fragmented figure tries to regain a structure for his life with the woman he finds in the room. The attempt at isolation fails, and when the character attempts to re-enter the world he is destroyed.

But because *Last Tango* is narrative cinema and not painting, and the creation of a sensibility different from Bacon's, it is more complicated than Bacon's painting: it is an attempt to offer an ideological explanation for some of Bacon's modernist premises. Yet it remains at the same time close to its source, not only to Bacon but to the painterly premise in general, to a notion of composition, of significant framing of figures and objects. In the previous films, camera movement had largely determined composition. Here Bertolucci develops methods of moving figures within the frame, or of bringing them into and out of the frame, which, in combination with the movement of the camera (Storaro's camerawork is at its most graceful in this film, articulating emotional relationships through the traversal of space between figures) and the cutting, relates information that often takes the place of, or is more important than, what is related by dialogue alone.*

An example of this compositional skill occurs in the film's opening sequences, during which – after Paul's first utterance – no dialogue occurs. The first post-credits shot is a crane down to the figure of Paul. He is standing beneath the Paris Métro, which is roaring over his head. The camera assumes a triple perspective: it is almost a substitute for the noise of the Métro itself; it acts as a surrogate for the spectator's own anxious look, and as an imposition by the author upon his character, swooping at him while being repulsed at the same time. For as the camera bears down on Paul, he raises his head, hands over his ears, screaming back at the noise: 'Fucking god!' There is a cut to a shot of the Métro, from Paul's point of view, a cut to a close-up of Paul, from the opposite direction, and the camera tracks back as he begins walking beneath the elevated structure. The camera has intruded upon an agonized figure, attempted to compose him, to set him before our gaze, as Bacon might one of his tortured figures. But the figure resists the composition. We are as yet unable to know anything but his despair. Through composition and its refusal, the film's two subjects – the character and the viewer – are left uncomposed.

But the desire for composition cannot be denied; without it cinema (and painting) would not be able to survive the anarchy that exists outside the frame. To create meaning, signifiers must be ordered, given form, held in place. Bertolucci pursues his character, forcing him to obey the gaze. As Paul walks, his figure bowed in a heavy overcoat, the camera tracks before him. Barely noticeable, in the background, in soft focus, is the figure of Jeanne. Just before that figure can be clearly seen, another cut is made, this time to a far shot of the Métro, including the bridge beneath it and the Seine. This functions as something like a conventional establishing shot, giving us a larger view, locating us in Paris yet at the same time still withholding information we want. Although the two major characters of the fiction have begun to be held in place by the frame, narrative has not yet begun – at least not in the way we expect it to. Only in retrospect, or on re-viewing these shots, does it become clear that in fact they are composing the narrative to come by delineating the central characters and adumbrating their relationship.

* Viewers should take caution: *Last Tango* is most likely to be seen now on videotape, the image of which is cropped. Bertolucci makes extraordinary use of the breadth of the non-anamorphic wide-screen ratio. With that ratio of 1:1.85 reduced to an almost square proportion, much of what is said here about composition will be evident only by imagining the wider frame.

When, in the next shot, Paul again dominates the frame, the space behind him is in clear focus and Jeanne is behind him. A couple can be seen walking by. Paul stops and nearly breaks into tears. His hands in his pockets, he makes a strong gesture, moving them away from his body in an indication of incomprehension (the gesture is typical of Brando; throughout the film the intersection of actor and character is strongly marked, so much so that it is interesting to speculate what both character and film would have been like if Bertolucci's original choice, Jean-Louis Trintignant, who played Clerici in *The Conformist*, had played Paul). At the moment of his gesture, Jeanne is quite near and can be clearly seen in the frame. She is wearing a white coat and fur, with a dark flowered hat which she holds on her head with her hand. She passes Paul, turning briefly to look at him. Her face barely registers any reaction, and she walks on ahead of him, neither character paying any further attention to the other. Bertolucci, however, pays attention to the visual dynamics of their first meeting and begins to foreshadow both their relationship and its end. As Jeanne moves off, Paul is put into soft focus as she now dominates our gaze. There follows a cut to Jeanne walking away, as if seen from Paul's point of view. But it is a false point of view, for with the reverse shot we see that Paul is looking in another direction and not at Jeanne at all.

The characters who will soon become the focus of the film meet and do not, in effect, see each other; though, by seeing them, the viewer is led unconsciously into the formative stages of the narrative. Uneasiness is provoked as Bertolucci continues to play on their coincidental crossings, charging them with meaning and withholding that meaning at the same time, developing what Roland Barthes calls the hermeneutic code, 'one of the forces that can take over the text ... one of the voices out of which the text is woven', which in this instance sets up *'delays* (obstacles, stoppages, deviations) in the flow of the discourse.'[32] The discourse of *Last Tango* is at this point still nascent. We can detect a 'voice' in the images but cannot yet clearly hear what it is saying, for the hermeneutic code promises that a disclosure will be made while at the same time holding that disclosure in abeyance.

As I noted, the reverse shot of Jeanne walking away from Paul under the bridge is not authorized by his point of view. She is part of the narrative under formation, but not yet controlled by it – and, in a sense, never will be. Paul looks away and then looks down. Bertolucci, however, must still pursue her, and there is another reverse shot of Jeanne from behind, and then a long shot taken from the side of the bridge. Traffic goes by; we can just make out Jeanne and, behind her, Paul. The camera executes a broad rightward track to the front of the archway formed by the Métro overpass, picking up Jeanne just as she walks through the arch. Paul is now seen in deep focus behind her. At this point there is a cut to something quite unexpected, something that adds to the enigma of these opening shots: a group of policemen standing around a police bus, the windows of which glow with the yellow Baconian light. The enigma is heightened by the editorial association of the police with Jeanne. We see her again as she enters the following shot – or rather part of her, for the composition is from a low angle as she continues on her walk; her head is beyond the top of the frame; to her left we can make out a street-sweeper. The police and their bus appear again in the following shot, this one from a high angle, looking through a fence above the street. There is no determining point of view for this, though again the figures are associated with Jeanne, who appears in the following shot, which begins to define her in less enigmatic terms. She gaily leaps over the street-sweeper's broom and leaves the frame. Her gaiety is contrasted to Paul's despair, for he is again behind her in this shot, indistinct in soft focus. Bertolucci cuts immediately to his face. He is weeping. While Jeanne seems to embrace the city, enjoying herself and in control of her surroundings, Paul continues to be oppressed by them. From the close-up of his face looking up, Bertolucci cuts to a low-angle shot of the Métro bridge, the camera tracking slowly to the buildings surrounding it. This is clearly Paul's point of view, since we see him again looking up, an alienated figure, almost crushed by the environment that oppresses him.

In the following shots, Jeanne comes to the apartment building on the rue Jules Verne (the street of fantasies) in which, eventually, Paul will engage her in his attempt to escape the world in a haven of anonymous sexuality, dissolving the self in sensation. Yellow light glows from the doorway of the building. Jeanne rings to ask about a room for rent. No one answers the doorbell and she leaves, walking down a flight of stairs, past the policemen and their bus, and into a bar to phone her mother. The sequence in the bar demonstrates another compositional arrangement that Bertolucci employs throughout the film. He divides the frame by means of doorways, glass, mirrors – objects that cut the characters off from physical contact with each other. The viewer must therefore actively relate the various parts of the divided composition, which are analogous to Bacon's two- and three-panel canvases in which a figure is seen in different perspectives, or different figures are juxtaposed in a painterly version of cinematic montage. For Bertolucci, the divided frame produces an internal montage, separating and connecting the figures simultaneously.

In this instance, when Jeanne enters the bar and goes to the washroom in front of the telephone booth, Bertolucci composes the shot so that the bar itself, with its patrons and their activities, are on the left of the frame, in dark, neutral colours; the washroom door is screen right, emanating the yellow light. Within that area, once Bertolucci cuts to it, we can make out a figure behind the glass of the phone booth. In the washroom itself, Jeanne confronts an anomalous and somewhat repellent figure, an old woman washing and inserting her false teeth (all these actions are presented in relatively short shots). The old woman provokes the first self-conscious reaction in Jeanne. She looks at herself in the mirror, making faces (reminiscent of Jean Seberg's reactions to her mirrored image in *Breathless*), showing some small degree of recognition about old age and decay, until a brief cut to the doorknob of the phone booth, and the sound of its opening, brings her and our attention back to the figure behind the door. It is Paul in the phone booth. In a following shot, with Jeanne in soft focus behind him, he leaves the washroom without noting Jeanne's presence. Bertolucci cuts back to the split composition of bar and yellow-lit door, as Paul disappears from the frame; then returns to Jeanne in the phone booth, this time pausing long enough to allow his camera to pan up her body as she exposes her leg from under her short skirt.

Not only the nascent narrative relationships, but the formal and stylistic structure of much of the film is limned out in these opening shots (which analysis tends to express in slow motion – they take up only about five minutes of screen time). The intensity of Bertolucci's gaze at his subjects, counterpointed by an equally intense interest in their surroundings, which provide relevant information about them and their state in yet another example of the lingering neo-realist influence upon his work; the careful compositional relationships between the characters; the schematized control of colour and light; the use of mirrors and distorting glass; the controlled tracking movements – all indicate an extraordinary, almost obsessive desire to extract significance from each shot. The non-verbal discourse begun in the image structure of the film's opening sequence continues throughout, creating an intensity and a lyricism always played discordantly, relating emotions that are charged and short-circuited.

The intensity is created by the short-circuiting, the narrative's refusal fully to discharge the emotions it creates, an effect achieved by continually drawing the viewer into a contemplation of its form, rather than permitting that form to disappear behind the emotions it generates. For despite its movement away from modernism, *Last Tango* still retains a reflexive structure. Through the strength of its images, through various aspects of its narrative structure, and through its analysis of the ideology of sexuality and patriarchal power, the text asks the viewer to contemplate the artificiality of the act of cinematic looking, and to consider the greater political ramifications of the

The intensity of the gaze: Jeanne and Paul in *Last Tango in Paris* (Maria Schneider, Marlon Brando)

ostensibly private emotions of the characters involved.

Some of the reflexive gestures occur by means of allusion and parody, through the painterly visual structure and through direct reference to the film-making process. The latter occurs within the film's secondary narrative, involving the relationship between Jeanne and her film-maker fiancé, Tom. Within the fiction, Tom is the foil of Paul and his passionate, self-destructive quest for a release from his despair. Tom is engaged not merely to Jeanne, but to making a film of their engagement. His resulting lack of emotional engagement contrasts with the intensity of Paul's relationship with Jeanne, or, more appropriately, his *use* of Jeanne as an object for emotional release. Her decision to marry Tom and adopt a safe bourgeois life signifies her ultimate betrayal of the passion Paul attempts finally, and too late, to offer to her.

The fact that Tom is not only a film-maker but is played by Jean-Pierre Léaud, whose very presence recalls Truffaut, Godard and the obsessive cinema-making of the New Wave, introduces a parodic element into the film's structure. No doubt Tom represents Bertolucci's last attack upon what he perceives to be the excesses of the early Godard and Truffaut films, the individual so immersed in his craft that he can only filter life through the lens of his camera. But in a more profound sense, Tom is neither Godard nor Truffaut but Bertolucci ('I was poking fun at myself rather than anybody else,' Bertolucci says of the character[33]). For just as Tom intrudes his camera into his own life and that of his lover (which is not life but fiction), so Bertolucci intrudes his camera into the agonies of Paul and Jeanne and the banality of Tom. Of course he does more than intrude: he creates the agonies, creates the characters (with Brando, in the case of Paul, colluding to make emotions and to embalm them on film). But then the author enters his own work via a character, and proceeds to make fun of that very character who signifies his presence. Bertolucci hints at all this through a little joke. After the first meeting of Paul and Jeanne in the apartment, their urgent love-making and decision to take the flat for themselves, Jeanne goes to meet Tom at a station. They embrace; his crew films them: 'If I kiss you, that might be cinema,' he says. As they talk and argue, Jeanne at one point pushes away the microphone which one of the crew has pointed at them. As she does so, the dialogue on the soundtrack that *we* hear fades out, until the microphone is brought back into position. For a moment, the film Tom is making is explicitly the film we see, just as the film Bertolucci is making is implicitly the film we see. If the apparatus were not present – and more important, if the intelligence that uses it to create the cinematic narrative of these fictional characters' lives were not present – we would neither hear nor see anything. There would be no *Last Tango in Paris,* which is not reality but film. *Ceci n'est pas une pipe.*

Another, more subtle, aspect of reflexivity occurs through a process of doubling characters within the narrative, who reflect each other and by so doing reflect upon their own status as characters in a fiction (as well as reflecting the subtle repetition of psychological pain that extends from one character to another and the continuing refinement of the doubles concept that had concerned Bertolucci since *Partner*). Paul has an almost literal double in the character of Marcel, his late wife Rosa's lover (played by the old neo-realist actor Massimo Girotti, who was the lover in Visconti's *Ossessione*). One of the film's important duets occurs when the two of them sit side by side, wearing the identical bathrobes Paul's wife Rosa bought for them, as they discuss Rosa's incomprehensible character, the camera panning up the wall to show where she attempted to tear off the wallpaper with her fingernails. Marcel is the passive side of Paul, the man content to sit in his room clipping newspaper items. Both men are enclosed, not merely during the sequence in Marcel's tiny room but in a larger sense, by their emotions. Paul attempts to expend his emotions in another room in the rue Jules Verne; Marcel is reduced by his. He is the shadow cast by

Paul and Rosa, and like the shadow cast by that other double in *Partner*, his presence in turn reduces Paul. The two of them become, finally, diminished within the enigma of Rosa (who has her own double both in the figure of Jeanne and in Jeanne's mother).

If Marcel is Paul's double, Tom is his Other. He is an individual secure in his life where Paul is deracinated, absorbed in external activity where Paul is trapped in subjectivity. Yet at the same time the terms are reversible. Tom can be seen as being entrapped within his vocation, staring into the mirror of cinema while Paul attempts to create a new symbolic order, a realm of the senses (observed by the eye of cinema). If Tom is the bourgeois romantic, enthralled by how he can make life into its own reflection, then Paul *becomes* the bourgeois romantic and attempts to rebuild his life out of the reflections of cinema. In a sense, he becomes a figure Tom might have created on film; both, in fact, become reflections of the form that creates them. Tom may begin as lyric tenor to Paul's tragic baritone, but by the end they are both Gene Kelly. Late in the narrative, Tom is filming Jeanne's selection of a wedding dress in preparation for their 'pop' wedding. In ecstasy, Tom runs out into the pouring rain, calling out to Jeanne in the only language he – and Bertolucci – knows; the language of cinema. 'You are better than Rita Hayworth,' he yells, 'better than Joan Crawford, Kim Novak, Lauren Bacall, better than Ava Gardner when she loved Mickey Rooney.' The crew packs up and leaves. Jeanne disappears. Tom pursues her in the rain and Bertolucci cuts to Paul in the entrance way of the apartment building in the rue Jules Verne. He has just come out of the rain and he does a little dance. Paul is the American in Paris, Tom the Parisian cineaste; both are singing and dancing in the rain.*

Once again we see Bertolucci creating an integral mix of influences. Painting, Verdian melodrama, American musical comedy, are all put at the service of a narrative that contains them and permits them to play off one another, holding together the dominant structure of the film. The counterpoint is discordant, the modernist urge pulls against the romantic, the characters' movement toward dissolution struggles against their desire to impress themselves upon the world, to achieve presence. Perhaps more accurately, the romantic urge becomes a middle term in the film's structure, played on by its two mutations, melodrama with its insistence upon the expression and the death of desire, and modernism, which seeks also the death of desire, but forces desire to examine its own reflection as it dies; forces the observer to

---

* The association between Paul and Gene Kelly is a conscious one. Cf. E. Ungari, *Scene madri di Bernardo Bertolucci*, p. 91.

examine that reflection as well. In *Last Tango* both melodrama and modernism impose on the romantic and attempt to destroy it. They impose on the spectator, one insisting that we enter the text and partake of the emotions it offers, the other insisting that we pull away and examine the structure of those emotions.

A clear example of this conflict occurs about midway into the film. Tom and Jeanne are in a boat, being filmed by his crew as he promises he will marry her in a week. He places a lifebelt round her, which she removes and throws in the water, where it sinks like a stone. Printed on the lifebelt is the name 'L'Atalante', the title of the barge in Jean Vigo's 1934 film of the same name. Vigo was a film-maker who gathered to him the romantic legend of the sickly, misunderstood artist, and whose films were either banned or held up in distribution (he made only four). *L'Atalante*, his last film, not seen publicly in its original form until after his death, is a romance of newlyweds (the husband's name is Jean) who take their honeymoon on the husband's boat. The bride comes under the tutelage of the wise old first mate (Michel Simon); she leaves her husband to wander about Paris, finally joining him again in a celebration of love reconciled.

Bertolucci had already made a reference to *L'Atalante* in *Before the Revolution*, in a sequence in which Fabrizio and Gina lie in different rooms, moving about in sexual desire for each other, as do the couple in a sequence in Vigo's film. In *Last Tango* the reference is more general and significant. Tom would preserve Jeanne's life with the security of marriage – a security that Paul has attacked. Jeanne, still under Paul's tutelage, rejects Tom's protective gesture, which is itself shown to be false by the fact that the lifebelt sinks. The statement is simple: there is no security in the myths of romantic love created by movies, an observation confirmed by the cycle through which the characters pass.

Paul has attempted to play a version of the Michel Simon role of Vigo's film, the man wise to the ways of the world. But unlike the Simon character he suffers too much, wants too much, and makes the fatal error of falling in love with the woman he attempts to tutor. Vigo, the conventional romantic, could not forgo a romantic closure to his film, the reuniting of his lovers. Bertolucci unites two of his lovers, Jeanne and Tom, though for Jeanne it is a union made of desperation. She turns to Tom as an escape from the sexual pressures and humiliations visited on her by Paul, whose role as tutor becomes confused with that of oppressor. Paul has attempted to leave his role of the anxiety-ridden, desolate man, ruined by love, seeking shelter in a Baconian space of sexuality removed from the world and from identity. He then decides to re-enter the world and become re-created by the romantic mythos that had been his undoing. When he does, it destroys him.

This movement is defined by the film's *mise en scène*, by its various allusive gestures, and is driven by the structure of the film's narrative. I have discussed the fact that Bertolucci uses a linear chronology for the narrative of *Last Tango*. However, he does not yield to the banality of conventional chronological structure, creating instead a complex of mutually enlightening parts, a sequence of discrete sequences which play against each other (in effect doubling upon each other), none of them reaching closure – though many do reach an emotional crescendo. Each of these sequences leaves a small gap, a fissure through which the spectator's perceptions and reactions may flow into or out of the following or preceding sequence, or be halted and made to start anew. Each sequence is connotatively strong and poses questions which the subsequent sequences do not necessarily answer. The hermeneutic codes set in motion at the opening of the narrative remain active throughout, and nothing is gained by the viewer without careful probing of the images and their narrative linkage.

A return to the early section of the narrative will indicate the effect. Paul and Jeanne leave separately after their first meeting in the apartment. Outside, she passes the police bus again, he walks along a bridge, under the Métro. Immediately following is the sequence of Jeanne's meeting with Tom at the railway station. The doubling process is set in action. The mysterious, powerful sexuality of Paul and Jeanne in the sequestered room is compared to the public, adolescent, cinephiliac relationship of Jeanne and Tom. But lest this somewhat comic sequence lessen the spectator's curiosity about Paul, Bertolucci follows it with the latter's visit to the place of his wife's suicide, a blood-smeared bathroom, the very appearance of which echoes Hitchcock's *Psycho*. The episode consummates the enigmatic, somewhat violent aura of the preceding sequences. Paul talks with the maid of the hotel in which he and Rosa lived, and which Rosa owned. The *mise en scène* and dialogue play against one another. The camera cannot avoid the blood-stained walls and glass, behind which it occasionally moves, distorting – after the manner of Bacon – figures on the other side. The viewer is overwhelmed by the sight of the horror, while the characters, almost matter of factly, discuss the police investigation. The maid gives Paul the razor that Rosa used to kill herself and talks to him about his life – information which is itself a weapon, forming the image of a wandering and rootless individual, a man with no centre (the information offered by the maid is made up of a biography of Paul as well as of Brando and the characters he has played in films: actor, boxer, bongo player, South American revolutionary, journalist in Japan, sailor to Tahiti, moving to France where he married Rosa, a woman with money and a hotel). As she talks, Paul glances out of a window and sees

The Parisian cineaste: Tom (Jean-Pierre Léaud) with Jeanne

in an opposite room an image that emphasizes the strangeness of the hotel and his own alienation, and which acts as a synecdoche for the relationships of sexual power and oppression that are beginning to emerge from the narrative. A black man plays a saxophone as a woman mends his trouser fly with needle and thread.

The sequence ends with the camera gazing upon the maid as she continues to clean up the blood. She smiles to herself enigmatically. The following sequence returns to the apartment on the rue Jules Verne. Jeanne enters and playfully stalks the room like a cat (later in the film, Paul will present this cat with a rat, tormenting her with a dead rodent in an episode that recalls the Bacon painting behind the credits with its rat in silhouette before the seated figure of the woman). Furniture is delivered and Paul directs its placement. He lays down the rules of the game: they will not know one another's names; they will create a world separate from the one outside, which they will attempt to forget. The response to this impossible demand is suggested by the visual treatment of the sequence, by the way Bertolucci places his characters, reflecting Jeanne in a mirror, isolating Paul by a window. Her gaiety and his despair still clash; the apartment remains not a

140

refuge, but a place of isolation. This minor chord is continued in a different key in the following sequence, where Paul visits his mother-in-law (played by Maria Michi, a neo-realist actress who appeared in two Rossellini films). Bertolucci separates the characters and separates the spectator from the characters. As their meeting begins they stand on either side of a door. The camera tracks between them, displacing their centrality in the frame, finally coming to rest on a word printed upon the door: 'privé'. And Bertolucci obeys the sign. We are not permitted into the recesses of the characters; no secrets are revealed, only the external moments of torment and misunderstanding. As the sequence proceeds, the two fight with each other over the mother-in-law's wish to have a priest at Rosa's funeral. The sequence ends with Paul closing the doors on the residents who, like the film's spectactors, have been eavesdropping on this private conversation that reveals hatred and frustration without revealing their cause. Each time a door is closed by Paul, the entire screen – our view of the proceedings – goes black.

These alternations between what Paul hopes will be the safe interior world of the apartment and the crushing despair of the outside world continue for the course of the film. The contrasts can be superficially

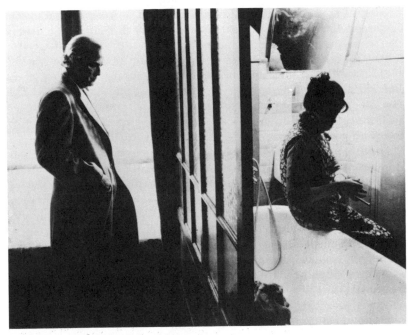

Paul at the scene of his wife's suicide

playful. Paul and Jeanne sit naked together in the apartment and make animal noises (Paul tells her a grunt would be better than a name). Bertolucci cuts to a gaggle of squawking geese at Jeanne's country house where Tom is making more shots for his documentary (the montage alludes to the cut between gossiping women and squawking birds in Fritz Lang's 1936 film *Fury*). The spectator learns more about Jeanne in these sequences in which she is apart from Paul than we ever learn about Paul himself, whose identity remains enigmatic throughout. Unlike Paul, this woman and her past pose no mysteries. She is the daughter of an upper middle-class family; her father was an army colonel who died defending France's colonial interests in Algeria. When, in the following sequence, Jeanne tells Paul about her father, how she adored him like a god in his shining uniform, Paul responds in typical fashion to her awe: 'What a steaming pile of horseshit. All uniforms are bullshit. Everything outside this place is bullshit.' But Jeanne is incorrigible on the subject of her father, and continues the story of his death in Algeria in 1958.

The introduction of her father is a major event in the narrative of *Last Tango*. He lurks as a ghost in its structure, haunting the major characters, eventually controlling their lives and deaths while becoming another double for Paul. The father is the political-social-ideological presence, just as Rosa, the other 'ghost', haunts the narrative as its enigmatic absence, the question posed by the text that is never answered. These 'ghosts' increase their control over the narrative as the film proceeds. The father's power is subtle and does not reveal itself fully until the final sequence. Rosa's continuing control over Paul undercuts all his attempts to separate himself from his past. His anguish over Rosa's suicide and his growing realization of the horror of his marriage turns his sexuality more cruel; he begins to use Jeanne as an object upon which to express his rage and frustration.

This becomes evident in another sequence between Paul and Jeanne. Paul has had a vicious fight with Rosa's mother-in-law which ends with him biting her hand and turning off all the lights in the hotel. During this interchange, Marcel — Rosa's lover — makes his first appearance. Paul introduces him with bitterness and sarcasm to the mother-in-law. Following this he returns to Jeanne and she discovers — without being aware of its significance — the razor with which Rosa killed herself. Bertolucci exercises an interesting Hitchcockian control over this sequence and its primary signifier of violence. Jeanne is in the bathroom naked when she discovers the razor in Paul's coat pocket (recalling Bertolucci's remarks in his Godard essay about rummaging in a lover's pockets 'in order to touch all the things that, as proofs of his treachery, become proofs of his existence'). Paul retrieves the razor and begins shaving (his very use of it is an action significant of masochism and self-hatred). When Paul enters the bathroom, Jeanne is at first hidden by his jacket and then placed in the background of the composition, reflected in a mirror, her presence reduced. In one shot, as Paul strops the razor, Jeanne's breast is in the foreground of the frame. Throughout she remains a naked, unsuspecting, vulnerable figure.* The suggested threat to Jeanne is momentarily undercut when she asks if Paul plans to cut her up. He answers, flippantly, no, for that would only mark her as his slave. She tells him that he hates women – a comment that uncovers one of the major problematics inherent in Bertolucci's and Brando's conception of the character of Paul, a problematic that is, for the narrative moment, shunted aside by Paul's response: 'Well, either they always pretend to know who I am, or they pretend that I don't know who they are, and that's very boring.' He digresses further from this momentary revelation of character by picking up Jeanne and whirling her about. He puts her down, says he thinks he is happy with her and walks out. She yells after him, demanding like a child that he do it again.

Paul attempts to evade the nature of his personality, to withdraw himself from the tensions established in this sequence and in the narrative as a whole. But the narrative itself does not permit such evasion. In the following sequence, Jeanne meets Tom in an underground Métro station. The music and the trains scream as the two characters scream at each other in a kind of displacement of the anger existing between Jeanne and Paul. Although they embrace at the end of the sequence, the violence that has marked the film from its beginning now emerges to overtake the desire of the characters to ignore it. While this violence is not fully realized until the end of the film, it pushes through insistently, emerging from the characters' despair.

After the episode in the underground we see Paul and Marcel together in the latter's room, wearing the identical bathrobes bought for them by Rosa. They talk in French, attempting to understand, hoping to reconstruct an image of the woman neither of them comprehended. The sequence is shot in deep yellow-orange light, which by this time has become an emblem of the tension between its promising warmth and security and the threat of anguish and hurt that always occurs within it. This sequence, and a later one in which Paul delivers a monologue over his wife's body, constitute the narrative's climactic moments. They are also the most moving and terrifying sequences in

* In the course of the sequence, Bertolucci uses the bathroom mirror to break up the figures, alluding to Bacon's 1970 triptych of a man shaving, *Three Studies of the Male Back*.

The impossibility of knowing: Paul's monologue over his wife's body

the film. Each expresses the gap of knowledge between Paul and the external world – and between the narrative and our attempts to comprehend it – the impossibility of his knowing himself or the woman he married and who killed herself. 'I wonder what she ever saw in you,' he says to Marcel in English as he leaves his double. He might as well be saying the words to himself. Later, after his agony over his wife's body – the presence that, with Jeanne's father, makes up (in Roland Barthes' sense of the phrase) the body of the text, forming its contours and our perception of it – after he has reviled her, when he has broken down in tears of pain, he cries: 'I'm sorry. I don't know why you did it. I'd do it too if I knew how.'

'I don't know . . .' The words that create the text's obliqueness. The words that, once spoken, create a downward spiral in the narrative which ends in self-delusion and death, that announce Paul's own 'suicide'. Paul's meeting with Marcel is followed by the sequence in which Paul sodomizes Jeanne while he reviles the institution and politics of the family (a speech I will deal with in more detail in the final chapter). After this, Jeanne and Tom meet on the raft and drop overboard the hopes of romantic love, the lifebelt of *L'Atalante*. Bertolucci then cuts to the apartment of Jeanne's mother, who is standing on the balcony, beating the dust out of her late husband's uniform. Jeanne proceeds to put on another part of her father's regalia, looking slightly depraved with her curly hair and adolescent face peering from beneath a military hat. She takes her father's gun, which she says he had taught her to use, and points it about the room. The father begins to assert himself. Later Jeanne will use his gun to kill Paul; it becomes associated with the razor, the instrument of Rosa's death which previously had threatened Jeanne. The two ghosts of the film begin to cohabit and assert their destructive force.

But at this point the assertion of these two absent figures is only suggested. Bertolucci continues to alter narrative sites and events in a grinding movement toward dissolution. As she leaves her mother, Jeanne announces her forthcoming marriage to Tom and joins him to plan their 'pop' wedding. When she returns to the flat in the rue Jules Verne, she finds a dead rat on her bed. Paul teases her with it, and she taunts him about her marriage; he bathes her, washes her feet, warns her of the snares of the kind of marriage and security she seeks, tells her that the man will only look to her as a refuge, force her to worship 'in front of the altar of his own prick' (the very thing Paul has been forcing her to do). Throughout this scene Jeanne is naked, except for a towel round her shoulders. Vulnerable to Paul's self-hating and self-revealing language, she stands far back in the frame, in front of a window. He insists (talking as much to himself as to her) that she is alone, and will only free herself of aloneness by staring death in the face. This is an introduction to Paul's penultimate moment of self-abasement, and his final abasement of Jeanne. He has her thrust her fingers up his rectum as he reviles her with Sadean language about embracing a dying pig.

The act is an introduction to Paul's confrontation with his wife's body, which is the confrontation with himself that he has been so desperately trying to avoid – his discovery that he was a kept man, one of Rosa's 'clients'. The revelation is presented almost tangentially, all but hidden in the emotional deluge which Brando unleashes during the sequence, and is clarified in a coda to the sequence in which another double appears. As the monologue with Rosa ends, Paul is in tears. There is a knock at the hotel door. 'I have to go, sweetheart,' he tells the corpse. 'Somebody's calling me.' A prostitute, one of the hotel's regular clients, is at the door with her customer. Paul refuses to let them in. Part of the scene is shot from the other side of the glass door of the hotel, so that the reflection of the prostitute's customer obscures Paul's figure on the other side of the glass. The prostitute yells at Paul and when the customer runs off sends Paul after him. He chases the client through the streets and beats him up. The reflections double upon one another. Obviously the whore's client reflects Paul's relationship to Rosa. In the preceding monologue he says he was one of her 'guests'. But more, Paul's body is refracted through everyone with whom he comes into contact, dissolved and mutated like the figure in a Francis Bacon painting. The more he humiliates others, the more he himself is damaged. The more Bertolucci mocks him (and the viewer), lest any fragment of romantic-melodramatic aspiration be left and believed in, the more he becomes trapped within the ideology of romance which finally destroys him. When the whore's customer escapes from Paul in the street (where the yellow light can be seen emanating from the background), the camera cranes above Paul to a shop sign. It reads 'La Bohème'.

The ironic mockery of romantic ideology turns into a fully formed indictment, created so subtly that it could be missed if the spectator fails to notice the structure that informs the emotional overlay of the text. *Last Tango* transgresses most of the codes of conventional, romantic cinematic discourse; yet in its final sequences it suddenly returns to some of these codes, momentarily re-creating its central character, and the viewer's response to him, within a discourse that seems familiar and comforting. Paul abandons the flat. Jeanne wanders through its emptiness, pulling down the sheet from the strange form that had dominated one end of it and discovering only a collapsing heap of junk. She invites Tom to the flat, hoping they will take it for themselves. They talk of the children they will have there, selecting names of individuals whose political passion could not be more different from their own romantic callowness. If they have a son they will name him Fidel, if a girl, Rosa (after Rosa Luxemburg, Tom says, unaware that it is the name of Paul's dead wife). They dance through the apartment, which, without Paul, is cold and barren. They quickly realize it is not for them.

When Jeanne leaves the flat Paul appears, this time following her under the Métro bridge where they first crossed paths. But this is not the despondent figure she passed unknowingly at the beginning of the narrative. Paul is now cleaned up, shaved, wearing a sports jacket. He has become the romantic suitor, insisting to Jeanne that their romance may now start anew. They go to a dance hall, where a tango contest is taking place.

In Bertolucci's films, the dance is a recurrent formal motif whose connotations vary according to context. In *The Spider's Stratagem* it is the site of defiance and treachery, as Athos Sr dances in spite of the fascist music the blackshirts have told the band to play. In *The Conformist* Clerici and Giulia go to a dance with Anna and Luca Quadri. Anna dances seductively with Giulia. Towards the end of the evening all the dancers surround Clerici, capturing him in a swirl of motion, creating another external sign of his entrapment within his own paranoia. *1900* contains two major dance sequences. The first, in which Ada, Alfredo's wife-to-be, is introduced to the peasant community of the Berlinghieri farm, ends with the fascists breaking up the celebration by burning down the school house. Liberation Day is marked by an enormous outdoor dance, the peasants swirling about the farm, carrying the red canopy they have been secretly putting together throughout the fascist reign. Caterina and her son Joe dance seductively in *La luna*. A community dance occurs at the end of *Tragedy of a Ridiculous Man*: an irritating mix of punk music and traditional Italian melodies, it forms the background for the meeting of old and new, when the son, presumably kidnapped by terrorists, is returned to his father. The dance sequence in *Last Tango* is the most complex presentation of this recurring signifier. Within it are enfolded all the text's latent and manifest ironies, and it reveals multifaceted connotations of community, ritual, celebration and stultification, of expression and repression.

Bertolucci creates a misleading montage throughout the tango sequence, cutting to the ludicrous dancers and their ritualized movements, as if in contrast to the free-spirited interchange between Paul and Jeanne, who get drunk and disrupt the proceedings. 'It's love,' Paul tells the outraged dance judges. 'But it's a contest,' a woman judge tells him. 'Where does love fit in? Go to the movies to see love.' Indeed. Paul bares his backside in defiance. But Paul's actions throughout this sequence are a parallel to the ritual of the dance, not a contrast. He has become the movie lover, the romantic leading man wooing the girl of his dreams. His very language (save for the profanity) becomes the discourse of the 30s movie suitor. He tells Jeanne – in a voice that begins to take on the flat Midwestern drawl of the character's origins – that he loves her and wants to live with her. 'In your flophouse?' she asks. 'What the hell difference does it make if I have a flophouse or a hotel or a castle. I love you, what the fuck difference does it make?' He cannot see difference. Like Marcello Clerici in *The Conformist*, he has become blind to what has happened to him, to what he was, to the very narrative that has created him. He has become separated from that narrative's structure, from its attack upon the codes of romantic melodrama – and the part he took in that attack – and has presumed to take on a life of his own, which is not his own but the very Other against which the narrative has been speaking. When he continues this discourse in Jeanne's mother's apartment, his skewed perceptions are manifested in a symbolic act: he puts on the military cap of Jeanne's father and asks, 'How do you like your hero, over easy or sunny side up?' (At the tango hall, offering Jeanne a drink, he said, 'Come on, just a sip for daddy'.) He has forgotten that heroism destroys, that the romantic assertion of self leads to the dissolution of self. He is blind to the fact that, in the gesture of putting on the hat, he assumes the role of controlling father: blind because the movie discourse of romance has consumed him. 'I ran through Africa and Asia and Indonesia and now I found you. And I love you.'

Before this, at the dance hall, Jeanne's despairing response to Paul's solicitations was to masturbate him. They sit at a table away from the crowd, and as she brings Paul to orgasm the camera pulls away from them, isolating them, withdrawing.[34] It is an act of disavowal, disapproval, linking back to an earlier sequence in which Jeanne attempted to prove her independence of Paul by masturbating herself. But the final act of disapproval and rejection is still to come. Paul runs after Jeanne through the streets, past the Hotel d'Orsay where Clerici had stayed in *The Conformist*, to her mother's apartment (the entrance door to the building and the apartment windows emanate the yellow light). He pursues her upstairs as she becomes more desperate and frightened. His donning of her father's cap is finally too much; the return of the repressed and of the oppressor leads to her final act of rebellion. The bourgeois order that both characters had attempted to deny reasserts itself and recoups the scandal of transgression. In the final act, Paul, who wanted no names to be spoken, asks Jeanne's name. As she tells him, she shoots him with her father's gun. Paul cries out, 'Our children, our children'. Brando inflects the character with a final gesture, sticking his wad of chewing gum under the balcony railing. Paul dies, lying in a foetal position on the balcony. From the rooftops of Paris, the camera cranes down to his figure and pulls back inside, where Jeanne is mumbling a preparatory speech for the police (the guardians of order Bertolucci referred to earlier in the film when introducing the two major characters). 'He tried to rape me,' she repeats. 'He's a madman ... I don't know his name ...'

4 Collapse and Renewal

'When people tell me their dreams, I find it very uninteresting.'
Douglas, Joe's stepfather, in *La luna*.

Last Tango in Paris is an attempt to find the name of romance and efface it; to investigate the psychology of a character who knows and suffers the traps of romance ('Our marriage was nothing but a foxhole for you,' Paul tells his dead wife) and who, despite the efforts of the narrative, falls into them nevertheless. By absorbing ideological and character analysis and its own reflexivity into a highly emotive form, the film insists that the spectator remain alert to the very things to which its characters are blind, and makes that alertness difficult at the same time. *Last Tango* is simultaneously seductive and distancing, inviting entry and denying it, expressing an intellectual and emotional intensity which Bertolucci had not achieved before and has not achieved since.

Nor perhaps cared to. *Last Tango* marks a climax in Bertolucci's film-making, the end of his first period of major formal experimentation. With it, the modernist urge is repressed, a repression that can be detected in the linear structure and emotive force of the film. In the following work, *1900*, the remnants of modernism can be found only through a dialectical analysis. Because of that repression, and the intra-textual clash of realism/neo-realism/socialist realism and the ideology of collectivity which those forms are asked to express, the film stands as a major turn in Bertolucci's career. Its failure, both commercially and to a certain extent textually, seems to have put him in a position once again to re-examine and reconsider the formal methodology of his work. He seemed unwilling or – given the movement of commercial cinema in the mid-1970s and his situation as a film-maker with an international reputation – unable to return to the modernism of the pre-*1900* films. At the same time he was unable to find a formal approach that differed significantly from the realist conventions of *1900*. The result was the textual failure of *La luna*.

On one level *La luna* can be seen as an attempt to return to the concerns of *Last Tango*. It eschews explicit examination of politics and tries to examine the intensive elements of the family in psychological pain. In fact, it seems to want to deal with those destructive potentials of the family that Paul evokes early in *Last Tango*; but it cannot find an appropriate form for its enquiry. Lack of perspective, of a determining structure, is its primary undoing. In interviews Bertolucci has insisted on the subjective nature of the film, proclaiming it as a psychological examination of himself and his audience, which draws upon the images of his own dreams, a displaced narrative of his psyche. Were this true (and, if one chooses to ignore the text itself, the author's own reading of his work cannot be gainsaid), the film could be seen as standing in a progression of authorial interests. *The Spider's Stratagem* and *The Conformist* concern themselves with a particular political period as filtered through the consciousness of their central characters. *Last Tango* concentrates on the psychological wreckage of its central character, playing personality against romantic mythology, investigating the destructive structures of romance and the ways cinema has invaded our unconscious. *1900* drops reflexivity for the conventions of the 'epic' film, and uses those conventions to create a text of the politics of the class struggle. While *1900* does concentrate on families and generations, it suppresses psychology (or more accurately, it reverts to conventional melodramatic psychology) in order to allow its politics to emerge clearly, just as *Last Tango* hid its ideological analysis within the psychological.

Seen in authorial progression, *La luna* might indicate that Bertolucci was creating an alternation of interests. First *Last Tango*, a 'subjective' film about emotions and familial politics, followed by an explicitly political film, an investigation and celebration of the left, followed in turn by another more 'subjective' work. But this is not what happens, for *La luna* has neither the intensity nor the complexity of *Last Tango*, neither the perceptual precision of *The Spider's Stratagem* nor the energy of *The Conformist*. It does expand upon the psychological clichés of *1900*, but without the political passion which informs that film. Lacking a carefully worked out formal structure, it is a film that constantly threatens to fall in on its own subjectivity without ever opening up to create a space in which the spectator might experience – to borrow a notion from Roland Barthes – a recognition, an enlightenment, a state of bliss *(jouissance)*. Such a state, a disgorgement of pleasure stimulated by the text, does occur in *The Spider's Stratagem*, *The Conformist* and, especially, *Last Tango*.

In these films, one might say with Barthes (substituting the elements of cinema for those of literature): 'All the signifiers are here and each scores a bull's-eye; the author (the reader) seems to say to them: *I love you all* (words, phrases, sentences, adjectives [compositions, camera movements, cutting, music], discontinuities: pell-mell: signs and mirages of objects which they represent) ... a marbled, iridescent text; we are gorged with language. ... [They are] the pledge of continuous jubilation, the moment when by its very excess verbal [cinematic] pleasure chokes and reels into bliss.'[1] Barthes contrasts the text of bliss with the text of pleasure, which is not as intense, allowing the reader spaces of rest. Texts of pleasure 'are perverse in that they are outside any imaginable finality – *even that of pleasure*'. As opposed to *Last Tango*, *1900* is such a text. We move through it, it moves round us, and we take our pleasure from it where we will. It creates a fantasy of political history within the conventions of the realist, epic film. Its duration, its *copia*, the sweep of its movement through time and the physical movement of the camera create 'the text that contents, fills, grants euphoria; the text that comes from culture and does not break with it [though, in fact, *1900* breaks with the dominant culture at many points], is linked to a *comfortable* practice of reading.' In contrast, the 'text of bliss' *(The Spider's Stratagem, The Conformist, Last Tango)* 'imposes a state of loss, [it is] the text that discomforts ... unsettles the reader's historical, cultural, psychological assumptions, the consistency of his tastes, values, memories, brings to a crisis his relation with language'.[2]

La luna aims to be a 'text of bliss', but only occasionally manages to offer pleasure; it hopes to discomfort and unsettle, but often only embarrasses the viewer with its excess. Desiring to investigate the psychology of domestic pain and confusion, it presents itself as confused and pained. The film does not bring to crisis the viewer's relation with language as much as it indicates a crisis in the author's relationship to his language. The formal authority so carefully cultivated and brought to fruition in *The Conformist*, *Last Tango* and *1900* here seems to be in the process of dismantling itself as it grasps for disparate formal elements which are not synthesized as they were in the earlier films.

On the level of its signifieds alone – the meaning (sporadically) generated by its narrative – *La luna* does manage to achieve a certain lurid coherence. Its tale of domestic disintegration, of a mother's sexual desire for her young, deracinated, drug-addicted son, of the rediscovery of the father and a hoped for but uncertain reconciliation, is carried forward without hesitation and without the authority of an enquiring point of view. Even the most unsavoury events – Joe piercing his arm with a fork because he has no syringe for his heroin; Caterina masturbating him – are rendered without distance, delineated without substance or subtext, offered for sensation without the support of insight. The discourse of the film, the arrangement of its signifiers, the authorial voice controlling the structure, the situating of the viewer in relation to that structure, are without potency. Visually, the film seems to be seeking a never discovered style. Storaro's glowing colours are present, his strong tracking shots creating an almost perpetual movement about the characters, but they seem not to inform the narrative, despite Bertolucci's claim that the camera movements in the film are of sexual import: 'a dolly shot forward always expresses the movement of a child moving closer to his obscure object of desire. . . . [Dolly shots upwards] are simply erections. . . . Like when we fly in our dreams, they reveal a specific sexual impulse.'[3]

The temporal construction of the film follows the linear continuity begun in *Last Tango* and *1900*, but does not work out the complex interlocking of sequences found in the former or the embracing of large temporal blocks in the latter. It is an ordinary linearity, a conventional progression of events that suggests a psychological predetermination of the characters rather than the dialectic of character and history which structured the earlier films. This is suggested in the long pre-credits sequence where Joe as a baby is seen alternately pampered, ignored, and sexually enticed by his mother, a sequence that begins with a provocative image of Joe sucking honey from her fingers. A phallic helicopter flies overhead; father and mother dance to a pop song as he pokes at her playfully – but symbolically – with a fish and a knife. A mirror is prominent, a self-conscious reference to Lacan and his 'mirror stage'.[4] Baby Joe gets entangled in his grandmother's knitting, signifying the unbreakable connecting web of an individual to its past. The image is recapitulated near the end of the narrative when the adolescent Joe returns to his father's house; here the grandmother gets entangled in the knitting as she goes inside to play on the piano the melody she played during the pre-credits sequence.

The image might suggest the controlling metaphor of the web in *The Spider's Stratagem*, a suggestion enhanced by the fact that Alida Valli, who plays Draifa in the earlier film, plays the grandmother here. The image is too explicit to recall the subtleties of the earlier film, but the suggestion is not accidental. The one modernist articulation that Bertolucci holds on to in *La luna*, with an obsessiveness that hints of desperation, is the use of allusion. The allusive and self-referential act had, as I have noted, been fundamental to his film-making practice from the very beginning. He picked up from Godard and others this method of recognizing and celebrating film history, of noting within the text itself the fact that film is born of film. From *Before the Revolution* to *Last Tango* the allusive acts had been wide-ranging and intricate, opening the texts and enriching them with multiple significations. In *1900* the process of allusion is at its most subtle. The film subsumes an Eisensteinian view of history as socialist progress within the combined forms of the Hollywood epic and the neo-realist observation of the plight of the poor. Eisenstein, Rossellini and David O. Selznick whisper behind the discourse of Bertolucci's celebration of the peasant left.

The voices behind the discourse of *La luna* grumble and speak discordantly, and those heard most often are Bertolucci's own. In the opening post-credits sequence of the film, set in New York, Joe's stepfather (played with extraordinary dignity by Fred Gwynne, an American actor best known for his work in television comedies), steps out on his New York balcony and discovers a wad of chewing gum under the railing. Within the fiction, the gum most likely belongs to Joe. But the external reference is not lost: at the end of *Last Tango*, Paul's dying gesture was to put his gum under the balcony railing. It is as if in *La luna* Bertolucci wanted us to recall a better moment in a better film. In this same sequence, there is a cut to squawking birds, as in *Last Tango*. Later, Caterina wanders through the same streets of Parma as Gina did in *Before the Revolution*. She and Joe then take to the road. They drive through the Berlinghieri farm of *1900*, Caterina remarking that they used to buy their bread there. Joe runs off to a café where he is served and entertained by none other than the salami curer (Pippo Campanini) from *The Spider's Stratagem*. Still sticking picks in the meats and offering the aroma to his guest, still singing Verdi arias, the character is almost literally transported from the earlier film to this one. Why? Gestures like these used to infuriate reactionary critics when they met them in New Wave films, bringing accusations of pedantry and the playing of 'inside jokes'. I think any viewer familiar with Bertolucci's canon would be delighted to recognize the character; but that *is* a self-indulgence for people familiar with the films. Perhaps Bertolucci felt that, in this film about a son in search of his father (which, after all, is the same basic 'theme' as *The Spider's Stratagem*), it would be appropriate to echo the earlier work, thereby creating a textual continuity that would counter the terrible discontinuity in the life of his young character. But this does not account for the other self-quotations.

I have a suspicion, borne out by comments made by Bertolucci, that these allusions were a way for the film-maker to comfort himself, to provide a retreat from the trauma of *1900* (once again one runs the risk of vulgar psychologizing). '*La luna*,' Bertolucci says, 'is not only the consequence of a disappointment. *1900* had enabled me to explore thoroughly, personally, the mechanisms and contradictions of production. ... I don't know whether the strongest element in *1900* is the Olmo-Alfredo story or rather the tale of the contradiction existing between the use of capitalistic, multinational means of production and a naive, edifying, grassroots vision. Without that experience, I never would have dared make *La luna*.' As a result, he makes a film about psychological production, and about his own emotional past. 'I had to accept all the risks involved in a descent into the past, and this descent included also the films of my past. A film about an incestuous fantasy must be punctuated by that violently auto-erotic and incestuous act of self-quotation.'[5] The validity of this statement lies in the fact that *La luna* is, by and large, a film for the solitary pleasure of its maker. If *1900* is a recuperation of cinema history in order to prepare for an alternative future, *La luna* is an attempt to recuperate Bertolucci's brief cinematic past in order to secure himself against the trauma of *1900*'s distribution and reception. These fragments he has shored against his ruin.

Self-quotation is not Bertolucci's only allusive gambit. Within two successive sequences early in the narrative there are no fewer than three allusions to films by other people. Joe and his Italian girlfriend go to a cinema in Rome. The film is a Marilyn Monroe vehicle, an excellent Technicolor *film noir* of 1953, Henry Hathaway's *Niagara*. The Monroe character, Rose, is married to a psychotically jealous older man (Joseph Cotten). She is unfaithful; he kills her. Excerpts from the film, dubbed into Italian ('When did she learn Italian?' Joe asks about Monroe), are intercut with Joe and his girlfriend engaging in sexual play in the toilet of the movie theatre. Monroe sings a sexy 50s ballad. In the midst of their own sexual experiments, the roof of the cinema opens over Joe and his friend (a surreal event which, I am told, is based on the fact that Rome cinemas did have movable roofs to cool them during the summer). A full moon hangs in the night sky, the sign of Joe's mother (an image which Bertolucci says came to him in a dream) to which Joe responds, as if hypnotized, 'I must go, I must go'. As they leave, Bertolucci cuts in a voice-over from the beginning of *Niagara*. The Italian surrogate for the Joseph Cotten character talks about the power of the waterfalls in words that could refer to the power of Joe's mother: 'Why should the falls drag me down here at five o'clock in the morning? To show me how big they are and how small I am?' He goes on to say (though this part of the speech is not quoted in *La luna*) that he could gain his independence if he had a little time.*

The point of the allusion is to present, in Marilyn Monroe, a female character whose power is similar to Caterina's. Bertolucci calls Monroe a Madonna. In the same sequence reference is made to a fictional character who also exercises a destructive power over her man. When Joe's girlfriend removes her orthodontic appliance so that she can kiss him, he reacts by making faces, recalling the Belmondo character in

---

* My thanks to Vittorio Felaco for telling me about Italian cinemas and helping me match the dubbed Italian to the original version.

Godard's *Breathless*. Bertolucci has claimed that *La luna* resembles *Breathless* in its freedom.[6] In fact, the film is a slave to its own melodramatic impulses.

In the next sequence an allusion is made to a male figure who dominates a woman to whom he is also enthralled. Joe goes to see his mother perform in *Il trovatore*, and glares at people in the audience when they start talking. As the applause at the end of the aria subsides, Joe goes on applauding, which prompts the audience to continue their ovation – a direct reference to the opera scene in *Citizen Kane*.

A critic could get breathless with his own pedantry in enumerating Bertolucci's pedantic allusions in *La luna*. But the text requires us to note its attempt to incorporate as much and more than it can handle. Before discussing the major allusive structure of the film, I want to cite one other reference, which is not an allusion to a particular film, but to the very structure that *La luna* lacks. Of all Bertolucci's works since *The Grim Reaper*, *La luna* has the least political subtext. To a certain extent, like *Last Tango*, it does attempt to examine the complex structure of sexual and domestic politics, in this instance the manipulation of an alienated, fatherless child by a powerful, vain and confused mother. But Bertolucci does not find the potent signifiers of patriarchy and matriarchy that appear in the absent figures of Rosa and Jeanne's father in *Last Tango*. He finds no equivalents for that film's intricate narrative structure, its complex interaction of character and spectator, its enquiring distance that forces a political perspective on its events. After the experience of *1900* Bertolucci may have wanted to subdue political reference. Certainly the one political figure introduced into *La luna* seems an anomaly, an additional fragmenting of the narrative's already uncertain form.

In the sequence in which Joe and Caterina are on the road, travelling from Parma, Joe drives off after his mother has fixed their car's flat tyre. A stranger stops to pick up Caterina. A well-dressed *borghese* in a white car, he insists on telling her that he is a Communist and not only knows Fidel Castro but has gone fishing with him (he shows her a photograph of Castro on a fishing boat). Caterina is unmoved by his unsolicited confession, but he insists that she should know this truth because after all, he says, she is American and he is a Communist, as if this information must shock her. In fact, it remains unclear who is trying to shock: the character in the fiction or the author of the fiction. Is this man speaking for Bertolucci, warning his American public of his politics, even though his politics are invisible in the rest of the film? Is it, perhaps, a joke, referring back to *1900*, the film he had hoped would convince even the most implacable anti-communist that the ideology was not the evil that Americans had been indoctrinated to believe? In the film, the comment goes nowhere; Caterina has no interest in the man or his politics, letting herself be picked up because she needs the ride and – once they arrive at the inn where they find Joe – to make her son jealous. The only thing the scene does is to make the character (played by Renato Salvatori, a prominent actor in Italian film, who also appears in *Tragedy of a Ridiculous Man*) look somewhat foolish. It is as embarrassing a moment as the appearance earlier in the film of Franco Citti as a homosexual trying to pick up Joe in a bar.

The sequence supports the impression of a film that threatens to break under the weight of its own confusions. There is the suggestion throughout of a film-maker unaccountably stuffing his text because he cannot find a coherent pattern or design, a form that will adequately express or transcend the banality of its Oedipal subject. In only one area does the allusive structure of the film cohere, and that is, once again, in the use of Verdi. But the coherence here is itself uncertain. Obviously, by creating an opera singer as his major character Bertolucci provides for himself the opportunity of consummating the operatic allusions that have occurred throughout his work. *La luna* turns out to be Bertolucci's opera, not only because he stages two performances in the course of the narrative, but because the excessive gestures and lunatic passions expressed by the characters are as overtly operatic as anything he has done. At the same time, the operatic allusions do not provide counterpoint and subtext for the main narrative, as they do in *The Spider's Stratagem*. Rather, they tend to form the *main* text of the film. Bertolucci devotes an attention to the film's musical structure that he neglects in its narrative. In the earlier films, knowledge of the Verdian allusions enriched the texts; here the viewer not familiar with Verdi is impoverished, because the allusions do not so much nourish the narrative as stand outside it, gaining strength from its diminished status.

'He was like a father to me,' Caterina tells Joe when they pass Verdi's house. A somewhat obvious remark in a narrative about the search for the father; yet it does serve as a useful place mark in Bertolucci's own dealing with Verdi, the figure whose works father many of his narratives. In this film, the son fully honours the father. Apart from the two performances that occur as part of the narrative, Verdi arias occur throughout the film.*

---

* And, for contrast, one by Mozart, 'Soave sia il vento' from *Cosi fan tutte*, played in a touching sequence in which Caterina visits her old and now senile opera teacher near Parma. The aria is a still and quiet point in a narrative that is always on the brink of hysteria – a fact, Martin Mangold says, that is true both of the film and the opera. Professor Mangold identified for me, and helped to determine the significance of, the incidental arias in *La luna*.

Sometimes, as in *Before the Revolution* and *The Spider's Statagem*, they embellish the narrative events or create an ironic contrast. At other times, they act only as a junction between the narrative and the Verdian text, the allusive relationship often forced. For example, at two points in the film we hear Gilda's aria, 'Tutte le feste al tempio', from Act Two of *Rigoletto*. Caterina sings the aria as she prepares to leave New York for Italy. Joe, against his will, is to be left behind – until his stepfather, Douglas, dies unexpectedly. The second time the aria is heard in Rome. Joe has just given himself an injection of heroin. A small leap in time is made and Caterina is seen looking out of a window of their apartment. There is a cut to the garden outside and the camera executes two lyrical tracks as Caterina walks through the garden calling after Joe. Each call of his name is synchronized to the rhythm of the aria. At this point its words so aptly express Caterina's feelings about her son that the relationship of operatic text to film narrative is almost banal: 'Every holiday, at the church,/As I was praying to God,/A young man, handsome and fatal,/Presented himself to my gaze … /If our lips were silent,/Our hearts spoke through our eyes./Furtively in the darkness,/Only yesterday he came to me.' As the sequence ends, the source of the music is shown to be a record upon which turns Joe's packet of heroin. In *Rigoletto*, Gilda is singing of her love for the Duke. Her father disapproves of the man and her daughter's affection for him. The expression of love, the allusion to the father, fit too obviously into the narrative of a woman who falls in love with her son who does not yet know his father.

Verdian references abound. The Prelude to Act Three of *La traviata*, the opera of a man's love for a dying courtesan, is played when Caterina leaves a sleeping Joe to rediscover her operatic roots in Parma. The events in the film are ironically the reverse of those in this particular opera. At the beginning of Act Three it is Violetta who is asleep and wakes to find her friend Annina beside her. In the film Joe wakes up to find that his lover-mother has abandoned him. In her place is her friend and would-be lover Marina (played by the same actress who is Rosa's corpse in *Last Tango*). But Joe goes to Parma, and like Alfredo in the opera, returns to his lover. When the two stop in the inn run by the salami-curer from *The Spider's Stratagem*, Caterina asks him for a room for herself and Joe. As she makes her request, he breaks into an aria from Act Two of *Il trovatore*, sung in the opera by the gypsy Azucena. The aria, 'Condotta ell'era in ceppi', tells of Azucena's mother, burned to death by the Count di Luna's father. Azucena took revenge, wanting to steal the Count's son, but somehow throwing her own son into the fire instead. 'She was led in irons,' Azucena sings, 'To her terrible fate;/With my baby in my arms,/I followed her, weeping.'

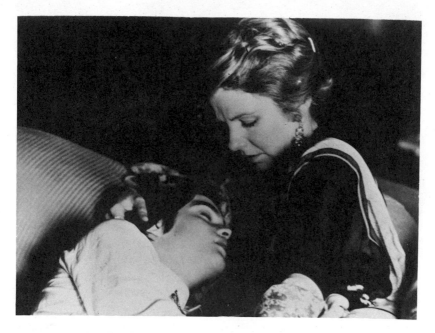

Confused sexuality: Caterina and her son Joe in *La luna* (Jill Clayburgh, Matthew Barry)

Like Azucena, Caterina is imprisoned – by her passions in this instance – and sacrifices her son, not to the flames but to her own confused sexuality. At this moment in the narrative the sacrifice seems about to be consummated. Once in the room, Caterina pulls Joe's face to her crotch. Bertolucci, however, does not see the act of incest through, and Joe pulls away from his mother's sexual hysteria. Acting like a chorus to the impending tragedy, the innkeeper provides the appropriate Verdian reference, for *Il trovatore* becomes a major allusive frame for the film. The first operatic performance Bertolucci stages is the end of the opera's first act. Caterina does not sing the role of Azucena but that of Leonora, loved by the Count di Luna, whose name – as well as the ramifications of the opera's story – must have brought the work to Bertolucci's mind (although it is equally conceivable that the opera itself suggested the narrative of the film). Though loved by the Count, Leonora is in love with his enemy, Manrico, who believes he is Azucena's son. However, when Azucena hurled her own son into the flames to avenge her mother, she stole and brought up Manrico, who is Di Luna's brother. Revenge is finally taken when Di Luna captures Manrico and Azucena. Leonora offers herself to the Count in exchange for Manrico, and takes poison. Di Luna sends Manrico to his death.

Azucena, herself about to die, tells the Count he has murdered his own brother. Gabriele Baldini writes:

> One can say of no other Verdi opera that the libretto fails to narrate; any attempt to run over the events of the plot very soon becomes meaningless because they all cancel each other out and become confused in the memory. It is a very special quality of this distinguished text, and derives not so much from individual complications as from the extremely elusive nature of the characters and events outside their musical setting (*The Story of Giuseppe Verdi*, p. 210).

The statement is quite applicable to *La luna*. It is by no means a 'distinguished' text, but like *Il trovatore* it fails to narrate. The overwhelming passions, the overwhelming sufferings of Joe, his sudden discovery of his father and the promised reconciliation of the family at the film's conclusion (a reverse of the death and dissolution that ends Verdi's melodrama), the recurrence of the image of the moon that raises it to the point of symbol with nothing to symbolize, all fail to link together outside a conventional melodramatic cycle. Unlike *Il trovatore*, however, there is no *other* text, like the music of an opera, or the carefully considered visual structure and synthesized influences of the previous films, to absorb and give form to the narrative shreds.

The problem is evident in Bertolucci's staging of the end of Act One of *Il trovatore*, in which Leonora mistakes Di Luna for Manrico and the two rivals fall to duelling. The sequence suggests, according to Bertolucci, Caterina's struggle with her own two lovers – her two husbands, Joe's natural father and his stepfather[7] – and he creates it in a stylized, almost ritualized form. The sequence begins in the middle of Leonora's aria, 'Tacea la notte placida/E bella in ciel sereno;/La luna il viso argenteo/Mostrava lieto e pieno', 'The serene night was silent/And lovely in the calm sky;/The moon happily revealed /Its full and silvery face.' The lighting on the stage is a deep blue, with the stars and moon painted on the top of the set (an image that recalls the sky above the cinema when the roof rolled open and which will be repeated late in the film, when Joe finds his father, a schoolteacher, whose students are painting an enormous picture of the universe on the school floor; Joe adds a multi-faced picture of the moon, and his father promises the children that when they return from holiday the whole painting will be hung from the ceiling).

Caterina sings her aria on a raised podium, points to the moon, and is then cranked down to stage level. The artificiality of the 'production' is foregrounded, its unworldly expressions of hermetic passion emphasized. When the Count di Luna sings his aria about the night and his love for Leonora, Bertolucci has Joe go backstage, and the artifice of the opera is further opened to scrutiny. Harpists play behind the scene; the stagehands go about their work, pulling flats, cranking a huge assembly of rollers that create the illusion of a waterfall on the set. Manrico throws down his lute and a stagehand reaches for it, so that, from the front of the house, it seems to disappear silently into the water. The prompter emphasizes key words for the singers, which Bertolucci chooses to reflect the emotional turmoil in the opera and the narrative it supports: 'jealousy' ('gelosia'), 'faithless' ('infida'). The point of view keeps shifting (again alluding to *Citizen Kane*), from Joe's wanderings backstage and in his mother's dressing room to the audience's view in front. At the end of the act, when the Count and Manrico duel, the camera is behind the singers. Caterina turns towards the spectacle, with a broad, exaggerated gesture, raising her hands above her head. Her operatic character recoils from the violence she has caused in her two suitors; her character in the film hides from the clash of fathers and the clash of emotions caused by her passion for Joe and his own struggle following the separation from his father.

Bertolucci elides the end of the act with the end of the opera as a whole by carrying its music over the following sequence, which takes place in Caterina's dressing room. There the narrative resumes in the more or less conventionally realistic style that marks the film, emphasizing its core problem. In Bertolucci's overtly modernist works, the operatic subtext informs the stylization of the entire work, so that film and opera become suspended in a dialectical relationship. Here they are in contradiction. The opera is presented as a bizarre, ritual-ized spectacle that would demand from an opera audience deep engagement in its hermetic and an acceptance of its melodramatics, as well as a belief in its almost mythic properties (cf. Bertolucci's com-ments on Verdi and myth quoted earlier). The narrative proper of *La luna* retains the foolish melodramatics but drops stylization and the distancing-ritualizing effects both of the opera within the film and of Bertolucci's earlier work. An argument could be made that *within* the film Bertolucci is consciously playing off two melodramatic conven-tions – the operatic and the cinematic, each with its own codes to structure audience belief. In fact, he has alluded to this: 'What counts is the melodrama itself. . . . It's a formula. It's finding the space where passions can go very far'.[8] If this is the case, the contrast does not work; the appropriate space is not found. The performance created by Bertolucci is too manifestly 'artificial', and he goes to great pains to reveal that artifice, particularly by showing the backstage scenes. The form of the film's narrative proper is too securely set in the conventions of classical cinematic realism, with comparatively little comment upon

La luna: Caterina/Leonora and her moon in *Il trovatore*

that form. One might say, modifying Baldini's remark about the opera, that *La luna* fails to narrate because all it cares to do is narrate. It finds no suitable form for its narration because, for the first time in his career, Bertolucci seems not to investigate the intricacies of discourse that create narrative information and textual pleasure. Instead of the pleasure of the text, he wants the pleasure of a movie. 'Really, I think the goal of a movie is pleasure. I want to feel free to have pleasure because it's what I always wanted to have when I went to see a movie. So *La luna* is no longer ashamed of pleasure. That's why I say the eighties look much better than the seventies.'[9] Coming out of his experience with *1900*, the left-wing Italian modernist intellectual attempts to speak the language – and make the film – of the Hollywood corporate producer.

In this light, the Verdian allusions become something of a perverse act, tantalizing in their presence, frustrating in their absence (in this 'movie' made for the pleasure of an English-speaking audience the operatic performances and arias go unsubtitled). They are hooks in the text by means of which Bertolucci wants to attach connotative material, but which he leaves all but empty in his conflicting desire to create a film unimpeded in its narrative progress.

But the film-maker's conflicts are the critic's material, and the wreck of *La luna* can be partially rebuilt by forcing the connotations of the operatic allusions back into the text. The strange narrative of destroyed children that informs *Il trovatore* operates throughout the film. Near its end, Joe tries to destroy himself. He has been attempting this physically, through his dope addiction. However, when he finally meets his natural father, Giuseppe – a schoolteacher and a gentle, understanding man who is a younger version of Cesare in *Before the Revolution* – Joe tells him his son is dead. Unable to reveal his identity, he acts as his own surrogate, conflating within himself various characters in Verdi operas with assumed identities – a phenomenon made more intriguing by the fact that father and son wear identical clothes and Joe steals Giuseppe's shoes.

Their meeting leads to the film's final and climactic operatic reference, *Un ballo in maschera*. Joe comes to the rehearsal of the opera at the Baths of Caracalla, where Caterina, in her despair, is refusing to sing, speaking her lines instead. When Joe first sees her, she is 'speaking' the aria in Act Three, 'T'amo, sì, t'amo', 'I love you, yes, I love you, and in tears/At your feet I prostrate myself.' She and Joe meet under the stage and they to come to an understanding, with Caterina telling him that she left his father because he did not like her singing and because (the irony is stunning in its heavy-handedness) he was in love with his mother. Indeed he still shares a house with her. Mother and son embrace; he puts over his head the veil that serves as her mask in the opera, thereby continuing to hide himself within her personality. When Caterina returns to the stage, Giuseppe comes to her. She points out to him that Joe is not dead but is there in the auditorium, watching them. Giuseppe goes to Joe and slaps him, a cathartic act that seems, ultimately, to relieve everyone's tension. Caterina begins to sing and, in a series of one-shots, smiles are exchanged between Joe, his father and mother. The film ends with a shot of the stage, the moon hanging brightly in the sky.

Un ballo in maschera has a plot almost as strange as *Il trovatore*. It takes place in 'Boston', whose governor, named Count Riccardo, is in love with Amelia, who is married to Renato. Riccardo is threatened by two conspirators, Samuel and Tom (referred to in *The Spider's Stratagem*). There is a soothsayer and attendant prophecies. Amelia's husband would kill her for her unfaithfulness, but has pity on her because of their only child. He decides it is Riccardo he must kill, and joins the plot against him. At the masked ball that ends the work (and the film), Renato stabs Riccardo, who, dying, reveals the innocence of his love for Amelia and pardons everyone. As with *Il trovatore*, the opera's narrative bears a rough and, as in Bertolucci's best use of Verdi, ironic analogy with the events and characters of *La luna*: the child caught between parents at odds with each other; the deracination (Verdi's mythical 'Boston' replaced in the film by an Italy that is a foreign world to Joe). The reconciliation which the opera pretends echoes the uncertain reconciliation offered by Bertolucci as a closure for his film.

As with his production of *Il trovatore*, Bertolucci takes delight in showing the backstage workings of the opera. Because the opera rehearsal and the film's narrative are here closely interconnected there is much less stylized rendering of the production than there was in the *Il trovatore* sequence. Caterina's refusal to sing affects the whole company. When Joe appears the rehearsal is interrupted, giving them time for a reconciliation. After Caterina has pointed out to Giuseppe that their son is indeed alive, sitting in the amphitheatre watching and applauding them, she begins to sing, picking up the score at the point where Amelia and Riccardo are singing 'Addio' to each other. Renato, the jealous husband, stabs Riccardo. As this action occurs, Bertolucci creates one of the cleverest moments in the film, relating more by means of one cut than he had in most of the previous shots.

On the stabbing of Riccardo, he inserts a brief shot of Giuseppe, now in the audience, looking at Joe. The entire Oedipal process is implied in this juxtaposition. In the operatic fiction, the father kills the man who loves his wife. In the *other* fiction, the father, who must assert his presence to remove the son's desire for the mother, appears and gazes at his child. In the opera, as Riccardo is stabbed, Caterina (now singing her role) cries, 'Soccorso! Soccorso!' 'Help! Help!' The chorus responds, 'Ah! morte . . . infamia . . .': 'Ah! death . . . infamy,/Infamy upon the traitor . . ./Let the sword tear him,/The avenging sword!' Giuseppe angrily slaps Joe, reducing him to tears. The father imposes his castrating power. But Bertolucci discovers in this a conciliating gesture and lets his own narrative follow the opera's lead. The dying Riccardo sings that Renato should be left alone; his wife is pure, 'I loved her, but I wanted her unharmed/Your name and her heart.' Amelia/Caterina sing of their guilt and remorse: 'Oh, remorse for love/That devours my heart,/Between a guilty man, dripping blood,/And the victim who dies!' The link is almost allegorical. Giuseppe is the guilty man who 'kills' Caterina's son-lover. The catharsis comes and Bertolucci intercuts Joe and Giuseppe in one-shots, smiling at each other as Caterina sings triumphantly on stage. 'In *La luna*,' he says, 'the characters' eyes launch a complex dynamic of glances, an interplay of objective shots and subjective points of view that follow the musical rhythms of *Un ballo in maschera*.'[10]

Curiously, Bertolucci at one moment claims that he wants his film to bring pleasure, and at another insists that pleasure is not necessarily to be gained by this moment of apparent reconciliation. The characters, he says, 'are in separate shots. . . . The recomposition and reconstruction of the family is what you want to see. But the movie is very open. The ending is very ambiguous. I didn't think afterward the three of them will go home to watch television.'[11] His recall of the cutting is almost correct, though there are in fact a few two-shots from behind Giuseppe to Caterina on the stage (and shots of Joe together with his girlfriend in the auditorium). But the ambiguity and openness are somewhat less than he hopes, and apparent only if one is aware of what is going on in the opera. In the narrative of the film, the characters' final reconciliation presents such a strong contrast to the previous emotional and physical violence that the notion of a 'happy ending' is both inescapable and uncomfortably abrupt.* However, amid the smiles, Riccardo dies in the opera, proclaiming his forgiveness. Bertolucci cuts to a long shot of the stage with the moon above it and rolls the credits. We hear Riccardo's dying call: 'Farewell . . . my children . . . forever . . . ah!/Alas . . . I die! . . ./My children . . . forev . . . (per sem . . .).' The words recall Paul's dying cry in Last Tango: 'Our children, our children.' The opera and the film end with a final chorus that indeed throws a pall on the entire proceedings. 'Notte, notte d'orror', 'Night, night of horror!/Night, night of horror!'

In both opera and film the conflicts are unreconciled. Parents remain tyrannical and the night of horror reigns, despite the fact that Bertolucci attempts also to show a night of hope. The contradictions in closure merely recapitulate the contradictions and schisms that run through the text. Bertolucci's desire to create a 'movie' clashes with his desire for narrative complexity. Unhappily, the contradictions become confusions. 'Pleasure' is mistaken for obviousness and the lurid is substituted for revelation.

The film does have its affecting moments. There is, for example, the sequence in which Caterina visits Mustafa, the baby-faced Arab who is Joe's drug supplier and the one character in the film with an emotional and (paradoxically, given his trade) moral centre. Caterina's visit to her former music teacher provides a point of repose and a contrast between an elderly man of reserve and distance and the hysteria of his pupil. The sequences between Joe and Giuseppe are full of insight into the tentative relationship of father and son. Although fraught with Oedipal connotations – Joe takes his father's shoes and is called 'Bigfoot' (Bertolucci says he was unaware of the play on Oedipus's name[12]) they also express the possibilities of a comforting relationship,

---

* And in another interview, Bertolucci contradicts himself: 'I like the idea of a happy ending. Every socialist movie has a happy ending.' (In Cineaste no. 1, 1979–80).

quite the opposite of the father and son relationships in Bertolucci's other films. Unfortunately these are relatively brief moments in a film whose lack of a controlling centre denies the spectator either pleasure or perception.

With *Tragedy of a Ridiculous Man*, his most recent film to date, Bertolucci seems to recognize the problems inherent in *La luna*. Control of form and perceptions returns, melodrama is eradicated, and there is now a revised modernism – a post-modernism which reflects an understanding that the modernism of the 60s and 70s is at an end. A number of important events occur, or re-occur, in this film. Explicit political and ideological analysis, absent from *La luna*, is carefully woven into a text that, once more, deals with parents and children, fathers and sons. The formal and stylistic structures which collapsed in *La luna* are recouped, caught, as it were, in mid-fall and remade. Structurally and visually, *Tragedy of a Ridiculous Man* is like no other Bertolucci film. One reason for this is the absence, for the first time since *The Spider's Stratagem*, of Vittorio Storaro. Because Storaro was not available (during this period he was busy photographing *One from the Heart* for Coppola and *Reds* for Warren Beatty) his place was taken by Carlo di Palma, who helps provide a colour scheme and movement pattern more restrained than in the previous films. Storaro's lush pastels are replaced by a cooler and more graded colour. While the camera still moves, these movements are tighter, smaller, shorter. Placement of figures in the frame, static composition and cutting take on great importance.*

But it is not merely the cinematography that marks a difference in *Tragedy of a Ridiculous Man*. The narrative and its construction are themselves restrained. Where *La luna* attempted to depict every action and reaction with the abandon of excess – without managing to achieve the delirium of excess, the hysteria that transcends melodrama as in, for example, the early films of Ken Russell – *Tragedy of a Ridiculous Man* withholds as much as possible. So much so that the elements of 'plot', the events signified by the narrative, are withdrawn to the point where some events are not easily or precisely perceived and understood, a phenomenon that becomes part of the film's ploy. This is a work of silences and dead times, of waiting, of rumours, uncertainties and deceits, of the space that exists between parents and children, of the mutual ignorance of their actions and motives. Bertolucci's comment about *The Grim Reaper*, which I quoted in relation to that film, is

---

* There are some references to the old style: at one point Bertolucci uses a sequence of disorienting Dutch tilts that are levelled to a horizontal position in the course of the shot, as he had done in *The Conformist*.

considerably more applicable to *Tragedy of a Ridiculous Man*: 'In a certain way, Antonioni is the abstract painter of time passing. In my film, however, the passing of time is whispered about like a secret, and the whisper is so low that almost no one can hear it.'[13]

The immediate subject of the film is 'terrorism'. But the inverted commas could not be more significant, for while this political phenomenon is the initiating element of the film's discourse, it remains, by and large, outside of that discourse – or buried deep within it. Terrorism informs the history that in turn infiltrates the text of the film. In contemporary history left-wing terrorism is a two-pronged attack, upon capitalism and upon the entrenched reformist and conservative communist and socialist parties. Desperate and doomed, it brings down the wrath of right, centre and old left. The result is often the entrenchment of reaction; while the causes and meanings of the terrorist intervention are buried in mass outrage. To make a film concerning this subject would be an act either of gross stupidity or of enormous bravery. If sympathy and analysis were given to the terrorist groups, the film and its maker would be doomed to the outrage; if the film were anti-terrorist in approach, it would join ranks with the unanalytical condemnations by the dominant ideologies of the West.

Two of the best known films on the subject made outside Italy tried, without a great deal of success, to combine the approaches of analysis and condemnation. Claude Chabrol's *Nada* (1974) attempts to depict its terrorists as figures from a spaghetti Western, their politics not quite articulated and their existence violently countered by a governmental authority more brutal in its reaction than the terrorists in their action. Rainer Werner Fassbinder's *The Third Generation* (1979) is more complex. His terrorists are essentially middle-class activists, somewhat crazed, torn by their own psychological turmoil, and unwittingly playing into the hands of the corporate forces they attempt to undo. The subject was apparently so painful for Fassbinder that the film all but buries it within a complex formal experiment in sound, movement and the portrayal of grotesque figures. In Italian cinema the subject has been broached by – among others – Francesco Rosi in *Illustrious Corpses* (*Cadaveri eccellenti*, 1976), a film which concentrates more on aspects of state terrorism than that committed by left-wing groups; and by Visconti in *Conversation Piece* (1975), where the subject is an excuse to examine the attraction of Burt Lancaster's staid, middle-aged art professor to Helmut Berger's ambiguous character of a young radical.

Bertolucci comes to the subject fully warned both by the history of the cinematic treatment of terrorism and by terrorism's own status as a frightening and despised attack on the body of the reigning ideology.

166

'To me,' he says, 'terrorism seems to be too important a thing to leave to the terrorists. Terrorism has affected people to such an extent that it seems to me impossible to make a film on Italy today without it being also, in whatever way, a film about terrorism. Terrorism, which has failed as a mass movement, has instead been very successful in socio-cultural change, in modifying psychological relationships between people.'[14] In this light we may recall Bertolucci's comment in 1967, made apropos of Godard's *Made in USA*: 'Political assassination is, by definition, always partial information that necessarily refers to a situation that exists outside, before and around itself: that is, politics.' In *Tragedy of a Ridiculous Man* Bertolucci is aware that, were he to address only the immediate signifiers of terrorism, he would only be offering 'partial information'. To fail to enquire into the intricate political and psychological relationships that surround the terrorist act would be to damage his project. This is why he places the subject simultaneously on the periphery and within the hermeneutic core of his film, con-centrating not on the politics and actions of terrorism, but on the politics of its 'victims' and on the psycho-political space that exists between the political activist and the political reactionary. This may also be a reason why the film is formally the most restrained and controlled of all his works to date. As if in response to the hysteria of Chabrol's and Fassbinder's films and the nonsense of Visconti's, *Tragedy of a Ridiculous Man* persistently distances itself from the events it creates, its text acting something like a cloud chamber in which traces of actions and reactions can be detected.

The film is elusive and recessive. Because of this it received minimal critical and commercial attention. Few people have seen the film, fewer have discussed it, and therefore some exposition of the events it tells needs to precede a discussion of its formal structure. The 'ridiculous man' of the title is one Primo Spaggiari, a late middle-aged owner of a cheese and sausage factory near Parma. On his birthday, ludicrously decked out in a captain's hat and a pair of binoculars given him as a present by his son (who refers to him in his birthday note as a perfect, blowhard businessman), he stands atop his factory and views what seems to be the pursuit and capture of his son by an unidentifiable gang. Because the event is seen from Primo's point of view the identity of the kidnappers is not clear, but it has the conventional significations of the terrorist act: a wealthy businessman is attacked, this time through his son, who is violently kidnapped, presumably to gain a large ransom.

The immediate response of Primo and his wife, Barbara, along with their fear and grief, is to find a means to meet the inevitable ransom demand. Barbara is especially obsessed with gathering the necessary funds, and both turn to the assets of their factory. But the factory is more than a means for this couple: it is a fetish. For Primo, it is his life; for Barbara, the inventory of their wealth. The first night after the kidnapping, when the police have made their initial investigation, searching the cornfield from which Primo's son was dragged by his attackers after his car was overturned (a place in which Primo seems to express genuine emotion, vomiting and weeping among the corn stalks), the couple sleep in the factory among the cheeses. Rather than return to their luxurious villa, overlooking the countryside, they seek refuge and comfort among the things that produce their wealth. Primo refers to the cheese warehouse as his Fort Knox, and Bertolucci ironically infuses the room with a golden light. But Primo's Fort Knox is not as rich in its holdings as he would wish. Business has been bad and it will be difficult for him to raise money from the factory's assets. What is more, his workers are not impressed by his calls for solidarity in the face of his troubles. In her growing anxiety, Barbara turns to other sources for comfort and financial assistance: her numerologist, who insists that Giovanni will be returned unharmed; and the town's rich usurers, a motley collection of petit-bourgeois businessmen whom she entertains. Sitting at a piano, looking for all the world like Joan Crawford in *Humoresque*, she attempts to auction off her wealth.

These elements are enough in themselves to constitute Bertolucci's notion of the ridiculousness of a family who reduce themselves to barter and trade to redeem their son. A legitimate question is raised, of course: what else are they to do in the face of such a trauma? If the kidnappers want money, and that money is difficult to find, a loving family will go to any ends to attain it. But there is something wrong with the cool ferocity with which they make the attempt; it is somehow devoid of passion and care, too full of self-righteousness. Most important, they cannot see who they are and why this is happening to them. Primo, so fooled by his own internal contradictions, cannot see how he can be the target of the wrath of the left. He evokes his peasant origins, speaks of how he felt like a socialist hero standing among the milk cans in his youth, reminds us of his work as a resistance fighter during the war. He is blind to the fact that his past is severed from his present; that as a failing captain of industry he stands for the acquisitiveness, the fetishism of goods and wealth that are anathema to the left. He is indeed their target, and he proves the accuracy of their aim. This becomes clear as two other figures move into prominence during the wait for the release of Giovanni.

One is Giovanni's girlfriend, Laura. The other, Adelfo, a friend of Giovanni who tells Primo that he is a worker-priest – though an odd priest who has on his bookshelf a copy of an autobiography by Maria

Tragedy of a Ridiculous Man: 'they cannot see who they are and why this is happening to them' (Ugo Tognazzi, Anouk Aimée)

Callas and Kenneth Anger's book of scandals, *Hollywood Babylon*. Both work at Primo's factory, and both are profoundly involved with the kidnapping. They toy with Primo, bringing him what they claim to be news and letters from Giovanni about his condition and the demands of his captors. Laura plays seductress, proving further how ridiculous Primo is, easily enticing him in the midst of his apparent misery. (Laura remains an intriguing and enigmatic character throughout the film, for it turns out that she has the greatest knowledge of events as they transpire, and is to a great extent controlling them.) Laura and Adelfo play with Primo because the entire event becomes a game, an elaborate plot to part a fool from his money, to aid the cause of the left, and to prove the ridiculousness of a man who, while proclaiming his love for his son, in fact loves mainly his factory and his position as boss. Adelfo and Laura convince Primo that Giovanni has been killed by his captors, but only Laura seems to know that this is not so. Ever the pragmatic businessman, Primo sees now a chance, if not to save his son, at least to save his business. He hides the news of the death from his wife, arranges with his business associates to come up with the ransom money, and (he believes) with the help of Laura and Adelfo to use this money to refinance his failing business. Primo believes that they go along with the plot because he promises to turn the factory into a co-operative, with himself as president for life.

The plan is hatched in the pig barns of Primo's factory, and as Primo elaborates it, Bertolucci intercuts shots of the slaughtering and skinning of pigs. It is an apt and ironical montage (in a sequence which I will examine in detail below), for Primo slaughters his conscience as easily as he has the pigs killed for his profit. And the irony doubles upon him, for it is Primo himself who, figuratively, is the pig being led to slaughter. (The metaphor of the pigs, and the presence of Ugo Tognazzi in the central role, associates this film with Pasolini's *Porcile*, a film about pigs, savagery and the rise of neo-fascism.)

Giovanni is not dead. Giovanni is in fact a leftist himself, a fact revealed when the police search his room and find left-wing posters and books; and the spectator is left to speculate why his parents never referred to or even seemed aware of their son's politics (even though, at one point, Laura tells Primo that Giovanni had considered kidnapping him). His kidnapping, it seems – though this is not clarified – was set up by himself and his colleagues, including Laura and Adelfo, with, perhaps, full knowledge of how his father would react. And react he does, still not telling his wife the truth, carrying through an elaborate plan of leaving a suitcase full of money in the woods (money he expects will be returned to him). Barbara takes it all very seriously, even threatening to shoot Primo as he bumbles through a beautiful autumnal landscape where the money is to be left. When they return home, Primo reveals the plot to Barbara, but it is too late. In a hall across the road from their villa, the people of the region gather for a dance. Primo goes to the dance with Laura and Adelfo, thinking that they will return to him the money he left for Giovanni's ransom. Punk rock music is played at the dance (the 'worker-priest' Adelfo does a frantic little dance by himself), followed by traditional Italian country melodies. Old and new meet in a cacophonous confusion. Giovanni appears, returned from his 'kidnapping', returned from the dead (Primo sees him at first almost as a spectre, as a pair of legs dancing, first with only one shoe on, then with both). Primo walks away, and the film ends as his voice comments upon the enigma of sons who die and are born again. He says he will leave this mystery to us; he prefers not to know. And Bertolucci irises in on him, isolating his distant figure on the screen.

Tragedy of a Ridiculous Man is a curious variation on *The Spider's Stratagem*. As in that film, a complex political ploy is played out between father and son, though the terms seem here to be reversed. In the earlier film a dead father produced a theatrical gesture that extended through time to his son. In *Tragedy of a Ridiculous Man* a son who is thought to be dead creates an elaborate game which traps the father within the contradictions of his own economic-political-psychological position. The ramifications of this game do not extend through the webs of history as they do in the earlier work, remaining locked within the bounds of a single family. On closer examination, however, the ramifications of the events are even greater here. Eschewing overt modernist forms, concentrating upon the linear progression of present moments, Bertolucci creates what is for him a new dialectical structure in which a contained and limited enquiry into the struggle of right and left is made to radiate through the entire social structure of Italy and the middle class of much of western Europe.

Within this structure it becomes clear that the film's narrative does not, finally, reverse the pattern of *The Spider's Stratagem*. The game may seem to belong to Giovanni and his colleagues; Primo may be portrayed as a fool outwitted by the left. But the game is possible only because Primo and all he stands for hold power. Like Athos Magnani Sr, he is the betrayer, of his past as worker and resistance fighter, and of his present as father. The only thing he does not betray is his status as owner. Like Athos Sr, he is the creator of his son, physically of course but also ideologically. Giovanni, despite the fact that most of what we learn of him is by suggestion and inference, is clearly not the innocent that Athos Jr was on his arrival in Tara. His politics, it would seem, are fully formed; but his clever outwitting of his father is possible only because of what his father is and continues to be. Athos Sr created a gap, a kind of black hole in history into which he, his son, and the entire community fall. The structure of ownership of which Primo is a part is not a gap but a continuing process of social and political betrayal, of the people he controls, of the family that echoes the structure of the corporation. When he believes his son dead, he does not mourn for long, but like a good capitalist exploits the event for his own profit. His son's blood, he says, will be the 'compost' which will start the regrowth of the factory.

There is a fine double edge honed here as the moral righteousness and moral corruption of the bourgeoisie are folded in upon each other and the moves played by right and left wind up in stalemate. Again, as in *The Spider's Stratagem*, the major players get trapped in the narrative they have created. In the end ownership and the patriarch remain. The son may have gained a temporary victory over the father, but the father's stratagems survive. While that temporary victory is of great importance within the total structure of Bertolucci's work – and I shall examine it more fully in the next chapter – the cyclical process of victory-defeat-victory of the middle class remains in control of the narrative.

With all this in mind, we can return to the formal elements of the film with a greater appreciation of the control Bertolucci exercises over this complex field of signifieds. As I have suggested, while the narrative connotations of *Tragedy of a Ridiculous Man* play counterpoint with *The Spider's Stratagem*, the signifiers, and their arrangement in the form and style of the two films, could not be more different. The temporal-spatial twists and distortions of the earlier film are here replaced by an almost obsessively linear construction, a cool, distanced observation of events; expressed, if not in real time, at least with the intense notion of time passing slowly, filled with the emptiness of waiting and expectation. There are none of the complex narrative juxtapositions of *Last Tango*, the indulgence in psychological realism of *1900*, or the melodramatic excesses of *La luna*. Through its restrained structure, the meanings the film generates are implicit, suggested, and Bertolucci attempts an interesting variation upon the perceptual experiments of his earlier works, creating a first-person discourse, allowing Primo to narrate events in voice-over. This gives him apparent control over what is seen, heard and done by filtering everything through his consciousness.

The Conformist attempted something similar, although its main character does not narrate the events directly and is himself so confused and unbalanced that the film's *mise en scène* takes on the hallucinatory aspects of an unbalanced personality. Primo is not neurotic. Unlike Clerici he has the comfortable awareness of a man who believes that he knows his place. Although in appearance he is an oafish, stumpy-looking individual ('I always have been ridiculous,' he says, looking at himself in the mirror, 'but with style'), he feels his soul and conscience to be clear and upright. He is an ordinary, vain man, in many ways the conformist that Clerici wished to be, but with all the obsessiveness of that character's personality seeming to be under control. His ordinary personality, his banal view of the world, inform the style of the film. He authors the gaze into the narrative.

In fact, like Athos Sr, he attempts to create the narrative – the plotting of events that will allow him to prosper from his son's death. And he creates the 'look' of the film, because it is his 'look' that relates and determines what is seen and interpreted, even though his interpretation is often incorrect. Here is where the first-person narrative becomes intriguing. Primo 'authors' the narrative, but he himself is 'authored' by the narrative in a double sense. The film is created by Bertolucci, of course. That creation in turn generates the narrative and the character who, in his turn, believes he creates events within a structure that is itself apparently predetermined. More subtly than in *Last Tango* the film entraps its subject within a space that the subject believes he controls. This illusion is heightened by the double view of things we, as spectators, are offered when Bertolucci presents us with subjective shots of what Primo thinks he sees – as in his observation of the kidnapping through the binoculars which his son has given him as a birthday present. More often, however, we see Primo and the events that surround him while listening to his commentary upon them. Shortly after the kidnapping, Laura, Giovanni's girlfriend, comes to visit the Spaggiari house. The camera tracks her into its modern, luxurious rooms as Primo's voice on the soundtrack comments, 'Let me tell you about Laura's visit. She mustn't know I'm watching.' The camera cranes up to the gallery above the room Laura is in, and the viewer can see Primo's feet pacing back and forth as he watches and comments on her. Of course Primo knows nothing about Laura, while she knows everything about him and the kidnapping (or, at the very least, the plans that are set in motion after the kidnapping). Sometimes we pull away from his point of view entirely, as in a sequence where the camera is mounted on the top of a car, between two loudspeakers. As if assuming a point of view of its own, or – as the viewer at first suspects – of the police, the camera eye prowls the streets, following Primo. The car, it turns out, belongs to the union; Adelfo has borrowed it to track down Primo and begin confronting him with the counter-plot that will prove to be his undoing. The point of view, in this instance, is of those forces to which Primo is blind.

This interplay of what Primo sees, thinks he sees and does not see determines the restrained complexity of the film. His middle-class view of the world generates its *mise en scène*. His utter lack of insight and comprehension, along with his businessman's cunning – morals come after sincerity, he says – and the use made of this cunning by the left, determine the film's other scene: the fooling of father by son and the patriarchal overdetermination which finally renders that gesture small and useless. Like most of Bertolucci's characters, in the end Primo sees nothing; the entire structure of the narrative he thinks he controls falls in on him. But unlike the characters who precede him, he survives – with neither morals nor sincerity.

The surface simplicity of the film becomes itself an illusion, hiding within it the subterfuge of misguided perception while it seeks out a clearer perception of its events by means of an important allusive subtext. Not Verdi this time, although reference to the composer is present once again. When Primo and Barbara walk through the autumn woods to leave the ransom for Giovanni, Primo tells her they have their season box at the opera and asks if she knows what the first performance is. He lets her know by singing a bit of an aria from *La traviata*. It is from Act Two, where Germont has come to ask his son, Alfredo, to leave Violetta and return home with him. 'Di Provenza il mar, il suol...', Primo sings. 'Who erased the sea, the land/Of Provence from your heart?/What fate stole you/From your splendid native sun?/Ah, recall even in your grief/That joy glowed for you there,/And that only there/Can peace still shine on you . . ./God led me . . . God led me!/Ah, you don't know how much/Your old father suffered!/With you far away, his roof/Was covered with shame . . .' 'Don't you respond to your father's love?' the aria ends. Primo believes his son is dead; Barbara thinks (or knows) he is alive. The aria is the father's climactic expression of bad faith, the lyrical expression of his manipulation of wife and child. Primo would be the proper middle-class father, like Germont; his expression of love for his son, however, is mere pretence. He does not suffer, though he is unknowingly covered with shame.

But the Verdi reference does not constitute a major structure in this, the most unoperatic of Bertolucci's films. The central influence comes from that figure Bertolucci had tried to cast off more than ten years earlier, Jean-Luc Godard, and a particular film of Godard's, *Tout va bien*, which had marked Godard's temporary return from the cinetracts he and Jean-Pierre Gorin had been making since the late 6os. Godard and Gorin called their film a 'materialist love story', and it places the relationship of Jane Fonda's American journalist and Yves Montand's frustrated film-maker within the context of a strike in a sausage factory. Both characters spend time with the workers of the plant and their boss, who is being held hostage. The boss is played with great comic fervour by Vittorio Caprioli, who plays the *maresciallo* (the police marshall) in *Tragedy of a Ridiculous Man* – with equal comic fervour, if less political resonance. The mutual infiltration of the romantic and political in *Tout va bien*, its drama of class and gender struggle, played out on a huge artificial set (suggested, Gorin admits, by the set Jerry Lewis created in *The Lady's Man*) generates a direct and simple political text. Individuals are played against the collective. The workers are always observed in groups, their spokespersons surrounded by their comrades. The 'stars' of the film are removed from the centre of the spectator's gaze and situated in history. It is a Brechtian fable for the times immediately following 1968.

Ten years later, filtered through a different sensibility, the Godardian influence appears as tracings beneath a different kind of political text. There is the obvious similarity through the actor who appears in both films and the sausage factory setting (though Bertolucci does not create an artificial set). There are peculiar visual similarities. As in *Tout va bien*, the interior walls of Primo's factory are painted blue and hung with pictures of the factory itself – a mark of the capitalist's fetish for his property. In homage to Godard's fascination with the graphic signs that re-present or substitute for actual objects, the sliding doorways to the Spaggiari plant are painted with an

174

enormous cow, a piece of photo-realism which, like similar graphics in Godard's films, mocks the illusory realism of the film image itself.

The most interesting tracings of the Godardian influence lie in the way Bertolucci deals with the workers in his film. In *Tout va bien* they were the most important characters. The workers in *Tragedy of a Ridiculous Man* are a fairly passive group. The only time they express themselves is when Primo makes a ridiculous call for solidarity in face of his son's kidnapping. At first that expression is negative, as Bertolucci cuts to their impassive faces, intercutting significant looks exchanged by Laura and Adelfo, who will stand out from the workers as major actors in the political drama. The workers react when, at his wife's urging, Primo tells his people that he will have to sell the factory. One worker says that their sons must live too. They threaten to occupy the factory. Primo's response is to mock them, and he ends the meeting with an odd (though perfectly accurate) statement that were this a co-operative rather than a private company, he would not be a *padrone* whose son was kidnapped. This nonsequitur is supposed to communicate an inescapable truth and obligation to the workers. But it merely signifies that Primo is aware of alternatives to private ownership which he only acknowledges at a time of turmoil. Bertolucci ends the sequence after this statement. Its lack of effect upon the workers is signified by the absence of a reaction shot of them.

Tout va bien stands behind *Tragedy of a Ridiculous Man* as a mark of difference. In acknowledging it, Bertolucci acknowledges a change in history. Unlike Godard's film (and unlike *1900*), the workers and their reactions are not of primary importance: factory workers in the early 80s were not quite as militant as they were in the late 60s and early 70s or before the end of World War II. Yet, at the same time, while the workers are physically in the background, they remain very much a part of the film's narrative. Once again, Bertolucci turns round the Godardian-Brechtian perspective. The collective spirit recedes, to be represented by the individual figures of Adelfo and Laura, who act, perhaps, as the residue of worker militancy. Bertolucci says that 'theirs is a utopian, ideal terrorism . . . I'd like to see practised by the youth of the FGCI [the Federation of Young Italian Communists]. I don't understand why what didn't work in 1968 because it was arrogant and unreal in relation to the working class should not, and could not, at least in part, materialize itself today. What do Laura and Adelfo do? Once they have obtained from Primo the ransom money, they think of using it to snatch the dairy factory from the boss's hands and turn it into a co-operative [something barely suggested in the film]. It's an idea that's a little reminiscent of 1968, but the fantasy of young communists should feed on ideas like this one.'[15]

Like *Tout va bien, Tragedy of a Ridiculous Man* suggests a political alternative, but much less directly and with considerably less optimism. The political 'terrorism' in Godard's film is presented openly, by means of the strike at the factory and the leftists' attack on the supermarket where they seize goods and give them away. The 'terrorism' of Adelfo and Laura is subdued, uncertain, and finally useless – despite the fact that they get Primo's money. The ridiculous man is at their mercy and they at his. As a group, the workers remain helpless. A few of their representatives are allowed to fight for them. Historically, all is not well. In its quietness, *Tragedy of a Ridiculous Man* echoes the dead level of political activity and the desperation of the late 70s, as in its energy *Tout va bien* had echoed the vitality and hope of the late 60s and early 70s. At the same time, possibilities of political action and change remain active precisely because the film does carry on a dialogue with its predecessor.

The result is a powerful but subdued dialectic. The film's structure is at the same time meditative and ambiguous, clear and direct. The intricacies of political action are all but eclipsed by the prolonged observation of those moments when nothing important happens – moments when Primo sits in his kitchen and joins his housekeeper as she dances to music on the radio, when he slices ham for lunch, relieves himself in an outhouse while waiting for Adelfo and Laura to bring him news; moments taken up by useless interviews with the *maresciallo*, who offers Primo medical advice or comments upon a Ligabue painting hanging on the wall (depicting a horse-drawn carriage attacked by wolves in Siberia – a painting which also appears in the credit sequence of *The Spider's Stratagem*). These uneventful times permit an intensive relationship to develop between film and viewer. The complexities of the narrative are suppressed, unstated; the spectator views them as if through the narrow end of a funnel, attempting to reach the hermeneutic of political action all but hidden at the other end. Hidden, but clearly waiting to be discovered.

Despite its overall quiet the film is not without its bravura passages, though even these are done with restraint. There is nothing here to equal the myth of the cave sequence in *The Conformist*, the moments of psycho-sexual intensity of *Last Tango*, the initial revolt of the peasants in *1900* or that film's scenes of fascist atrocities. But there is in fact no desire to equal them. The centrepiece of *Tragedy of a Ridiculous Man*, in which Primo hatches his plan to use the ransom money for his son to save his factory, is understated, depending, more than anything else in Bertolucci's work so far, upon a subtlety of framing and cutting to make its point. The director who, in 1964, wanted editing removed from the film-maker's vocabulary, here uses it with finesse, alluding

Uncertain 'terrorists': Adelfo and Laura in *Tragedy of a Ridiculous Man* (Victor Cavallo, Laura Morante)

with it to the film-maker for whom editing was the primary structural device of cinema: Sergei Eisenstein.

This particular sequence takes place among the pig barns of the Spaggiari works (it is interesting that Primo rarely refers to the sausage-making part of his trade, preferring to concentrate on the 'cleaner' cheese operation: he is not aware, for example, that his own employee, Adelfo, works with the pigs). The sequence begins with Primo and Laura standing before the enormous cow painted on the wall and sliding doors of the plant, the image of Primo's trade, realistically portrayed – but just an image, as Primo himself is a false image of the man he thinks he is. The two of them enter the pigyards, where animals are heard squealing for the remainder of the sequence. The colour throughout is a dull blue-grey.

As they enter the yards, Bertolucci begins, through his cutting and framing, a kind of hide and seek game among the participants, counterpointing them with shots of pigs looking, running, being prodded, fed, slaughtered. Primo runs, calling after Laura. There is a cut to a shot of pigs looking about; a brief shot of Adelfo, represented only by his boots among the stalls; then a cut back to Primo, who walks across the frame while, in the distance, through the rear window of the pig barns, Laura can be seen walking in the same direction. The camera shifts focus to her and Bertolucci cuts to a shot of Adelfo looking up, and from his perspective Primo can be seen walking past a back window, followed by Laura who walks by an *intermediate* window separating the barn in which Adelfo stands and the barn on the other side, the window of which Primo passes. Adelfo moves out of the frame and Bertolucci cuts to pigs running through the stalls. He pans up to Laura, standing at the rear window of the barn. He cuts then to Primo, himself looking through a window, then to Laura, continuing the cutting so that a découpage is created that forms a fugal counterpoint of passings, of people looking for, and at the same time avoiding, each other; seen, but not making contact. The fugue is punctuated by shots of Barbara, Primo's wife, seen in profile or in silhouette, looking, listening. It is never clear whether she is privy to what is going on or merely present and oblivious to the conspiracy Primo is trying to hatch. In the rest of the film she gives no indication that she has overheard the plot, and she forces Primo to proceed with the ransom plan as if Giovanni were alive (which, of course, he is).

Around them all are the pigs, being led to their troughs, grunting and complaining. Primo, Adelfo and Laura finally do meet one another, at which point Laura states that Giovanni is dead. Adelfo reluctantly agrees, turns away and comments that the pigs squeal as if they are being slaughtered rather than being fed. In fact they are being fed in order to be slaughtered. Adelfo remains nervous about the plot, for he is still uncertain whether Giovanni is in fact dead. He seems reluctant to take part in the hoax being planned. 'A hoax?' Primo cries in indignation. 'Against whom? You? Her? Those of you who work here? Those who lend me money. . . . Money that has to be paid back in three months or two or one? A hoax?' The pigs are led out of their stalls. 'I officially declare,' Primo states, 'that the billion ransom will go to Spaggiari Inc.' Laura is seen on the left of the screen, Primo in shadow on the right, Adelfo in soft focus in the rear. Primo yells at Laura, 'You don't know shit!'

And Bertolucci cuts to a slaughtered pig hanging upside down by its feet, blood spattered on the wall, the dripping of blood on the sound-track. This is followed by a shot of Barbara walking among the barns in silhouette. Bertolucci returns to the three conspirators, cutting between them, sometimes isolating them in one-shots, as Primo elaborates his plan. Laura will forge a letter from Giovanni with instructions on how to deliver the money. He believes she can do it, for after all she and Giovanni were in the same class together. There is a cut to a close-up of Barbara, as if she were listening to the conversation. She turns away, her face hidden by her hat, and Bertolucci cuts to the most violent image in the film: a dead pig in a skinning machine, its carcass rolled about again and again. He follows this with another shot of Barbara, the camera tracking into her shadowy figure.

Laura runs off, yelling 'Giovanni is dead!' And as Primo leaves the stalls his voice-over commentary takes the place of direct dialogue, elaborating the plot. He will collect the ransom as if Giovanni were alive and reinvest it in the factory. In his monumental self-delusion he says that Laura's and Adelfo's acceptance of the plan proves his son is dead. 'His death would save the factory.' Laura reappears, looking strong and conspiratorial in a red sweater and dark glasses. Primo's back is to the camera as his voice-over continues: 'I was a peasant again like my father ... my grandfather. My son's blood was my compost.' Adelfo is seen looking at them. As they walk off together, Primo speaks to Laura, saying she is like Giovanni – he did not understand Primo's world either. 'We're at war here,' he says. 'I know, I fought with the partisans.' Bertolucci intercuts shots of the three of them. Primo says Laura and Adelfo think they know about terrorism, but they know nothing about partisans. He walks off and Laura enters the frame, saying, quietly, 'Harakiri!' She walks around Primo and, in close-up, repeats the phrase. The camera arcs round Primo and Laura. 'What nice kids,' he says in voice-over. 'Sons of bitches!'

The sequence is a complex creation of the lineaments of self-delusion, the presentation of a man so completely blind to what is going on about him that he believes he sees all with the clarity of age and wisdom, while all he remains is the old freedom fighter turned capitalist; the father turned usurer of his son's life; the apparent victim of terrorism become the terrorist of free enterprise, a soldier in the war of the circulation of capital. He is, finally, the pig being led to slaughter.

But the montage links all the participants within the metaphor of slaughtered animals. Adelfo and Laura lead the parents on, abetting their destruction by manipulating their ignorance of who their son is and confusing the roles all are playing in the terrorist game. But the parents remain the final slaughterers, and Primo the ultimate terrorist, 'killing' his son so that his body may act as fertilizer for the growth of the factory. And they are the slaughtered, for the domestic unit is destroyed by placing it within the charnel house of capital. The association with Eisenstein becomes clear. In the montage at the end of *Strike*, the slaughtering of workers by police is intercut with the slaughtering of animals in an abattoir. Here the pig montage represents perhaps a more subtle killing: of conscience, of the ability to make connections between the political, the moral, the financial; of the domestic and paternal imperatives that reactionary ideologies always preach.

Finally, the sequence represents an important reassertion of Bertolucci's formal control, a rediscovery of montage, of a rhythm constructed not only within but between shots, and of suggestion. As a whole, *Tragedy of a Ridiculous Man* asserts a major change in formal structure. The film is Bertolucci's chamber piece, non-assertive though experimenting still with the problems of perception, exploring, as always, the politics of the domestic unit and the larger politics of the capitalist enterprise. It represents a moment of pause and regrouping, a search for expression after the disaster of *La luna* that would not simply repeat those cinematic forms he had already proved he could fashion so well. The work also manifests a bravery that should not be dismissed. For a film-maker of international stature, whose work after *Last Tango* met with both critical and commercial displeasure, to choose and make so subtle a film which recalls the tenets of an earlier modernism and which all but guaranteed a small commercial response took, I think, some courage. *Tragedy of a Ridiculous Man*, while manifesting on its surface the realist conventions to which most film-makers had returned by the late 70s, remains linked to the tradition of Godard, and – with all its differences – to Bertolucci's own work of the early 70s. A text of quiet and demanding insight, shorn of emotional excess, honed of direct statement, it is a film of intellectual rigour, requiring in almost Straubian fashion the attention of its audience at a time when much film-making was giving the audience everything and nothing. Not, to return to Barthes' categories, a text of bliss, but of intermittent, worked for pleasure.

5   In the Name of the Son, the Father and the Dialectic

> I knew that my films were going to be non-religious, secular, bourgeois films, permeated with an uneasy conscience.[1]

This concluding chapter ought to be called 'the return of the repressed'. In examining the formal structures of Bertolucci's films, I have attempted to withhold, as much as that is ever possible, discussion of their contextual elements. As in all acts of repression, the task could not be a complete success, particularly when dealing with narrative form that speaks to us, through character and actions, of things that happen both within its fictional world and within the larger world from which the narrative comes and to which it is attached. Any discussion of form, narrative form in particular, demands that the substance of form – what the form is creating – be taken into account.

In that accounting, however, many things were left out, and here I wish to concentrate more fully on 'substance', examining some of the problems, obsessions, themes, ideas and conflicts that run through all of Bertolucci's works. Here, the Freudian notion of the 'return of the repressed' becomes doubly appropriate. Bertolucci is a Freudian. All his works deal with some aspect of the Oedipal conflict, the struggle of father and son, the threat of castration, the repression of desire. Repression is therefore a major subject of the films. But so is *oppression*. Bertolucci is a Marxist. His major work concerns the domination of capitalism or fascism and the various struggles against their order in the broad political sphere or the world in microcosm that is the couple and the family.

In serious film-making and film criticism of the past few years, the conjuncture of Marxist and Freudian/Lacanian analysis has created important advances in the understanding of the interaction between the text and the culture from which it emerges, as well as the interaction of text and spectator. But such a conjuncture did not come easily and has itself had a long history of repression. Marxists have long resisted the Freudian project because it represented a bourgeois individualism which was thought to be inimical to the Marxist model. In the quest for a new collective order there appeared to be no room for an ideology of the individual which was in fact part of the social and political modes of production that the new order sought to overthrow.

Georg Lukács, a Marxist but no blind anti-Freudian, expressed the problem in relation to the general aesthetic movement of the West in the twentieth century. He wrote that the modern bourgeois intellectual was in danger of retreating into a 'hermetic seclusion', which would engender 'the cult of the unconscious, depth psychology, myth-making of the inner life.'[2] He worried that literature would lapse into 'psycho-physiological pedestrianism'[3] at the expense of a proper understanding of how the individual is formed by the character of the social-economic forces that overdetermine him or her. This notion of ideological-social-economic determination is at the core of Marxist thought, succinctly stated in the 'Preface to *The Critique of Political Economy*', where Marx writes: 'The mode of production of material life conditions the social, political and intellectual life process in general. It is not the consciousness of men that determines their being, but, on the contrary, their social being that determines their consciousness.' Certainly, strict adherence to this premise would preclude the Freudian insistence on the primacy of individual consciousness and unconsciousness, concentration upon individual neuroses, the eternal recapitulation of the Oedipal process, the trauma of castration, the obsession with sexuality. In short, all those elements of individual development that appear to negate the external determining factors of social being.

Freud was not concerned with 'the mode of production of material life', but rather with the mode of production of the inner life of each individual. His work was the validation of nineteenth-century romanticism and its insistence upon the primacy of the individual psyche, and therefore a validation also of bourgeois ideology and its seemingly contradictory insistence on the conformity of each psyche to the productivity and well-being of the dominant class. Freud's studies of human behaviour, his perception that aggressive tendencies needed to be controlled by 'civilization', despite the repressions and neuroses that would occur, lead him, in his later writings, to a distinctly reactionary stance. Of communism he wrote (in 'Civilization and Its Discontents', 1930): 'I am able to recognize that the psychological premisses on which the system is based are an untenable illusion. In abolishing private property we deprive the human love of aggression of one of its instruments . . . but we have in no way altered the differences in power and influence which are misused by aggressiveness, nor have we altered anything in its nature.' He was certain that other instruments of aggression would be found. This and other statements betray a profound pessimism, a belief that human behaviour is immutably determined from within the individual – the opposite of the Marxist dynamic.

But given the force and influence of the Freudian project, and the applicability of its insights to an understanding of the interaction of individual behaviour and the capitalist structure, it was inevitable that Marxists would attempt some kind of rapprochement. In 1964 (the year of Bertolucci's *Before the Revolution*), Louis Althusser published an essay in the French Communist Party journal, *La Nouvelle Critique*, entitled 'Freud and Lacan'.* The essay attempted to demonstrate that, through the intervention of Jacques Lacan, and particularly his situating of the analytical project within the realm of language, Freud's work is given a scientific and materialist standing. 'Lacan has shown,' Althusser writes, 'that [the] transition from (ultimately purely) biological existence to human existence (the human child) is achieved within the Law of Order, the law I shall call the Law of Culture, and that this Law of Order is confounded in its *formal* essence with the order of language' (in *Lenin and Philosophy*, p. 209). The transition into language is a movement into ideology, which is controlled by language. Through the entry of the individual into the linguistic-ideological realm, we are able to analyse how the individual and the culture interact; even more, how the individual becomes subject to the dominant ideology into which he or she is born (the 'symbolic' realm, in Lacan's model). The initial phase of this movement involves the Oedipal process, in which the individual is 'given' gender, pulled from the protective realm of self and mother, and thrust into the symbolic realm of the patriarch, the realm of the phallus, of language and of power.[4]

'The Oedipal phase,' Althusser writes, 'is not a hidden *"meaning"* which merely lacks consciousness or speech – it is not a structure buried in the past that can always be restructured or surpassed by "reactivating its meaning"; the Oedipus complex is the dramatic structure, the "theatrical machine" imposed by the Law of Culture on every involuntary, conscripted candidate to humanity, a structure containing in itself not only the possibility of, but the necessity for the concrete variants in which it *exists*, for every individual who reaches its

---

* Althusser was by no means the first to seek such a reconciliation. Within the Freudian coterie, individuals such as Theodor Reik, Wilhelm Reich and Herbert Marcuse had sought a bonding of Freud and Marx. But Althusser's standing as a major Marxist philosopher made his intervention a most important event in the history of the debate.

threshold, lives through it and survives it.'[5] Through Lacan, Althusser makes the Oedipal phase a part of the 'social being' which determines consciousness. In his turn, Bertolucci makes obsessive reference to the 'theatrical machine' of the Oedipal phase, and in all his works seeks to discover the various ways it imposes the 'Law of Culture' upon individuals and how those individuals live through or succumb to it.

Before we move on to Bertolucci's place within the intersection of Marx, Freud and Lacan, however, a few more points need to be made about Lacan and the Oedipal phase. Lacan is himself no Marxist. Michael Ryan has labelled him 'a clever fundamentalist, rather conservative, clearly antimarxist, roundly antifeminist, and theocratic', although he does admit that 'a radical theory of the human subject or of ideology can be derived from Lacan's work'.[6] That is, of course, precisely the point. Despite what his own politics and intentions might have been, Lacan's work has *served* political analysis, film studies and feminism through the linguistic model he constructed and through his metaphor of the individual as a subject who moves among other subjects, one signifier among many in a chain made up of differences between the self and the Other – the 'I' which to another 'I' is a 'You'. Lacan provides insight into the agony of differentiation, the imperative that the self recognize that it is not a self to other selves. His model speaks to the need to be sexed (or gendered), and in that process (the Oedipal process) the need to discover – despite one's sex – that the phallus, the structure of the patriarchy and its language, controls all psychic and, by extension, all social and political activity. Such insight provides powerful tools for analysis of the individual and his or her position in the social order. Via Lacan the critic can proceed well beyond a vulgar Freudianism to a broad examination of the conflicts that exist between the individual and the collective, the psyche and the society.

Within Lacan's notion of patriarchal power and its control of language (the symbolic order, culture, ideology) we can rediscover Marx's concept of the social order and its modes of production that determine and oppress the individual. However, what Marx knew, what Freud and (implicitly) Lacan seem to deny – and Althusser reasserts – is that the control and oppression are *created* rather than natural forces. Freud and Lacan would have us believe that the Oedipal phase, for example, is an inescapable event through which all must pass in order to become functioning, semi-functioning or non-functioning subjects of the symbolic order. But in fact the Oedipal phase is only a construct, a metaphor that has been allowed to achieve the status of reality. Gilles Deleuze and Félix Guattari, in their important, difficult and occasionally crazed book *Anti-Oedipus: Capital-*

184

ism and Schizophrenia, point out how the metaphor has become a tyrannical device.

> We do not deny that there is an Oedipal sexuality, an Oedipal heterosexuality and homosexuality, an Oedipal castration, as well as complete objects, global images, and specific egos. We deny that these are productions of the unconscious. What is more, castration and oedipalization beget a basic illusion that makes us believe that real desiring-production is answerable to higher formations that integrate it, subject it to transcendent laws, and make it serve a higher social and cultural production; there then appears a kind of 'unsticking' of the social field with regard to the production of desire, in whose name all resignations are justified in advance. Psychoanalysis, at the most concrete level of therapy, reinforces this apparent movement with its combined forces. . . . We are compelled to say that psychoanalysis has its metaphysics – its name is Oedipus. And that a revolution – this time materialist – can proceed only by way of a critique of Oedipus, by denouncing the illegitimate use of the syntheses of the unconscious as found in Oedipal psychoanalysis.[7]

If not a full circle, at least a full dialectic occurs. Marxism attempts to embrace Freudianism, then perceives a tyrannical force within it that opposes both individual and collective development by creating the metaphysics of Oedipus. As a result, a new relationship needs to be made. Deleuze and Guattari find it in a peculiar concept of schizophrenia, somewhat related to the work of R. D. Laing.

In his own work, Bertolucci keeps searching for ways to express the conflicts, the possible resolutions and more pressing irresolutions of the Freudian and Marxist projects. In particular, his films express the great desire of every Marxist – which is also an expression of the great lack – to articulate the existence, perhaps in history, always in the imagination, of a collective, anti-bourgeois order. At the same time his work expresses the existence of the oppressive force that prevents the formation of that order: the patriarchy, the castrating father who would render both the individual and the collective impotent within the confines of his ideology.

The conflict is presented within both macrocosm and microcosm, within the individual's relationship to culture and to family. In Bertolucci's films, the male individual must confront the oppressive social order, which he may embrace, as Clerici does in *The Conformist,* or attempt – unsuccessfully – to resist, as does Athos Jr in *The Spider's Stratagem* or Paul in *Last Tango in Paris.* That order is always an extension of the father, and all Bertolucci's male characters (and sometimes female, like Caterina in *La luna*) must work through the Oedipal conflict. As a result, all of them, with the possible exception of Giovanni in *Tragedy of a Ridiculous Man*, come out of it scarred, deformed or dead.

An image in *1900*, Bertolucci's central statement about generations and the politics of the patriarchy, encapsulates the problem that is worked out in various ways throughout his work. The old *padrone*, Alfredo, is the patriarch of the Berlinghieri family and farm. He carries within him the tradition of oppression, the nineteenth-century mode of relationship between owner and worker which, as much as Bertolucci may despise it, is still recognized as something less inhuman than what will occur in the twentieth century with the rise of fascism. Old Alfredo is played by Burt Lancaster, chosen, Bertolucci said, because he, along with Sterling Hayden, who plays old Dalco, the patriarch of the peasant family owned by the Berlinghieris, stands for the patriarchy of the old Hollywood and 'the melodrama of the 19th century'.[8] Even more appropriately, the Burt Lancaster character is an extension of the character he plays in Visconti's *The Leopard*. His class has changed in *1900* – he is a bourgeois rather than a nobleman – but like his former incarnation old Alfredo is a proud man unable to absorb the changes in the society around him, changes he believes are for the worse (in many ways *1900* is an ideological, if not chronological, sequel to *The Leopard*, concentrating on the opposition of bourgeoisie and peasant rather than of nobility and bourgeoisie).

In one sequence, early in the film, the entire Berlinghieri family is eating a dinner made up of the frogs that young Olmo – who will come to represent the new, independent socialist peasant – has caught. Old Alfredo, who despises the family he has sired, sits in the next room, aiming his shotgun at them, pretending to destroy the group who will soon inherit his wealth and land. He is joined by his grandson, young Alfredo, who will grow up to be Olmo's friend and class enemy, the relationship between them forming the narrative crux of the film (in this sequence young Alfredo vomits when he is forced to eat Olmo's frogs). The old man and the young boy play, sharing the shotgun, until young Alfredo's father – old Alfredo's son – Giovanni comes to force his son to table. He grabs young Alfredo by the shoulder; old Alfredo grabs Giovanni by the shoulder; the three stand for a moment in a straight line, in tableau, two generations weighing down on the third, young Alfredo at the end of the line (he will sire no children), a conduit of patriarchal order, frozen, immobile, ineluctable.

I said earlier that Bertolucci examines both the larger and the smaller aspects of Oedipus. This needs to be redefined somewhat within the notion of 'weighing down' which is present in this image from *1900*. With the exception of *La luna*, which cuts away much political resonance, Bertolucci is not so much concerned with the clinical aspects of the Oedipal process as with its larger social-political ramifications, the burden of the father borne by the son, and ultimately the weight of all fathers borne by every child when he or she enters the 'symbolic stage' of the I and the Other, of language, law, culture and ideology. Like Althusser (and Deleuze and Guattari), Bertolucci attempts to politicize Oedipus. Thus the figure of the father is often either an active absence or a symbolic presence. In *1900* Alfredo and old Dalco die early in the narrative. Giovanni becomes a figure signifying the landed gentry's acquiescence in fascism. Olmo becomes the symbolic patriarch of the peasant movement. Clerici's father is in a lunatic asylum, and his son looks to fascism for patriarchal guidance. The fathers of Athos in *The Spider's Stratagem* and of Jeanne and Paul in *Last Tango* are dead, yet each exerts a powerful ideological presence. In *La luna* Joe's father does not appear until the end of the narrative, his absence being the major cause of traumatic events. Only in *Tragedy of a Ridiculous Man* is the father fully and continuously present, a fact which, as we shall see, leads to ironic results.

The father may be a surrogate force (as is fascism for Clerici) or a surrogate guide, as is Cesare in *Before the Revolution*. Cesare is the unique instance of an anti-Oedipal figure, an older man who attempts to guide the younger man into a new symbolic order, into political consciousness, into the maturity of the Marxist intellectual's concern with history and the place of the individual in it. 'Maturity is all,' he reminds his young pupil, quoting another Cesare, the writer Pavese. Fabrizio's actual father is a slug-like bourgeois, barely present in the narrative, except as the bourgeois force pulling his son in the opposite direction to Cesare, into his own confused individuality.

In this process of politicizing Oedipus, the name and power of the father is expanded, atomized into many different, often conflicting forces. In *The Conformist* Clerici's natural father is, as I said, in a lunatic asylum, driven mad not by the spiritual and political blindness that afflicts his son, but by the pain of having seen too much. He was an old fascist supporter; he once met Hitler. Like a figure from Conrad – or Shakespeare – the horror of what he has seen and known has forced him into a knowledge too great to be contained by normal behavioural restraints. The asylum Bertolucci creates for him is a huge white stadium, an open space which is the blank enclosure for a man whose blinding vision now permits him only to see the world in the single perspective of death and sadness. He writes obsessively and calls out three words: '*strage e malinconia*', 'slaughter and melancholy', raising his arms in a grand and self-destructive gesture to his keepers, who wrap him in a straitjacket.

Clerici's father is the operatic and too fully sighted opposite of his son. Despite the straitjacket he is unrestrained in his madness, where his son is rendered blind and repressed, the melancholy murderer about whom his father laments. Unlike his father (before he is strait-jacketed) his movements are rigid, stiff and puppet-like, not broad and embracing. Clerici's father, in his excess the demonic opposite of Cesare, might have shown his son a way to enlightenment; but Clerici chooses instead another guide, the totalitarian father, the great castra-tor that is fascism. Jacques Lacan writes about the movement of the subject into the realm of language and the dangers that movement entails. His words apply nicely to Clerici's condition: 'first and foremost it was the appeal of the void, in the ambiguous gap of an attempted seduction of the other by the means on which the subject has come compliantly to rely, and to which he will commit the monumental construct of his narcissism.'[9] Clerici never moves beyond the monu-mental construct of his narcissism. He absorbs the ideology of the Other, of fascism in this instance, and pretends it is him, whereas in truth it only cuts him from himself and makes him his own Other.

There are other fathers in *The Conformist*. There is Professor Quadri (who is, among other things, Bertolucci's surrogate for his own aesthe-tic father, Jean-Luc Godard), the weakest of guides, who cannot quite father himself through the various roles of a one-time teacher of a present fascist, a resistance fighter, a lover of bourgeois life in the temporary safety of Paris. And there is Manganiello, the father who accepts no nonsense, and who, with the physically blind Italo, is the representative of the patriarchal regime, the Law of Order – the club and the word.

To repeat, the essential point in understanding Bertolucci's treat-ment of the Oedipal scene is that he rarely separates it from the political. The concepts of father and patriarchy, *padre* and *padrone*, teacher and oppressor are profoundly linked.* The father owns the child as the boss owns the workers and the fascist state its people, each exercising power through the symbolic threat of castration. Like Rainer

---

* The pun on *padre* and *padrone* was clearly not lost on Paolo and Vittorio Taviani, who made a film in 1977 about a peasant family in which the father is tyrant to his son, using the words as its title. They followed *Padre padrone* with *Il prado (The Meadow*, 1979), whose subject is also the relationship between father and son. The son is played by Fabrizio Forte, who played the son in the previous film; his father by Giulio Brogi, who played Athos Magnani, father and son, in *The Spider's Stratagem*.

Werner Fassbinder, though perhaps without his exacting subtlety of insight, Bertolucci understands clearly that – despite the tenets of bourgeois ideology – the family and the state, private life and the structure of the society at large, are never separated; on the contrary, they continually reproduce each other.

No film better presents the phenomenon than *Last Tango in Paris*, even though, at one level of its narrative, it seems to deny it. In the denial, however, is the confirmation. In Paul's attempt to create a world of sexuality isolated from the outside world, to deny social identity and lineage by refusing names, to retreat from the symbolic realm of the I and the Other, he not only brings down the wrath of the father with devastating results, but manages to point up the linkage between state-patriarch-father-family-individual with an effect perhaps more subtle than in those films in which Bertolucci deals with the problem more explicitly. The relationships between interior and exterior worlds is clearly stated early in the film through the images of the police – the representatives of state order – which are intercut with Jeanne's initial appearance. The intervention of her dead father and the colonial oppression he represented brings about the film's final catastrophe. But the presence of the patriarchal order is manifested in other ways, most clearly in the behaviour of Paul himself.

In his desperate attempt to separate himself from the horror of his wife's suicide, in his anger and withdrawal from the domestic scene, he would act as its destroyer. He is violent in his reaction to his mother-in-law, more violent in his relationship with Jeanne, who, beginning as the object of his release from the pain of domesticity, ends as the subject of his pain. When he sodomizes her, he makes her repeat with him a litany about the family and its function as destroyer of the individual, repressor of the spirit. 'A holy institution, meant to breed virtue in savages,' he begins. 'Holy family ... church of good citizens ... where the will is broken with repression ... where freedom is assassinated by egotism ... the family ... you fucking family....' Lost on him in his despair and anger is the fact that in condemning repression, he is acting it out by hurting the woman who has become the symbol and object of his rage. Lost on him too is the fact that he is repeating the role of cruel father breaking the will of his daughter-lover (as cruel in a different way as his own father, who, he had told Jeanne, made him go out on a date with his shoes and socks smelling of cow dung). Later, when she taunts him with her engagement to Tom, he tries to warn her away from her romantic notions about the sanctity and security of marriage, telling her she will only become a refuge for her husband, implying that she will merely recapitulate the function of the woman in the capitalist mode of production – as keeper and protector of the man, as reproducer of the social order.

If Paul, in his agony, keeps shifting Jeanne as signifier of woman, daughter, wife, mother, object of sexual abuse, warning her of the dangers inherent in all those roles, simultaneously creating her in those roles, he himself also shifts. From his role as angry destroyer of the patriarchal structure, he decides to become part of its apparatus; from his role as instructor of its dangers (an odd version of Professor Quadri, and who, like the Professor, gets killed for his pains), he becomes an actor in its melodrama. He assumes the role of romantic lover, and in so doing revitalizes the ghost of the father. His donning of the Colonel's hat in his final confrontation with Jeanne in her flat, before she shoots him, is not merely a symbolic act, but one in a string of gestures Paul makes as he falls back into the very world he wished to escape, but to which he capitulates and recapitulates. He becomes the patriarch with all the rules and authority, all the demands for obedience. In response Jeanne, who herself wishes to join that world through her marriage with Tom – the safe bourgeois whose pretence to difference is perfectly transparent – becomes, for an instant, the revolutionary, and destroys Paul. Paul attempted to break the dominant ideology with the thrust of his penis, and ended being castrated – indeed executed – by the very ideology he attempted to defy. From sexual anarchist to romantic movie hero-father-lover to a corpse crouched in the foetal position, he moves through a seemingly ineluctable cycle of revolt, self-deception and oppression. He may not follow the stages of Oedipus as Freud marked them out; in fact he seems to move in reverse. But the results are the same. In death as in childhood he becomes suborned, placed in the hierarchy.

All Bertolucci's male characters are symbolically castrated by the patriarchy – the social structure of capitalism. Athos Jr is unmanned by the ghost of his father in *The Spider's Stratagem*, who entraps him and history within the web of fascist spectacle and melodrama. Joe, in *La luna*, suffers a peculiar kind of castration by being denied his identity as child and turned into a surrogate father-lover-husband by his mother. I noted earlier that *La luna* appears to be the most 'non-political' of Bertolucci's films, the most dedicated to a purely psychological-psychoanalytical pursuit. But if we follow through the notion of politicization of Oedipus, even such a confused and explicitly 'personal' film as this must be examined in a political light (as, in fact, Bertolucci has insisted it must). *La luna* can be read as a film about control, about the very oppression and breaking of the spirit which Paul speaks of in *Last Tango*. In her own sexual confusions, Caterina manipulates her son, transgresses the power of the mother (which in the life of the child, of course, precedes the power of the father), attempts literally to enact the Oedipal scene, breaking the will of the child by enforcing her sexual needs upon his confusion and helplessness. In the Freudian scheme, the success of the Oedipal conflict lies in the son's ability to repress his desire to possess the mother and enter into the dominant and dominating realm of the father. Caterina denies 'normal' development by an imposition of her own will.

A dialectical reading of the film might suggest that by denying the 'normal' processes of the Oedipal conflict, the son could be initiated into a freer, *less* repressed existence, precisely because the need to repress Oedipal desire sets in motion the continuum of repressions that make up human life. But in fact Caterina's activities repress all desire in her son, except the desire to die. Once again, a chain of repression takes command. Just as Caterina is exploited by her own fears and insecurities – as well as by her vocation, the world of commercial grand opera and its hangers on (the one point in the film where she commits a genuinely maternal act and calls a doctor to help her son in his withdrawal symptoms, the doctor pulls out a Polaroid camera to take her picture) – so she exploits her son. The lack of the father permits the presence of the mother to overwhelm the child. (The argument as to whether Bertolucci has presented a feminist perspective on this process through using a woman as his central figure will be examined later.)

Perhaps the strangest 'castration' resulting from the father-son conflict occurs in *Tragedy of a Ridiculous Man*, where the son, for once, manages revenge against the father. We are given no explicit details of the relationship of father and son in the narrative. What is implied, however, is that the son attempts to destroy the father, in perhaps a miniature re-enactment of the myth Freud develops in *Totem and Taboo* – the slaying of the father by the outcast sons. Giovanni 'kills' his father politically and economically by knowing and playing upon his weaknesses. The 'tribe' – in this case the leftists who apparently help set up the plot – trick the father, even to the point of offering him the son's lover (reversing the myth Freud sets up). Laura all but yields to Primo's sexual advances, which she seems, at first, to do out of her own sense of loss at the disappearance of Giovanni (it is never explicit at what point the two representatives of the leftist group, Laura and Adelfo, know precisely what is occurring). In retrospect, it is also possible that she plays with Primo sexually, forcing him to reveal his own foolishness. This is clearly the case later in the narrative when Primo dictates to her the note that she will write in Giovanni's hand, which sets up the pretence for the delivery of the ransom money. They sit opposite each other in the chairs which Adelfo, the worker priest, uses for hearing confession. Laura removes her sweater and throws it at Primo. 'My God, what tits!' exclaims Primo in voice-over. The peasant turned *padrone* is capable only of a crude sexual response, while the son, through his surrogates, is setting up the trap that will undo his father's financial and moral life.

In the previous chapter I mentioned that *Tragedy of a Ridiculous Man* seems to reverse the structure of *The Spider's Stratagem*. Here it is the son who enmeshes his father in the history, the mode of economic, social and psychological production, which the father has, if not created, certainly perpetuated. In both films 'interior', domestic history, the familial relationship of father and son, plays analogously or dialectically with exterior history. They are never separated; one always imposes upon, reflects, affects the other. As a result, Giovanni's victory is an illusion. He may have bested his father, exposed the man's ridiculousness, 'castrated' him of his wealth. But as I noted, wealth and ownership continue; the son returns to the family, to his friends, his father, his mother. The last shot in the film is an iris in upon the father, diminished to be sure, not triumphant, but enduring. If Freud's *Totem and Taboo* does indeed form the film's hermeneutic, Giovanni also endures – as the guilty son who will recapitulate his father's rule.

Bertolucci has indicated his recognition of this cycle in a remarkable comment about *Tragedy of a Ridiculous Man* in which he addresses the character of Primo, and perceives a link between this Resistance fighter turned capitalist and the socialist hero of *1900* which suggests the relationship of Primo and his son:

> In a certain sense, Primo is Olmo, forty years later. He is the father who has become the boss, a boss who is a partisan, a communist and a farmer. Primo's political project is grafted on to a complex, sinister and tragically ridiculous reality which is Italy today, a confused reality which nonetheless still contains some pockets of resistance. Thus the political project of Primo, who once was Olmo, confronts the political project of Laura and Adelfo, who are a little bit the continuation of Leonida, the little boy in *1900* who threatened the *padrone* at gun point [in the frame narrative that begins *1900*, Leonida is the boy who is careful to wipe his feet before entering the house, holds Alfredo at gunpoint before his trial and cheers Stalin]. Laura and Adelfo, like Leonida many years before, represent the continuity of rural communism that doesn't hesitate to arrest the father [*padre*] when he becomes the boss [*padrone*].[10]

The cycle of rebellion and repression moves ineluctably as the son destroys the father who attempted to destroy him only to assume the father's role in his turn. 'It must be confessed,' Freud wrote, 'that the revenge taken by the deposed and restored father was a harsh one: the dominance of authority was at its climax. The subjugated sons made use of the new situation in order to unburden themselves still further of their sense of guilt.'[11] None of this is explicitly stated in *Tragedy of a Ridiculous Man*; it lies rather as a suggested, subtextual threat to the film's dominant discourse of filial victory – an important victory, despite the failure it carries within it, and one to which I shall return.

The relational complex of father and son, the symbolic act of castration that places the individual within the repressive community, the way this eternally repeated process acts as both metaphor and metonymy for the life and the politics of the culture at large is expressed no more fully than in *1900* – the film to which one must continue to return for an understanding of all of Bertolucci's central concerns. Here the psychological is subordinated to the political, where it acts as the base upon which the superstructure of history and class struggle may be built. To be sure, this structure is not built with total assurance. The film's realist narrative construction and Bertolucci's use of 'known' stars impose on its narrative the necessity of playing personal relationships against the historical, the filtering of political observation through the personalities of the leading figures – Alfredo and Olmo – and their personal attachment one to the other. Although cliché sometimes threatens insight, the tension derived by counter-pointing conventional psychological melodrama against unconventional political statement often results in a mutual enlightenment of the two discourses, particularly as paternal-filial-marital relationships are connected to the broader field of history and political progress.

With the exception of Jacob in *Partner*, the peasant Olmo in *1900* is the only male figure in Bertolucci's work who has no known male progenitor. He is a bastard. Alfredo's lineage, on the other hand, is quite clear; he is the last in the line of an old land-owning family. Within the psychological model Bertolucci is so fond of – as well as the model dictated by the historical structure of the film – young Alfredo represents the patriarchy, although it is a representation he struggles against, defying his father, aligning himself with the more 'liberal' tendencies of his grandfather. There is a patriarchal structure in Olmo's culture, but this is pointedly more relaxed, communal and emotionally comforting in the face of the physical discomfort of the peasants' life. Old Dalco is the nominal patriarch of the peasants, doubling, within his own class, the role of old Alfredo, acting as Olmo's grandfather and guide. The relationships formed on both sides therefore appear to suppress the father. Alfredo and Olmo are each more closely connected to their grandfathers than they are to their immediate progenitors; and the grandfathers are themselves closely allied, despite their class differences (sharing, for example, a hatred of church

193

Patriarchs: Alfredo and Dalco in *1900* (Burt Lancaster, Sterling Hayden)

and priesthood). These personal alliances, as well as the class antagonisms, are echoed in the friendship of Alfredo and Olmo.

The patriarchal structure is therefore somewhat skewed, and the Oedipal conflict to a certain extent passed over, at least within the development of the individual personalities. But in the interplay of political and personal development, Bertolucci tries an interesting act of transference. Olmo's 'father' is, in fact, the Berlinghieri family who, in political reality, are the patriarchs of the entire peasant community. In turn, Olmo becomes a political 'father' to that community. Through it all Olmo and Alfredo continue a brotherly relationship, strained to its limits by the imposition of the ultimate patriarchal structure, fascism, represented in the film by the destroyer, Attila.

This explicit politicizing of the psychoanalytical model leads to some interesting conflicts and mutations. Bertolucci creates two symbolic orders, the capitalist and the socialist – each with their own modes of discourse – with a third, the fascist, beginning as an extension of the first and overwhelming both. Freud's and Lacan's model of the symbolic order applies only to the patriarchal form of capitalism, so an opportunity is offered to Bertolucci to speculate upon how the psychological structures might operate in a new field. The communal apparatus of the peasants allows them to circumvent the destructive aspects of the bourgeois model. There is little symbolic castration in their child-rearing (old Dalco denies only one thing to Olmo: the possibility of becoming a priest). Fatherless, Olmo develops fully, strongly, and with a clear sense of the necessity of political struggle against the owner who would perform that act upon them. Olmo comes to an understanding of this very early, in a sequence in which, during their pre-socialist formation, the peasants are forced to enact a kind of auto-castration.

A hailstorm has ruined half the crops. Giovanni, the new *padrone* who has taken over the title from the dead Alfredo, demands that the workers take half pay. One answers with a response that clearly foreshadows a growing consciousness: 'When we harvest double we don't get double pay.' Giovanni speaks the entrepreneur's gibberish about how he is the one making the biggest sacrifice, how he should fire everyone, especially the day laborers. He makes fun of the peasant who spoke up, telling him his ears are large enough to hear what he is saying. The man promptly removes a knife from his pocket, slices off one of his ears, and presses it into Giovanni's hand. Old Dalco tries to pull young Olmo's hat over his eyes so that he will not see. But Olmo, even at this age, is not Marcello Clerici and will not be blinded. He pulls his hat back up and looks at the terrifying event.

This symbolic castration represents the peasants' anger and impotence, directed at themselves rather than at their enemy. But even though misdirected, it is an open and defiant act, a mutilation performed consciously, rather than a symbolic castration that is enacted upon the child, without his consent, in the Oedipal stage. Rather than repressing desire, it signals the birth of desire and presages a more useful rebellion which occurs when the peasants withdraw their labour, an act that forces the patriarchs into the field to do the work. Once they do act collectively, the peasants remove, if only temporarily, the owner's potency and control.

With the advent of World War I, that control is quickly reasserted, but against a force which, though never strong enough to overcome its enemies, applies a resistance against which the patriarchal order must continually struggle. The struggle is aided by the middle class giving birth to its fascist offspring (in *1900*, the local fascist organization is, significantly, formed in a church), who, upon maturity, acts as the ultimate castrating father, symbolized in the figure of Attila, the foreman of the Berlinghieri farm.

The character of Attila has been criticized as too 'one-dimensional', too much the embodiment of unadulterated evil. But Bertolucci's point is that fascism *is* an unadulterated evil; and, within the psychoanalytic

'The ultimate castrating father': Alfredo confronts the fascist Attila in *1900* (Robert De Niro, Donald Sutherland)

model, its major representative must signify the ruthless, destructive father (Attilio, incidentally, is the name of Bertolucci's father). Alfredo, politically and emotionally weak, attempts, at the prodding of his wife and Olmo, to control him, but becomes more his cowardly brother than his master. The most he can do is permit Olmo to take his father's gun for protection – in a sequence in which Alfredo wears his dead father's coat. He remains the patriarchal representative. Even though he goes a bit further in attempting to repress Attila, barring him from the house, his gestures remain half-hearted and cowardly. He tells Attila that the gun is stolen, thereby enraging the fascist. Outside the house Attila remains uncontrolled. During the wedding of Ada and Alfredo, Attila and Regina (Alfredo's cousin, whose advances Alfredo has always rejected) go off to make love in an abandoned shack. There, Bertolucci has them enact a ritual that is a curious refraction of the sodomy sequence in *Last Tango*. Regina pulls off Attila's boots and proceeds to enact fellatio upon him as he recites a litany: 'Italy is my master, I serve only her [the gender confusion here may be the result of the dubbing, or it may indicate the nationalistic frenzy that, for the fascist mind, melds the country into both father and mother]. That is what we marched for. The rich, they take and they steal and they ...

they eat, and they eat well, and they are rotten. We fascists, we eat crumbs and we gain strength. Alfredo Berlinghieri, you and all parasites will pay the bill for the fascist revolution, and the bill will not be cheap ... the bill will not be cheap. Everybody will pay, everybody, rich and poor, gentry and peasant, they will pay with money and land and bread and cows and cheese and blood and shit ...' He ejaculates, and Regina asks him if he will love her forever.

Unlike Paul, Attila is looked after sexually by a woman excited by his power. And even though, like Paul, Attila attacks the repressive family of the upper bourgeoisie (he still speaks the petit-bourgeois discourse of early fascism which disguised its nature within a populist appeal to the disenfranchised), in fact he cries for the formation of a new family, an all-inclusive, avenging and destroying family that will break the will with repression. The 'family' metaphor is pursued as Attila discovers a young boy apparently spying on them. Regina would have the boy play 'best man', indulge with them in a wedding game. The sequence is intercut with another 'game' occurring outside: Alfredo's bride, Ada, gets caught in Olmo's hunting net. Upper-middle and peasant class meet in the beginning of a political relationship that will destroy Ada's marriage and damage the friendship between Olmo and Alfredo. In the shack, petit-bourgeois fascist and his middle-class lover begin a relationship of death.

Olmo and the fascist *squadristi* in *1900* (Gérard Depardieu)

197

Attila has been sodomizing Regina; we see the little boy pushing his shirt into his trousers (in the original version there are signs of blood on rags and on the gloves which Regina has put on the boy). Obviously they have committed some sexual atrocity upon the youngster. But the worst is to come, as Attila grabs the child by the legs and whips him about the room, bashing his head on its walls, splattering the screen with red. Here is the final castration of the child: the removal not merely of desire but of life itself. The child, Patrizio, is made witness to fascism's 'primal scene' and it results in his death. Attila and his *squadristi* attempt to blame the death on Olmo, and nearly beat him to death. His friend and class enemy, Alfredo, looks on and does not intervene until the very last moment.*

The violence committed by Attila upon the child and Olmo represents in miniature the greater psycho-political connotations of fascism, which diminishes the lives of all its members and removes life from those who oppose it. Its version of the Oedipal scene is its restraint of the 'child' – the people it rules – from community and selfhood. Fascism castrates desire, equates love of self with love of state, and makes the state apparatuses the 'symbolic' realm into which all must enter. In fascism, the 'symbolic' and 'mirror' stage of development become confused and overlap. There is no 'I' and 'you', but only the 'I' of state authority, in whose image all must see themselves. All become 'best men' to their own blood wedding with fascist ideology.

Other intersections of psychology, political ideology and history are investigated through the relationship of Alfredo and Olmo, and the relationship between Olmo and the peasant community. Alfredo becomes caught between his various familial allegiances. He is not a peasant, of course, and although Olmo remains his friend and receives a modicum of his protection, he never receives his support. Alfredo is not even a whole-hearted supporter of his own culture. He prefers the 'decadent' life of the urban bourgeoisie to the country life of the *padrone*. Despite his dislike for the fascists, he is too close to his class to remove them from his farm. He becomes, finally, that most impotent form of political entity, a centrist liberal, attempting to understand and placate all sides, powerless to affect any of them. His indecision and his politics force his wife to leave him, permit Attila and his fascists to slaughter the peasants, and lead finally to his trial by the peasants on Liberation Day after they have murdered Attila.

At this point in the film further transferences occur which fit the Freudian/Lacanian model so well that they transgress the film's

---

* Attila and Regina marry and have a son, whom they name Italo – the name of the blind fascist propagandist in *The Conformist*.

political analysis and become (perhaps unconsciously) a way for Bertolucci to evade a satisfying closure, bringing into question the penultimate scenes of Alfredo's trial and the peasants' celebration of fascism's end and communist victory. The celebration is successful as an expression of collective joy. The trial, and the political events that occur following Liberation, are not. Their failure is partly a result of Bertolucci's need to respond to history, for there was no clear post-war communist victory in Italy. But another aspect of the failure can be understood by noting how, consciously or not, Bertolucci allows his obsession with the Oedipal process to stand in the way of possible alternatives to the representation of history.

Put most simply, in the closing sequences of the film, Olmo moves from activist leader and voice of the peasant collective to their 'father'. He tells them what to do. Some of his paternal advice is quite appropriate. He prevents them from killing Alfredo, partly because of his strong attachment to Alfredo as a friend, partly because he announces his decision as a dialectical principle: the death of the *padrone* will be proved in the living but powerless (and childless) figure of Alfredo. Another act, however, is much more serious in its repercussions, both historically and within the psychoanalytical model set up in the film. After the trial of Alfredo, a representative body of the Committee of National Liberation – the coalition group of anti-fascists that included Liberals, Christian Democrats, as well as Socialists and Communists – arrive at the farm. They insist that the collective give up their arms. Much to their dismay and anger (fully expressed in the full-length version of the film), Olmo convinces the peasants to follow the Committee's orders. In effect, he cuts short the revolutionary movement and acts as the castrating father by having them give up their guns. As banal as the iconography may be, he does make the peasants throw away the symbols, in fact the actual instruments, of their potency. His action predicts the failure of the revolutionary movement in the post-war period. In fact, for a variety of reasons, a left-dominated Committee of National Liberation did not survive. The order to hand over arms was initiated by the Americans.[12] The political history of Italy since the war has largely been one of weak centrist governments having to deal with or fend off pockets of power held by the Communists in various cities and communities.

The film, however, offers no analysis for Olmo's actions, except for the suggestion that he is protecting the peasants from the armed Committee. But the more one attempts to understand what goes wrong at the end of *1900*, particularly from a psychological as opposed to a political perspective, the more it becomes clear that Olmo, the film's 'hero', becomes its villain by turning into the castrating 'father'. This may also explain the film's unsatisfying and somewhat foolish final sequence, in which Bertolucci attempts to turn the tragedy of the loss of the revolutionary moment into an allegorical political comedy. Breaking the realist conventions pursued throughout the film, he depicts Olmo and Alfredo moving into old age as they continue their struggle in a literal sense, fighting and wrestling, repeating their childhood game of lying between the rails as a train crosses over them (though now only Alfredo lies on or between the tracks).

Certainly Bertolucci meant the sequence to signify the continuing struggle of classes and the endless repetitions of history – two points that the final sequence manages to turn into clichés which belie the revolutionary fervour of the film. Moreover, this final sequence further transforms the political passion of the film into the psychological and the allegorical. As the new revolutionary child, Leonida, weeps and watches, the two figures become fathers to their own childhood, in what is represented as an endless cycle of growth and regression (this is clearer in the American version of the film, in which the intercutting of the characters between their youth and old age is emphasized; in the original version, the characters remain old throughout most of the montage). Indeed, as Bertolucci has pointed out, in one shot old Alfredo is seen lying *across* rather than between the rails, as if he and the class he stands for are about to commit suicide.[13] Indeed, the film ends with a shot from an earlier sequence in which a train bedecked with red flags, carrying the youngsters from the strikers' demonstration in the city back to the farm, runs over a young Alfredo as he lies between the rails. Yet despite all this, despite the weak Eisensteinian montage that includes a cut to a mole emerging from the ground (the emergence of consciousness that begins blind – 'I was ignorant as a mole,' said Puck, the dispossessed landowner in *Before the Revolution*); and despite the fact that Bertolucci has claimed that 'the rapport between Olmo and Alfredo is ... a rapport born of necessity, as was the historical compromise [the Italian Communist Party's attempt, in the 70s, to work with the ruling party]',[14] the allegory of struggle, revived consciousness and a hoped for victory of the peasant class is too weak to overcome the despair, the uncertainty and the comedy with which it is created.

'The *padrone* is alive,' Alfredo proclaims when the Committee of National Liberation leaves. He is, unfortunately, correct. The owner-father (in fact two fathers, Alfredo and Olmo) survives, and by the end of the film the peasants are nowhere to be seen. The spirit of revolution is reduced to these two suddenly comic figures. More than reduced, for within the context of the fiction the revolution cannot be permitted to endure. By the end of *1900* Bertolucci seems to become weighed down

The revolution fails: Olmo and the peasant collective in *1900*

by historical reality and at the same time so intent upon splitting his
consciousness between Alfredo and Olmo, allegorizing both the class
struggle and a struggle between Freudian and Marxist analysis, that
the revolutionary project gets lost in the process.

I must emphasize the two different problems at work here.
Bertolucci, as I said, is responding to the historical reality of events in
Italy after the war. There was no communist revolution. By choosing a
realist form with which to present this history, Bertolucci is forced to
end his film in an impasse. Had he perhaps chosen a more Brechtian,
more abstract form, as does, for example, the Hungarian Miklós Jancsó
in his film of peasant revolt, *Red Psalm* (1971), or the Brazilian Glauber
Rocha in *Antonio das Mortes* (1969), he might have been freer to
elaborate a greater, or differently perceived, victory for his peasants *in
the face of* historical reality.

The second problem emerges from the very choices Bertolucci makes
from the paradigms offered to him by realist convention. He makes the
wrong choices, moving into the area of psychological-allegorical
fantasy which is, paradoxically, a traditional method of closure for the
realist film-maker. Since history – up to the point of the film's making –
can resolve nothing, Bertolucci chooses to close his film with nothing
resolved; or worse, he falls back on a reactionary psychological discourse which speaks to the ineluctable cycle of freedom and repression
that is the Oedipal process. Around the margins of these two problems,

Bertolucci is able to sketch in a *desire* for historical difference, an optimism that is realized in the collective action of the peasants, in their revenge against the fascists and the celebration of their liberation.

1900 received a fair amount of criticism from the European left for its optimism, for Manichean Stalinist tendencies, for its utopianism. But all these potential problems are obviated by its closure, its failure to resolve the issues it raises. In advance of the critical onslaught, almost in anticipation of it, and in spite of the film's actual text, Bertolucci defended his work on the basis of 'willing' a notion of historical victory in the face of despair. He takes the notion from the most important figure in Italian communism, the founder of the Italian Communist Party, Antonio Gramsci. In an early interview, while the film was still in production, Bertolucci said that it was necessary, in the face of the tragedies of history, to maintain and express an optimism, to enforce (he quotes Gramsci) an 'optimism of willpower and pessimism of intelligence'.[15] Unfortunately, by evoking that source Bertolucci reveals his problem.

In *The Modern Prince*, Gramsci wrote:

> If one applies one's will to the creation of a new equilibrium among the forces which really exist and are operative – basing oneself on the particular force which one believes to be progressive and strengthening it to help it to victory – one still moves on the terrain of effective reality, but does so in order to dominate and transcend it (or to contribute to this). What 'ought to be' is therefore concrete; indeed it is the only realistic and historicist interpretation of reality, it alone is history in the making and philosophy in the making, it alone is politics.[16]

This is the 'politics' which Bertolucci tries to create, or imagine, in *1900*. Within the codes of cinematic realism, he tries to 'dominate' and 'transcend' the existing reality, drawing from history a vision of a new history in which the progressive forces move to victory. However, Bertolucci neglects some important caveats offered by Gramsci, who goes on to write that 'no society sets itself tasks for whose accomplishment the necessary and sufficient conditions do not either already exist or are not at least beginning to emerge and develop'.[17] In the period covered by the film these conditions were certainly developing. But, Gramsci continues, 'no society breaks down and can be replaced until it has first developed all the forms of life which are implicit in its internal relations.' At the end of the war, capitalism had still not developed all the forms implicit in its internal relations, a fact demonstrated by Italy's subsequent political and economic development and the emergence of counter-revolutionary forces after the disbanding of the Committee of National Liberation. Precisely because the 'internal relations' of capitalism continued to develop, Bertolucci could not bring his 'will' to transcend 'reality', and concluded by dissolving his utopian project into psychological and allegorical struggle.

'A common error in historico-political analysis,' Gramsci writes, 'consists in an inability to find the correct relation between what is organic [i.e., the 'relatively permanent' structure of social groupings in a society] and what is conjunctural [the 'occasional, immediate, almost accidental' elements]. This leads to presenting causes as immediately operative which in fact only operate indirectly, or to asserting that the immediate causes are the only effective ones.' The results of such an error are either an 'excess of . . . doctrinaire pedantry' in the first case, or 'an excess of "ideologism"' in the second. 'In the first case there is an overestimation of mechanical causes, in the second an exaggeration of the voluntarist and individual element. . . . The dialectical nexus between the two categories of movement, and therefore of research, is hard to establish precisely. Moreover, if error is serious in historiography, it becomes still more serious in the art of politics, when it is not the reconstruction of past history but the construction of present and future history which is at stake.'[18]

In the case of a film about revolution it is not only the art of politics which is at stake, but the politics of art. In *1900* Bertolucci, while avoiding an excess of doctrinaire pedantry through the visual strength and 'realist' melodrama of the film (the former providing an aesthetic authority for the text, the latter a digressive pattern that tends to move 'pedantry' into the acceptable structures of convention), cannot avoid a certain 'ideologism' and clearly indulges in an exaggeration of the 'voluntarist and individual element'. The conflict between Olmo and Alfredo, the concentration upon Olmo as socialist hero, the romantic and sexual involvements of both characters with prostitutes, wives and lovers, and finally the inability to come to terms with the 'construction of present and future history', disable the film.

The 'dialectical nexus' between the essential and the peripheral is never adequately developed and, in the end, Bertolucci confuses rather than relates. Sex and politics, individual psychology and collective action are placed at equal levels. The 'individual element', the 'mechanical cause' is allowed too much emphasis, until it takes over at the end of the film. The eternal wrestling match of Olmo and Alfredo, the time-lock of their game on the rail tracks, approach that 'pedantry' Gramsci warns against, and allow the film and its audience to forget that it is 'the construction of present and future history which is at stake'.

As I have indicated, I believe *1900* will prove to be Bertolucci's most important, if (after *Partner* and before *La luna*) least satisfying work, both for what it succeeds in doing and for what it fails to do. Perhaps it will stand for the fact that, finally, the 'realist' mode is impossible for the creation of a speculative and celebratory political narrative. Or, on the level of content, that Bertolucci's talent – as with most of the major European, left-oriented film-makers and writers of the latter part of our century – lies in exposing and analysing bourgeois ideology, not in fashioning visions of a revolutionary society.

With this we return to a crucial political problem that Bertolucci poses in most of his films, directly or indirectly: the role of the middle-class intellectual in the arena of left-wing revolutionary struggle. Because this is not just his concern or obsession, it will be helpful to compare Bertolucci's handling – and sometimes mishandling – of the problem with that of some of his film-making contemporaries. It will be helpful also to link this problem with another concern touched upon in the course of this study: the structure of melodrama as it appears in the work of Bertolucci and some of his contemporaries. The process will help uncover some of the unresolved tensions in Bertolucci's films and clarify the formation of content in his work.

This route of comparison is somewhat circuitous, and it will take us along that dangerous border between the psychology and politics of the creator and the work he or she creates. We must begin, as always, with Godard, who started his film-making career by attacking the middle-class forms of his art, breaking down the narrative and generic structures that had satisfied filmgoers by not questioning their assumptions. Godard introduced the problematic of the way one 'sees' film and interprets it. Using the Brechtian apparatus, he attempted to throw the burden of interpretation, of positioning, back upon the viewer. Without the comforts of linear exposition, conventionally motivated characters, closure that brings to the narrative the illusion either of finality or a satisfying ambiguity, Godard's films in the mid-1960s offered the most sustained attack on the comforts of cinema as the escapist art of the masses and the conduit of the dominant ideology.

By breaking down the dominant forms, the first wave of Godard's films offered methods to alter expression and perception. I have pointed out that this project of radically altering the form and function of commercial, theatrical film was a political act, and that it provided other film-makers – more traditionally revolutionary in that they belonged to societies that had either undergone Marxist revolutions or were in pre-revolutionary situations – a methodology for a new cinema. The film-makers of Eastern Europe and the developing countries in the mid-6os, for example, were able to use the Godardian-Brechtian mix to express their countries' past and present history in ways that demystified the expression and created a didactic aesthetic which was at once political, engaging, distancing.

But for Godard himself the situation was more difficult. In the late 6os, the radical form of his films became more and more expressive of his own growing radical, Marxist perspective. Matters of class and alienation, in the fundamental Marxist sense of alienation from the means of production, analyses of the basic structures of capitalist society, mingled and finally merged with the formal patterns that continued developing, altering, reflecting upon themselves. Throughout this period, Godard persistently, subtly assumed some aspects of Bertolucci's Fabrizio in *Before the Revolution*. A discourse of self-doubt can be heard, no more clearly than in *Two or Three Things I Know About Her* (1966), where Godard's own voice keeps questioning himself, his images, the world they may or may not be creating or undoing. The romantic residue of the middle-class artist is present and indulged. Godard attempts to expunge it in *Weekend* and in *One Plus One*, but finds that the only way to escape it is to escape commercial narrative film altogether, and to escape himself – or his viewers' image of him. He withdrew into the 'collective' of the Dziga Vertov group to create a series of cinetracts which probe the methodologies and adequacies of image and sound in the making of revolutionary film. The project was an extension of what he had aleady started in *Le gai savoir*, an extension, in fact, of the work he had been doing since *Breathless*, except for the fact that the political urgency or – depending on one's view – obviousness of these later films is stronger than in his earlier work.

But the problems these films created were greater than any they attempted to solve. No one was ever unaware that they were Godard's films, despite his pronouncements that he was no longer to be considered a star. More problematic still was whether a viewer not already committed to the Marxist perspective, and particularly to the Godardian investigation of that perspective, could approach the films with any hope of enlightenment, with any hope of being moved. The lessons that the Latin American film-makers had learned were lost upon their master. The 'Dziga Vertov' films were still the work of a middle-class intellectual trying to come to terms with his art, with his own means of production, with his own ideology, as well as with his personality.

But if Marx is correct and it is the social environment that determines the consciousness of an individual, it could not have been otherwise for Godard. The events of May '68 had an enormous effect on him and his work. But when he attempted a return to theatrical film-making with *Tout va bien*, his historical moment had past. Although he and Gorin had some success in distributing the film themselves – taking it, along with *Letter to Jane*, a brilliant semiological investigation of its star, Jane Fonda, with them on a tour of United States college campuses – the film brought little public attention in comparison with the work of the 60s. The moment of cine-modernism was over; and Godard – for this and other reasons – retreated for almost ten years, experimenting with video, making a series of films for French television, still pursuing his obsessions with the image and the power and ownership of communication. He returned to commercial film-making in the early 80s, much of the thrust of his earlier experimentation softened, made more subtle, chastened perhaps.

He was asked in interviews why he had returned. Because, he said, he was tired of being alone. In *Sauve qui peut (La vie)* he quotes Marguerite Duras to the effect that making films is easier than doing nothing. The need of the intellectual to prove him or herself in work, the need of the artist for community, is overwhelming. That Godard returned to theatrical film is one sign of the Marxist intellectual's anxiety to prove that he or she can, must, enter the field of action. Besides, another set of historical circumstances had developed, for when Godard did reappear in the early 80s, a group of film-making intellectuals were recreating a cinematic community similar to the one he had left in the late 60s. The German cinema had emerged as the most recent enclave of intellectual film-makers (like those of the French New Wave not exclusively leftist, although the best of the group always maintained some political perspective in their work), and it was as if their appearance offered courage and competition to Godard, especially since two major figures of the movement – Wenders and Fassbinder – owed much of their artistic development to him.

Another of these figures, Jean-Marie Straub (a Frenchman who did much of his early work in Germany), is perhaps the only example of a leftist film-maker who has never seemed troubled by the contradictions inherent in his position. From *Machorka-Muff* (1963) and *Not Reconciled* (1965), he has refused all contact with realist conventions, abandoned from the start all hope of reaching that mythical field, the large audience – the working-class audience in particular. His films are made for another kind of worker, the intellectual worker, already convinced that ideas *are* as important as action – or are certainly a prelude to it – and who is ready to engage in a struggle not with the ruling classes, but with the ideological forms and substance of their productions, particularly as represented in film. Straub, in collaboration with his wife Danièle Huillet, circumvented most of those external categories set out by Terry Eagleton – the general and literary-cinematic modes of

206

production, and the general ideology – dealing instead only with the authorial and aesthetic ideologies as they are manifested in the cinematic texts, which challenge every mode of cinematic apprehension, every known relationship between viewer and film. 'Work' for the viewer of a Straub-Huillet film exists within the intellectual struggle between the signifiers of the film and the viewer's codes which these signifiers continually attack and negate, demanding a continual reconstruction and comprehension of the *function* of the viewer-text relationship.

It could be argued that Straub and Huillet should not be considered 'theatrical' film-makers at all, that they have chosen an elitist form of expression which has consciously removed them from the field of left-wing directors who are trying to come to terms with the struggles of the intellectual in a mass art, each of whose creations must fight for an audience. An audience who, it must be noted, for the most part could not be less interested in turning to film for Marxist interpretations of history. Certainly Straub and Huillet bear no comparison at all with Bertolucci, who, as we have seen, has continually searched for means to approach that audience and who has said: 'I believe that those who continue with that kind of elite cinema are seriously sick, sick with the fear of reaching huge audiences. They are people who never drew a mass audience and who never will, at least not through the movies.'[19] (The paradoxes and realities of film-making are often startling. In his quest for new forms Bertolucci made *Tragedy of a Ridiculous Man* which, in its withholding of information, in the spareness of its images and its desire to concentrate on empty spots of time, comes as close to the mode of Straub and Huillet as any 'commercial' film-maker is likely to get.)

One German film-maker, Rainer Werner Fassbinder, does provide an interesting comparison to Bertolucci's dilemma as a leftist intellectual working within an essentially bourgeois medium, searching for a form to express the conflict and an audience who will respond to that form. Fassbinder started making films somewhat later than Bertolucci, but made up for it by turning out about six times as many. Like Bertolucci, Fassbinder began as a follower of Godard (and of Straub as well). Like Bertolucci, he disowned the Straubian approach: 'Films from the brain are all right, but if they don't reach an audience, it's no good. . . . [Straub] tried to be revolutionary and human in an inhuman way.'[20] Like Godard – and unlike Bertolucci – he worked his way through a number of genres, trying them out, seeing how they would fit his own intellectual mould. Unlike Godard, but in a curious way like Bertolucci, he adopted one genre, the inclusive one of melodrama which he used, manipulated, twisted, analysed and remade until it became an almost encyclopaedic discourse, enabling him to speak the history of twentieth-century Germany.

The melodramatic base for Fassbinder was Douglas Sirk; for Bertolucci it is Giuseppe Verdi. The political base for Fassbinder was an anarcho-Marxism, a contempt for the bourgeoisie, an understanding of the working class, a suspicion of the organised left; for Bertolucci it was Italian Communism, with its Gramscian call for intellectual enquiry and for intellectual leadership to emerge from and for the working class. Unlike Bertolucci, Fassbinder abjured, as far as possible, his bourgeois roots. In his films he never undertook individualist, Freudian interpretation of character and event, insisting instead that character be understood in the context of history and environment, a perspective that turned his use of melodrama into a complex, dialectical process. Fassbinder was gay, part of a subculture that, for an intellectual, could provide a direct experience and understanding of repression which in turn could clarify the existence of repression on all levels of society.

Fassbinder is a point of reference for the work of Bertolucci; Pasolini a point of contact. Pasolini is the initial influence on Bertolucci's career, and also a figure against whom the political-psychological struggles in Bertolucci's films can be measured. In his best work, Pasolini's anti-bourgeois sentiments are clear. *Teorema, Porcile* and *Salò* are sustained attacks on the middle class. In these and other Pasolini films workers or peasants or the subproletariat are presented, sometimes in surprising guises, as anarchic or savage figures, functioning as destroyers of the assumed comforts of the bourgeoisie. Fassbinder's work, which does not have the mythic pretensions of much of Pasolini, is deeply committed to the extraordinary and banal struggles of the working class in Germany and its conflicts with history and with itself. However, with the exception of *1900*, the working class in Bertolucci's films seems to exist only as a point of reference. Like Godard, Bertolucci is much more comfortable concentrating on middle-class characters. Even as reference, though, the workers and peasants form a dialectical presence, whispering through the discourse of the film.

There is the workers' celebration in *Before the Revolution*. In *Last Tango* there is the street-sweeper whose broom Jeanne leaps over, and the laughing, all-knowing black concierge at the apartment building on the rue Jules Verne. There are the inhabitants of Rosa's hotel who intrude upon Paul's agony, and the maid who cleans up the blood after Rosa's suicide. In *Tragedy of a Ridiculous Man* the faces of the workers demand our attention, although they remain largely in the background or are glimpsed, almost guiltily, by Primo as he scans his property through binoculars. At the Spaggiari home a maid is seen behind a window or, along with other domestic help, going about her business in the kitchen. Another maid, in *The Conformist*, suddenly commands the viewer's attention when Clerici visits his fiancée and her mother. As the desperate *borghese* and his adopted family sit down to an elegant lunch, Bertolucci suddenly cuts to a brief close-up of their maid in a doorway, eating a bowl of pasta as she watches the strange trio. For a moment they are visually placed in the perspective of the class they abuse, dominated by a figure whom they otherwise dominate.

In every instance, these figures tend to undercut the overt or potential melodrama of the narrative at the peripheries where they stand. They are engaged in work rather than self-enquiry or tortuous relationships and therefore represent, in a sense, the narrative's better judgment, or at least its dialectical pole, its response to the nascent melodrama of the central characters. When, in *1900*, Bertolucci attempts to foreground the peasant class, they are brought immediately into the melodramatic centre of the text. Because of the film's realist structure and the imperative of that structure to concentrate upon individual turmoil, and because in this film Bertolucci gives overt attention to the oppressed and their attempts to overcome their condition, he cannot avoid an emotional excess. Here all figures and groups are given equal prominence within a historical milieu of struggle. With the perspective reversed, some perspective seems to be lost.

But one must always be careful in speaking of Bertolucci's 'melodrama'. With the exceptions of *1900* and *La luna*, the usual structures of that form are held in check by the controls of the overriding modernist elements. In *1900* an attempt is made to place the violence suffered by the peasants and the passions of their victory within a political context that deflects the spectator, if incompletely, from the personal to the ideological. In the other films *(La luna*, as always, excepted) the centrifugal force of melodrama – its attempt to pull everything into its hysterical centre – is always countered by other elements: temporal distortions; complex allusive structures; visual articulations that pull the viewer out of the narrative; and, most important to our discussion here, ideological imperatives that divert melodramatic intensity into a more extensive examination of character and psychology within the social formation.

Again a comparison with Fassbinder is helpful. Politically, Fassbinder sees the world as a hierarchy of the oppressed. Each of his conspiring, childish, vulnerable characters passes his or her misery down the line. Bertolucci's politics do not permit such bleakness. More than Fassbinder's, his films create for the spectator structures for ideological comprehension and analysis. Something must be built into the narrative that offers a promise of political restructuring (despite the absence of central working-class figures in many of the films). Even *Last Tango*, which ends with the death of the central character, avoids the despairing void of late Fassbinder, partly because of the vitality of its visual and narrative style, mostly because its hermeneutic, its political subtext of the father-state relationship, enlightens the otherwise despairing melodrama of the narrative. In other words, within his melodrama Fassbinder builds implicit relationships between the individual and capitalism or fascism, linking the microcosm of the individual with the larger political ramifications of ownership and repression. Bertolucci attempts to define those connections within the text itself through perceptual play and ideological analysis. The viewer must infer the analysis in Fassbinder's texts; read them in Bertolucci's.

In a sense, Fassbinder's mind is always made up. His use of melodrama as a form against which to play his complex social analysis, the certainty of his dismal vision of individual and social collapse, are clear from one film to the next. Melodrama is the means for Fassbinder to provide structure for his characters and destroy them at the same time. For Bertolucci, melodrama resides as a kind of hysteria, waiting, wanting to break through into his characters' actions. Occasionally it does, but usually as an inflection, as a remark upon the character or the events surrounding him or her – the murder of Quadri and his wife's desperate attempt to rouse Clerici to her aid in *The Conformist*, for example. Bertolucci will often imply melodrama, as I noted above, through the visual articulation of the action: the broad movements of the camera in *The Conformist*; the low tracking shots among the swirling leaves when Clerici visits his mother; the exaggerated Dutch tilts; the expressionist lighting patterns. The *mise en scène* of this film is melodramatic, even though the acting, for the most part, is not. Nor is the narrative situation *in itself* melodramatic, even though the ideology of fascism which surrounds that situation is so in the extreme. This is even clearer in *The Spider's Stratagem*, where the narrative formation works to mystify events, to create a hermeneutic that pushes the viewer away from the diegetic space of the film and prevents him or her from the identification with the main characters so necessary to melodrama. Those characters do not move through the conventional structures of melodramatic form (though they occasionally employ melodramatic gestures). However, the very hermeneutic that is revealed – the betraying father, the creation of a spectacle that turns everyone into an actor and history into an act, the elision of that history into the plot of an opera – is a melodrama. And that melodrama is, again, an aspect of fascism and its grandiloquent, paranoid distortion of history.

The melodrama of fascism is defined through its ideology of spectacle, sacrifice, the proving of self-worth by transcending the self for the state and incorporating the state within the self. Some of these elements, particularly those involving sacrifice – and including other peripheral matters such as the enclosing of the woman within the family* – are familiar to us in the melodrama of classic American cinema: an observation not lost on Fassbinder, who mutates that form into an expression of its own ideology. Bertolucci, as I say, does not so much imitate movie melodrama (with the exceptions of *1900* and *La luna*) as investigate the melodramatic roots of fascism itself. In the earlier films, and occasionally in *1900*, he is secure in his perspective and plays out, through the antitheses of melodrama and antimelodrama, a key opposition in the struggle between fascism and the left. He alludes to the left resistance movement as a collective activity, persistent and committed, self-effacing rather than self-sacrificing, dedicated to putting an end to the destructive melodrama of the dominant regime. The point is quietly made in *The Conformist*, in the sequence in which Clerici buys some flowers from a woman on a Parisian street – violets from Parma. At which point the woman and a group of children with her begin singing, gently but persistently, the 'Internationale', and pursue a confused Clerici down the street. The withdrawn hysteric, the man who has, paradoxically, become a fascist in order to control his emotions, to channel them into an 'acceptable' outlet, is driven to distraction by a quiet act of assertion by his political opposites. The moment is repeated more broadly and in a less overtly political context at the dance, where Clerici is encircled by the collective revellers, an active group entrapping the passive figure. The image is repeated again near the end of the film when the liberated Romans swarm around him. In *1900*, the peasants' resistance to the strikebreaking army, their revenge against Attila and the mass celebration that follows, constitute the major signs of the collective expression of individual passion, however shortlived.

In *The Spider's Stratagem*, the melodrama which exists as a persistent spectacle when the left betrays itself to fascism retains the dialectic in a different fashion. Father and son remain locked in the 'mirror stage', each negating the other while unable to separate from the other. The film's spectator is allowed to perceive the necessary break and understand how collective resistance can easily be subsumed to individual will.

---

* Nicos Poulantzas writes about German fascism: 'In fact it can be said that the national socialist party's most favoured cell was not the factory, the street or the local community, but the family itself' (*Fascism and Dictatorship*, p. 347).

Ending the 'destructive melodrama' of fascism: the peasants hunt down Attila in *1900*

The melodramatic aspects of *Last Tango* follow a still different route. The film is set in the 'present' and concentrates upon the agonies of a single individual, charging its images with angst and desire, discharging them by, curiously, reverting to the very melodrama it portends. *Last Tango* works against melodrama by using that form as a means of self-commentary (thereby coming as close as Bertolucci ever does to Fassbinder's methodology). Paul is the question mark of melodrama, the uncertain, emotionally blasted figure, who would destroy the oppressions of melodrama – particularly as represented in the family – by his complete withdrawal. By becoming reborn as the romantic-melodramatic male, Paul causes his own fall, commits the very suicide he tells his dead wife he wishes he could commit, and allows the oppressive order to continue. He becomes the world he tried to destroy, which, as at the end of *1900*, continues to exist. The ghost of the father – the ghosts of all fathers – continue their reign. Jeanne will marry Tom; the bourgeois world will proceed, as it does in the larger political sphere of post-war Italy prefigured in *1900*.

Melodrama, as Peter Brooks suggests (in *The Melodramatic Imagination*), profoundly emotionalizes political and familial conflict, moving it towards sacrifice and the fall into oppression. In Bertolucci's work this is a twofold process. As an internal structure it defines the political dialectic of right and left. As an external structure, it defines the other dialectic – or the other melodrama – that overdetermines the films, the struggle of the Marxist bourgeois intellectual who wants to make left-wing cinema. The conflict may be stated in many ways. Pasolini addresses it bluntly:

> I too, like Moravia and Bertolucci, am a bourgeois, in fact, a petit-bourgeois, a turd, convinced that my stench is not only scented perfume, but is in fact the only perfume in the world. I too am thus endowed with the characteristics of aestheticism and humour, the typical characteristics of a petit-bourgeois intellectual. This is not a run-of-the-mill confession, but purely and simply a statement of fact.[21]

Perhaps more a statement of self-loathing than of fact, and considerably stronger than Bertolucci's own statement that he is a maker of bourgeois films permeated with an uneasy conscience. But no matter what the degree of self-awareness and self-hatred, and no matter where expressed – within the films or outside them – Bertolucci is strongly contained within the contradictions of his social origins and his political commitments.

One major example of these contradictions is the post-production history of *1900*. This was to be the film that clearly stated Bertolucci's political commitment, 'sincerely dedicated', he says, to the Italian Communist Party. Their response was no more favourable than most others.[22] The political, editing and distribution problems created by the film precipitated an intellectual and emotional crisis. Alberto Grimaldi, the film's producer, turned, for Bertolucci, into the castrating father. 'Grimaldi did not respect the rules of the western Oedipus myth in which it is the son who tries to kill the father. As in certain oriental cultures, it was the father who tried to kill the son.'[23] Bertolucci forgot that the father's subduing of the son's desire is a form of castration. He came out of the experience 'with broken bones, bruised, but more mature'.[24]

That 'maturity' turned out, in fact, to be a withdrawal, a momentary fear of political discourse. *La luna* is a film in which the Marxist gives over completely to the Freudian, as if that voice, unencumbered by a political dialectic, might provide security. Only in *Tragedy of a Ridiculous Man* did Bertolucci rediscover his voice, finding a means to enfold the political and the psychological within each other judiciously, quietly, without the hysteria and melodramatic conflict of the previous film.

Obviously this calm did not come easily. Bertolucci's films express the conflict between political commitment and intellectual-emotional self-analysis more acutely than the films of Godard, speaking the tensions and uncertainties of their creator both explicitly and implicitly, in form and substance. The most overt statement of the conflict appears in *Before the Revolution*, where Fabrizio is caught between an acknowledgment of the Marxist analysis of history taught to him by Cesare and his own emotional and sexual turmoil which are determined by his family and class. The film expresses an agonized meditation on the difficulty – in this instance the impossibility – of an individual bred and formed by one ideology shifting allegiance to another ideology that calls for a repression of self in the service of collective action.

A more implicit expression of this conflict appears in *The Conformist* through the character of Professor Quadri, the Resistance fighter who suffers the brutality of fascist retribution against a figure on the left. Many writers, myself included, have followed Bertolucci's lead in linking this figure to Godard. In the film Quadri is given Godard's address and telephone number. The assumption is that, once again, Bertolucci was doing battle with his teacher/father, the figure from whom he learned so much and against whom he needed to rebel. Here Godard is re-created as a character whose politics seem to be correct (he is an anti-fascist), but whose methods, withdrawing from the field of struggle by exiling himself to Paris and indulging in a comfortable life, are questionable. An analogy could be drawn between Quadri's actions and Godard's withdrawal from his struggles within commercial cinema into the self-indulgences of the late 60s and early 70s cinetracts, a refusal – which Bertolucci found unacceptable – to deal with the mass audience. The result is that Bertolucci inscribes his own intellectual and cinematic uncertainties, his own psychological-aesthetic struggles, his own fears and Oedipal concerns, in a character he treats ambiguously at best, murderously at worst.

Within the context of·the current argument I would propose an alternative reading and suggest that Quadri is not so much a surrogate for Godard as for Bertolucci himself. In order to understand this, we must re-examine the relationship between Bertolucci and Godard. In my discussion of *Partner* I noted that Bertolucci attempts to 'murder' Godard by imitating him so closely that, like the doubles at the end of the film, the man and his Other, Bertolucci and Godard, consider a kind of joint suicide in order that a new, unfettered Bertolucci may arise, having shed one more patriarchal figure. The symbolic act was impossible, of course. Fathers and the patriarchal structure remain dominant – a phenomenon emphasized in *The Spider's Stratagem, Last*

Tango in Paris, 1900 and *Tragedy of a Ridiculous Man*. Bertolucci never gets rid of the influence of Godard, his dislike of and discomfort with Godard, and his admiration for Godard. He could not lose sight of the fact that, like himself, Godard was struggling with the problem of the bourgeois intellectual undertaking revolutionary work.

In this light Bertolucci might well have regarded Godard's movement out of commercial cinema with a certain jealousy and admiration, as well as disdain. ('I'm Marcello and I make Fascist movies,' Bertolucci once told an interviewer, 'and I want to kill Godard who's a revolutionary, who makes revolutionary movies and who was my teacher.'[25]) Godard's movement was, after all, a strong expression of aesthetic and political will. Godard did attempt to throw off his technical, stylistic, personal accomplishments as a subjective film-maker in order to become part of a collective that made didactic films about the possibilities of political film-making. His attempt was to realize in practice his often quoted remark that the time had come not to make political films but to make films politically.

Now, in fact, Bertolucci's reaction to all of this was to indulge in another act of imitation that contradicts his statement about not using cinema as 'a machine-gun'. In 1971, between *The Conformist* and *Last Tango* – that is between the two most commercially viable films he had so far made, as well as between a film that dealt directly with politics and personality and a film that would deal with politics as seen through the metaphor of sexuality and domestic relationships – Bertolucci tried his own hand at collective political agitprop. Under the auspices of the Italian leftist unions, he made a thirty-five minute film for the Rome municipal elections called *La salute è malata o I poveri muoiono prima* ('Health is Sick, or The Poor Die First'), a well-turned documentary on health care, women's rights and the living conditions of the Roman poor. The film is in a 'vérité' style, with conversations and debates, footage of marches, visits to hospitals and slums, interviews. It was shown, Bertolucci says, from a projector on the roof of a car, 'in the streets, the walls being our screens; the shadows of the passers-by walking and stopping to watch were added to the ones in the film'. He also refers to it as 'a rather ugly film', as if denying his desire and ability to leave the realm of the subjective in order to create work for public use.[26]

This documentary stands as an important reminder of Bertolucci's political affiliation. Despite the fact that he now attempts to dismiss it, the film was clearly something he wished to do. In another interview he recalls that 'once, in 1970, I was offended by a leader of the PCI [the Italian Communist Party]. We were having dinner and I told him that I wanted to do a political film, a documentary. He replied, "Look, the people need a poet more than a politician." At the time, the idea really aggravated me, I got really pissed off. But I have to say that today I agree.'[27] In the early 1970s Bertolucci could still wish to make politic-ally committed documentary films and yet respond ambiguously to the work that Godard was doing at the time. The phenomenon of *La salute è malata* further manifests the problems of the middle-class, left-wing artist plagued by the contradictions inherent in his intellectual life. He wishes to be an activist and to do direct political work, yet is both willing and unwilling to give up his primary talents. The problem lends weight to the notion that Luca Quadri in *The Conformist* is a surrogate for Bertolucci himself.

Like Bertolucci, the Marxist artist with an international reputation who knows the necessity of doing good works for his political cause, the fictional Quadri, a celebrated Italian anti-fascist who leaves Italy for Paris (while his comrades who remain are jailed and murdered), attempts to do good works from his position of safety. He pamphleteers and proselytizes, trying to convince his former pupil that the latter is not really a fascist. Quadri is on the correct side – as is Bertolucci – yet does not live as the people on that side are meant to live. Like Bertolucci, he enjoys a reputation and a bourgeois life. In fact, Bertolucci once called this character a bourgeois anti-fascist, his ideology 'not based on ... class struggle, but ... on a liberal vision of democracy'.[28] In response to the conflicts the character generates, his creator has him destroyed. Quadri represents too many things. He is, finally, more misdirected aspiration than a character. And because he does not reach the aspirations of his creator he must fail, as, perhaps, must his creator himself, who aspires to be ideologist and entertainer, intellectual, communist and cinema celebrity. Quadri, finally, is not only a reflection of Bertolucci but, like Godard, an image he wants but is unable to attain. So he tries to obliterate the image.

Yet another figure informs Quadri, adding to the complexity of the character's function in the film and for Bertolucci. Palmiro Togliatti, the late leader of the Italian Communist Party, recalled a description of a professor at the University of Turin when Gramsci was a student:

> There was something volcanic in his lectures. ... Every now and then he would turn his head toward the window to the left, and the light that fell on him, together with his laugh and the curly locks on his forehead, gave him a strange look, the look of an angel or a devil who was showing us the way. It was a new morality that he taught us, whose supreme laws were complete sincerity with ourselves, the spurning of convention, and sacrifice for the cause to which we had dedicated our lives.[29]

216

Bertolucci is likely to have known this quotation and perhaps used it to form his portrait of Quadri. The description of the light illuminating the figure may have influenced the myth of the cave sequence analysed earlier.

More important, the figure described may have been transmuted by Bertolucci into the man Luca Quadri ought to have been, the man Bertolucci, perhaps, might like to be himself: Antonio Gramsci. (It is certainly no coincidence that Bertolucci makes Quadri a hunchback, like Gramsci.) Antonio Gramsci is the heroic figure of Italian communism to whom both the fictional Quadri and Bertolucci might well aspire. Unlike Quadri, Gramsci remained in fascist Italy and was jailed until just before his death. Unlike Bertolucci, Gramsci did not express conflicts between individual aspiration and collective need; in fact his writings point to how they may be joined. His life and work became an almost mythic force, the unattainable object of desire to which any left-wing intellectual becomes subject. In *The Conformist*, Quadri becomes not only the surrogate of Godard and Bertolucci but the shadow of Gramsci, and he cannot survive the tensions between the committed intellectual left, the centre and the right which finds advantage in any weakness the left may demonstrate. Quadri, in the end, acts as a reflection, or a refraction, of an aspect of that struggle between desire and fulfilment, politics and personality, idea and action that makes up the melodrama of the life of a left-wing bourgeois intellectual.

Earlier I quoted a rather self-hating comment by Pasolini regarding his status as a petit-bourgeois. In a more subdued frame of mind Pasolini remarked that 'it is just as necessary and legitimate for the left-wing intellectual to express his own ideological and sentimental crisis as to contribute overtly to the class struggle.'[30] The remark may err on the side of self-defence, just as the other remark errs on the side of self-condemnation. Yet it is one way out of a conflict that can lead to paralysis, and one way of defending Bertolucci's own examination of his role through his films. The statement helps explain the political conflict inscribed into the character of Fabrizio in *Before the Revolution*, and helps in the analysis of the more profound inscription that occurs in *1900*.

Here, obviously, is the film in which Bertolucci hoped the conflicts would be resolved, or at least be contained within a text whose ideological certainty is determined from the outset. Yet what the text reveals is one more act of enquiry, another expression of the 'ideological and sentimental crisis' from which the author wants to withdraw, but which manifests itself at almost every turn. At the same time, it is a text that reveals just how 'necessary and legitimate' the crisis is for a middle-class, communist intellectual who attempts to express the reality of the class struggle in a form that will reach a large, middle-class audience. I have discussed the latter problem at some length; here I want to examine some of the ways in which Bertolucci limns out yet another area in which to express the conflict of thought and action, the crisis of self-knowledge and the crisis of history.

In *The Conformist*, Luca Quadri embodies in one figure the ambivalences of and about the left-wing intellectual. In *1900*, Bertolucci attempts to solve the problem by splitting it in two, creating separate characters whose narrative functions might allegorize and make static the dynamics of the conflict. At one pole is the figure of Alfredo, son of the middle class, undone by doubts and suffering brought on by a political and psychological paralysis. He is a later version of Fabrizio, living perpetually before the revolution. Unlike Fabrizio, he is unable to entertain, even on an intellectual level, the possibilities of revolutionary struggle. Imprisoned by his class, trapped in the mazes of its ideology, he is unable to act in any positive way to curtail the fascists and combat the history in which he is carried along.

At the opposite pole is Olmo, the strongest and most self-contained character Bertolucci has created, because he is politically the purest and least troubled. The historical turmoil that surrounds him, the attacks upon him by the fascists, his banishment from the Berlinghieri farm, the indecisions and inconsistencies of Alfredo's actions, seem only to swirl about him, affecting him but not causing him to waver. Like Alfredo, Olmo is also fathered by Fabrizio. But where Alfredo remains stuck within the bourgeois patriarchy, Olmo is born free of it. Olmo is a speculative figure, a peasant unencumbered by the urban middle class and a nostalgia for the present. He is a bastard offspring of history, which he attempts to change.

Up to a point, Bertolucci can allow these two characters to coexist without contaminating each other. The ideological certitude (or uncertainty, in the case of Alfredo) that determines their existence in the fiction protects them, or more accurately protects Olmo, who is untainted by Alfredo's decadent life. In a rather egregious sequence (whose carnality is much reduced in the American version) Alfredo and Olmo visit an epileptic prostitute. Olmo is at this point living with Anita, the woman who is his ideological equal and who carries his child. He is therefore secured from the unsavoury decadence of Alfredo even while partaking of it. The sequence takes on the aspect of a temptation. Olmo is offered initiation into Alfredo's world, seems to fall, but emerges untainted and unaffected.

The prostitute reappears much later in the narrative, at a low point in the relationship between Alfredo and his wife, Ada. They are spending an unhappy Christmas Eve in a workers' bar, where Ada has gone to find comfort in an alien atmosphere. The prostitute, Neve, is a lost figure, though happy in her self-sufficiency. She stands as a comparison to the failure of a middle-class marriage. It is a melo-dramatic moment: the return of Alfredo's past, the contrast between the endurance of the humble and the moral and political decay of the wealthy. By means of such open melodramatic contrasts. Bertolucci attempts further to secure himself against the internal conflicts of left and middle-class sympathies. Through much of the film he is able to express the conflicts externally, simply, without ambiguity: good versus evil, political commitment versus indecision, city decadence (homo-sexuality, whoring, cocaine-snorting) versus rural simplicity, happiness versus the corruption of happiness, left versus middle and right – all become directing signs to the correct and incorrect paths.

If this sounds easy, it is the result of a need for easy resolutions within a form that demands resolutions be expressed by means of dichotomies. Melodrama is a form of security, and ideological security is what the film seeks to express. Security and division are not necessarily the same as simple-mindedness. Bertolucci can work out the contrasts between his characters and their ideologies with moving effect and to narrative advantage. This is particularly true in those sequences which contrast the relationships of Olmo and Anita, Alfredo and Ada. Before they marry, Alfredo brings Ada home to the Berlinghieri farm where they attend a peasant dance. Ada plays blind, an act that was of significance earlier, when she wished to close her eyes to the rise of fascism and the appearance of the *squadristi* in the city. Her attitude, along with that of Vittorio, her 'guardian', Alfredo's uncle – a homosexual, an attractive if apolitical and amoral individual who thinks nothing of buying cocaine from a local fascist – becomes a synecdoche for the general blindness of the bourgeoisie to the political events which not only surround them but existed because of them. It resonates back to Clerici's symbolic blindness in *The Conformist*, with links even further back to *Before the Revolution*.

When Ada continues her blind act among the peasants, it appears only as an obnoxious affectation, of which she suddenly becomes conscious, at the same time as she becomes aware of the difference in the life and attitudes of those around her. This difference is represented first by Anita, who embarrasses her, and then by the strange image of a peasant dancing with and kissing a life-sized mannequin whose legs he has tied to his own so that it will accompany him about the dance floor. In the midst of this activity, as Ada attempts to apologize to the peasants for pretending to be blind, a terrible event occurs. The fascists burn down the Casa del Popolo, a meeting house and schoolroom where Anita teaches the peasants (portraits of Marx and Lenin, hammer and

The blindness of the bourgeoisie: Ada (Dominique Sanda) among the workers in *1900*

sickle adorn the walls). As the peasants leave the dance hall to attend to the catastrophe, Alfredo and Ada are left alone and start to make love. The fire, the peasants attempting to put it out, Alfredo's deflowering of Ada are intercut, resulting in a montage that clearly separates Alfredo's concerns, his *ideological determinations*, from Olmo's and Anita's. The sexual activity alone does not constitute the separation. Bertolucci the Freudian attempts not to separate the sexuality of his characters from their other emotional and intellectual activities. It is often a manifestation of them. Earlier, when Olmo returns to Anita after his outing with the epileptic prostitute, she first beats him and then pulls him to her to let him perform oral sex (in the school building, beneath a heroic mural of a man carrying a red banner) as a sign of their attachment to one another. His love and contrition are meant as a contrast to Alfredo's pleasure-seeking, just as the latter contrasts with the communal effort of the peasants to save their comrades from the fire. (One cannot totally disregard some cynicism here: the sexuality is also part of the film-maker's attempt to reach the mass audience he craves.)

Bertolucci extends this sequence into a fine expression of the authority of his political commitment. The narrative moves from the fire to the funeral procession for the four people who were killed. Olmo and Anita lead the oxen who pull the cart carrying the corpses, draped in red. In the deserted town streets they call out for others to come and honour the dead. Anita is in despair that no one will join their mourning. As he attempts to cheer her, strains of the 'Internationale' are heard on the soundtrack. People march into the square and Bertolucci cuts to the procession, now joined by many people and onlookers wearing red scarves and bandanas. The dead have been placed in proper caskets. The sequence ends with a high shot of the square and the procession, intercut with shots of the onlookers (including troops) and of Alfredo and Ada, also looking on. Bertolucci makes a transition from the square to a tailor's shop, where Attila is being decked out in a fascist uniform. Attila proceeds to demonstrate, by smashing with his head a cat tied to a post, the proper treatment of communists.

The film contains many powerful set pieces like this: Attila's murder of the child; Olmo's rousing speech to the dispirited peasants (like the funeral sequence much foreshortened in the edited version); the *squadristi* shooting down the peasants in the mudfields. But the clarity of ideological vision begins to trouble the viewer. One yearns for complexity, the formal, intellectual and emotional intricacies of the preceding three films. We become troubled by the contentment and certitude of the film, the way it always takes the right side. And so, apparently, does Bertolucci. In the final sequences, as I have indicated, the ideological uncertainties, the displaced Oedipal material, the difficulties in separating fictional clarity from historical reality seep in, and the text reverts to the ambiguities it has attempted to repress.

It is a truism that art grows out of conflict. The model set up by Terry Eagleton, incorporating the external modes of production, the author's place within them, his or her own ideology, the aesthetic forms chosen, and the text that is the site of the tensions produced by all the other structures, attests to the extensiveness of that conflict. Eagleton's model also helps to make clear why *1900* is so placid a work, for its conflicts are mainly external. That is, within the text Bertolucci attempts to create clear, unambiguous ideological confrontations, which break down in the end. Meanwhile, the unforeseen melodrama which overdetermines *1900* takes place between the text and the commercial modes of production which were unable to contain it. The resulting irony is that the one film in which Bertolucci does try to resolve the conflicts of the left-wing bourgeois intellectual fails on many counts.

'Today,' says Bertolucci, 'I am for a cinema and an audience that do not fear emotions, and the spectator I am looking for is one who is capable of surrendering to the unconscious process of film and of participating in that process.'[31] This is the voice of an intellectual who seems to have given up attempting to come to terms with conflict and ambiguity, who no longer seeks 'to express his own ideological and sentimental crisis', but rather to use his mode of expression to provoke the pleasure of surrender of both film-maker and viewer to the tyranny of the cinematic process (recall Bertolucci's earlier statements regarding *La luna*, that it is a film 'no longer ashamed of pleasure'). This would be a rather frustrating statement if it implied that Bertolucci would continue to create 'unconscious' films like *La luna*, with its signifiers of ruined lives and desperate passions which the spectator is asked to accept with a minimum of analysis. Fortunately, with the appearance of *Tragedy of a Ridiculous Man*, it became clear that the statement was not going to be acted upon. Bertolucci might imply by such remarks that he wishes to be part of the Hollywood entertainment machine, but his intelligence, his desire for film to be an analytical process requiring an analytical response on the part of the spectator, have by and large spared him his wish.

Tragedy of a Ridiculous Man initiated another struggle between the modernist demands for the analytical distance that must be created between the spectator and the text and the conventional realism that began appearing in the later films. By seeking this new rapprochement, Bertolucci discovered another means towards the resolution of ideological conflict that has concerned us in this part of our discussion. Recognizing with this film that Marxist aspirations within the restrictions of a capitalist society need to be examined objectively and analytically – coldly – Bertolucci is able to avoid expressions either of individual schizophrenia or of a Manichean split between good and evil. His recognition, in the comment quoted earlier, that Primo is a version of Olmo grown older, makes clear that Olmo is not, nor could ever be, a pure and consistent socialist hero. This is a major insight that enables the film-maker to turn the ideological struggle into a dialectic rather than a set of oppositions.

In the earlier discussion of *Tragedy of a Ridiculous Man* I argued that its notion of victory for the son and for the left was quite tentative, part of a continuing cycle of repression and liberation. But it is important to emphasize at this point that the opportunity for victory *is* offered, no matter what restrictions are applied, and that this is the first such victory present in Bertolucci's work. The son does gain temporary power over the father; the capitalist impulse is short-circuited, turned against itself; the left triumphs for a moment. *Tragedy of a Ridiculous Man* contains a curious kind of structuring *presence* (to reverse the usual critical category). The central figure may once have been a resistance fighter, even perhaps a leftist; but he is so no longer. Nor is he a tormented bourgeois intellectual, a despairing bourgeois anarchist, or even a fascist. Primo is the ridiculous figure of a peasant turned petit bourgeois, a small-time capitalist who manifests no ideological conflicts, whose central concern – like all capitalists – is the financial condition of his factory and the circulation of capital within and outside it. His ridiculousness is that of a satisfied ordinariness, and his narrative function is to demonstrate the strength of his position, its presence *and* its vulnerability. The structuring *absence* in this film is the left, whom we only hear about or see through the ambiguous figures of Laura, Adelfo, and the almost invisible son, Giovanni. The voice of the left is quieter in this film than in any of its predecessors (recall how in *La luna* a figure is suddenly dropped into the text, declaring himself a communist to an uninterested Caterina, as if Bertolucci suddenly realized there had been no other opposition voice). In that quietness is its force; and in the lack of implied or overt melodrama a victory for the left, however tentative, may be perceived.

Another victory over psycho-political conflict is suggested, though this too is highly tentative and fragile. *Tragedy of a Ridiculous Man* indicates the possibility – the illusion, perhaps – of either overcoming the imperatives of Oedipus or at least understanding them as something more than an inescapable psychological model. Much more than in the preceding films, the Oedipus process is perceived as a social-political phenomenon. Once again Deleuze and Guattari (in their book *Anti-Oedipus*) provide a useful insight:

> what a grotesque error to think that the unconscious-as-child is acquainted only with daddy-mommy, and that it doesn't know 'in its own way' that its father has a boss who is not a father's father, or moreover that its father himself is a boss who is not a father. Therefore we formulate the following rule, which we feel to be applicable in all cases: the father and the mother exist only as fragments, and are never organized into a figure or a structure able both to represent the unconscious, and to represent in it the various agents of the collectivity; rather, they always shatter into fragments that come into contact with these agents, meet them face to face, square off with them, or settle the differences with them as in hand-to-hand combat. ... And the unconscious is indeed at issue here. If in fact there are structures, they do not exist in the mind, in the shadow of a fantastic phallus distributing the lacunae, the passages, and the articulations. Structures exist in the immediate impossible real.[32]

The forces of repression do not reside only in a psychological/domestic cycle, but also, perhaps especially, in one imposed upon the child from outside, from 'the immediate impossible real', or, as Bertolucci says, 'the sinister and tragically ridiculous reality which is Italy today'. Sons and fathers do indeed struggle, and that struggle does move in phases of dominance and repression between one and the other. But in *Tragedy of a Ridiculous Man,* more strongly than in the previous films, that struggle is recognized as part of the larger political conflict of which the domestic unit is only one fragment. *Padre* and *padrone* merge, are separated and merge again. I have noted that Bertolucci has always attempted to politicize Oedipus; here he indicates a desire to displace the complex from the psychological to the political plane.

Roland Barthes writes: 'The text is (should be) that uninhibited person who shows his behind to the *Political Father*.'[33] Whether *Tragedy of a Ridiculous Man* is an indication that Bertolucci can indeed create such a text remains an open question. I have pointed out that *Tragedy of a Ridiculous Man* reflects at every point the oppressive side of its liberating force. I have suggested also that Bertolucci seems too caught up both in his own political conflicts and, more important, in the desire to work within commercial structures – aesthetically and economically – to create such a text. And we may recall what happened to his character Paul, who in *Last Tango* showed his behind to 'the Political Father' only to turn into that father and be destroyed. Bertolucci's talent lies, finally, in creating inhibited texts which speak within, to and about the organized power that forms the dominant ideology, that 'complex of superstructures, of which the intellectuals are, precisely, the "functionaries"', as Gramsci says.[34]

Never a 'functionary' of the superstructure in the strict sense, Bertolucci flirts with it, desires it, at the same time as he desires its overthrow. He is, ultimately, a practical left-wing artist, recognizing the interplay of social and psychological forces upon individuals, wanting to present his ideas to as many other people as possible in as many different forms as possible. He seems to understand that he needs to take into account, as well as account for, the realities of the given modes of production, and attempt to use them to whatever advantage they will allow themselves to be used; to play intricate dialectical strategies, and hope that, eventually, neither the intellectual, the artist nor the dominant ideology but the spectator will emerge with significantly altered perceptions.

At this point in his career, it is impossible to tell how the various strategies will work, if at all. Bertolucci has made mistakes and miscalculations. He abjured modernism when it became a recessive mode in contemporary film, and then attempted to return to it in modified form with *Tragedy of a Ridiculous Man* when the modernist urge was over in cinema at large. At the time of writing, he is planning to make a film in China – a fascinating prospect. With all the turns and changes in his work, and despite the misjudgments he has made, Bertolucci has not yet created an uninteresting film. His love of formal experiment, his insistence upon using cinema to evoke a recognition – if not a revelation – of the prevailing cultural and political apparatuses and their repressive functions, keep him aligned with the best work in the shrinking field of committed, political film.

One substantial problematic in Bertolucci's work remains to be examined. In his obsession with the patriarchal order and with the reproduction of oppression through the relationship of fathers and sons, Bertolucci often neglects close analysis of the situation of women in his films. More than neglects, he often places them in inferior or, worse, destructive roles. It might be argued that Bertolucci ought not to be singled out for special criticism in this area. The film-makers with whom I have most often compared his work – Pasolini, Godard, Fassbinder – are hardly models of feminist insight (though Godard has been making efforts in this direction since the early 70s). But this is, in fact, not the point. Any film may benefit from a feminist critique.

From this perspective, as from so many others, one finds considerable conflict within Bertolucci's films; and I can only treat it very briefly here. Most of the films contain unusual female characters, and rarely are they treated in a conventional manner. At the same time Bertolucci does not build narratives in which women are placed in central or unequivocal roles of strength; and without exception his female characters are either at the mercy of, or must make use of, their sexuality in order to survive as individuals within the fiction. Only sporadically, and only in some of the films, does Bertolucci attempt to create a female discourse, to permit a female 'voice' to dominate at least part of a text. When he does, that 'voice' remains overdetermined by the male characters and their activities. A central example of this has already been cited. Jeanne's comment to Paul in *Last Tango* that he hates women constitutes a major insight of the film, a point of perception that could reorder the text. But that text is, finally, unalterably ordered by the male voice; and Paul's response – 'Well, either they always pretend to know who I am, or they pretend that I don't know who they are, and that's very boring' – deflects the entry of another voice, another point of view.

The female discourse is deflected and buried while the female figure is elevated – as it is in the most conventional cinema – and made the object of the gaze of both the male characters within the narrative and the male spectators of the narrative. This occurs even when that figure is attempting to free herself from the gaze. In Lacanian terms, Bertolucci does not see women separated from the discourse of the patriarchy, from the symbolic order, from the concept of 'woman as *the* object, the fantasy of her definition',[35] a definition made for her by the male discourse, a place which, according to Lacan, she chooses to occupy. Lacan writes:

> I would say that it is in order to be the phallus, that is to say, the signifier of the desire of the Other, that woman will reject an essential part of her femininity, notably all its attributes through masquerade. It is for what she is not that she expects to be desired as well as loved. But she finds the signifier of her own desire in the body of the one to whom she addresses her demand for love. Certainly we should not forget that the organ actually invested with this signifying function takes on the value of a fetish. But for the woman the result is still a convergence onto the same object of an experience of love which as such . . . ideally deprives her of that which it gives, and a desire which finds in that same experience its signifier.[36]

This may be no more than over-elaborated language for the desperate Freudian cliché of 'penis envy', but it does explain the dilemma in which many of Bertolucci's female characters are placed, sometimes despite the directions these characters attempt to take in the fiction. Bertolucci's women tend to seek a kind of phallic authority for their being, to worship at the altar of the prick (paraphrasing Paul's warning to Jeanne and her desire for a secure marriage). The comment seems to express a problem inherent in all the films in which female characters appear ready for self-containment, only to fall into, or use, sexuality as a means of escape, an expression of their psychic confusion, as revenge. In only a few instances is sexuality a normal component of a female character in Bertolucci's films; too often it becomes a substitute, even an excuse for alternative modes of behaviour which Bertolucci seems unable to perceive as possible.

In *Before the Revolution*, for example, he attempts to create, in the character of Gina, something of a freed woman (perhaps fashioned after Truffaut's Catherine in *Jules and Jim*). But this freedom – like Catherine's – is bound by sexuality, by a desire that cannot be met, that 'deprives her of that which it gives'. (There is a lovely and significant image in the film that represents this dilemma: Gina has had an afternoon affair with a stranger. She walks with him in the street and meets Fabrizio, who is jealous and anxious. The two men disappear in soft focus behind her as she looks over her shoulder

'A freed woman'? Gina (Adriana Asti) in *Before the Revolution*

towards each vanishing figure, alone and unfulfilled.) The character wants to be free, but her quest is reined in by sexual dependence. She sleeps with her nephew, Fabrizio; she has casual affairs; she speaks in despair with a lover on the phone; it is suggested that Puck may have been a former lover. When Fabrizio makes his inevitable choice and marries Clelia, Gina transfers her loss by desperately hugging Fabrizio's younger brother, smothering him with embraces, embarrassing in their obvious sensuality. This is the image that ends the film. In her sexual freedom Gina finds only its opposite, an imprisonment to an oppressive sexuality that does not fulfil desire. This is hardly a novel perception on Bertolucci's part. The woman enthralled by sexuality, indeed determined by it, constitutes a major oppressive force in cinema. The male voice finds it difficult to put female characters into roles other than either the maternal or the figure of uncontrollable sexuality.

In *La luna*, Bertolucci attempts to combine the roles. This is the only one of his films that has a woman as a central character. Caterina is the centre of the gaze throughout the film (to borrow Laura Mulvey's point about the visual and psychological situating of women). She is a figure of enormous power, a diva, in command of her art and, one would hope, her life. But in fact her power and control is destructive to herself and those around her. Somewhat disingenuously, Bertolucci said of Caterina: 'I wanted a woman who is very autonomous, very independent, without the support of a man. Of course, there is a problem for a woman so creative and maternal – it's impractical in terms of time. It's a problem that should be faced by the liberated woman.'[37] In fact it is a problem that must be faced by a 'liberated' male. The division between the 'creative' and the 'maternal' may be more of a problem of the male perception of women than it is for the women men presume to speak for.

Bertolucci apparently cannot conceive of a woman who is able to be worker and mother. The tensions within the character make her collapse inward upon herself. She is not only the centre of the spectator's gaze but, within the fiction, the centre of her own gaze which in turn engulfs her son, Joe. He becomes her sexual object, a 'replacement' for the love she cannot find through 'normal' means. She left her first husband, an Italian, who did not like her career and was too attached to his own mother. Her second husband dies, and even though she expresses a feeling of freedom, the loss – it is implied – creates a lack which she cannot fill with her work. As in *Before the Revolution*, incest emerges as a major thematic in the film; more oppressively here, for the anodyne attraction of aunt and nephew is replaced by the destructive sexual attraction of mother for son. The destruction is, of course, twofold. In relation to Joe, it amounts to child abuse. For Caterina, it is an extraordinary oppressive force, signifying the inability of the female character to assume a role in the patriarchy. She desires the phallus, here in its most taboo form: her own son, whom she all but forces to re-enact the Oedipal crime. In the Freudian-Lacanian model, he must be 'saved' from this by the power of that other owner of the phallus, the father. But in the body of the film there are no men present to 'save' Caterina or Joe. Between the death of Joe's stepfather, Douglas, and the rediscovery of his real father, Giuseppe, there are only homosexuals – Caterina's friend, Edward (and her woman friend, Marina, who imposes upon her with a leering sexual gaze and climbs into the shower with her); the Franco Citti character who attempts to seduce Joe in a bar – and another child, the angelic and quite self-contained Mustafa, Joe's 'connection'.

The movement of Caterina through the narrative of *La luna* is depicted therefore as demeaning and without conclusion. She is presented alternately as vulnerable, manipulative, selfish, corrupt, and consistently lacking female completion by the male figure. She is not even permitted a conventional beauty, for visually Bertolucci treats her poorly. In the end, he is unable to do anything with his character but return her to the patriarchy, re-enter her into the safe domestic triad. Michael Ryan sums up this movement with nice precision:

> The continuity of male power demands reproduction, but the female is a moment of discontinuity in the line of direct descent from man to man. From this point of view, phallocentrism appears as a form of centering. ... I am reminded of Bertolucci's *Luna*, a recent example of what Deleuze and Felix Guattari might call the 'oedipalization' of woman. The wayward son, who has almost been seduced by his mother, is straightened out in the end by a slap from his father, who has been absent, himself a 'victim' of his own mother's love. Male bonding is re-established through punishment, and in consequence, the mother ... regains her voice. Potency is restored on all levels. The last scene has the men sitting in the audience smiling complicitly at each other, while the mother, once powerful, now looks debased and vulnerable, singing on stage with her mouth grossly distended, her deep throat exposed, and her arms outstretched – an allegory of feminine sexuality as seen from a male perspective.[38]

Two things need to be added to Ryan's observation. Although Bertolucci insists that, in the final sequence, the characters are not seen together in one shot, we do see Caterina from over Giuseppe's shoulder. Perhaps more significantly, we also observe Joe and, seated behind him, his Italian girlfriend Arianna – a grouping which suggests that Joe will now enter the realm of 'normal' sexuality. In the film's final shot, the moon, that great maternal symbol, reigns over the renewed domestic scene. Caterina is completely destroyed. The narrative will not permit her to exist as mother, opera singer, or a woman independent of male sexuality. If it had, interesting, even terrifying questions might have been raised about the dominance of the patriarchy. In its closure, the narrative stops whatever transgressions it might have suggested. The woman is returned to her conventional, and therefore safe role as the object of male adoration.

La luna is peculiarly straightforward in its confusions about the female figure; clear in presenting that figure bound within the dominant male structure. The film dodges its own hermeneutic, refusing even to be implicit about the potentials for freeing its character from that structure. *Last Tango* is Bertolucci's most ambiguous text in this regard, so much so that one's ability to determine the woman's role in the film keeps shifting with each viewing and each consideration of its emotional and political intricacies. While there is no question as to the formal and contextual success of the film in expressing the agonies of sexuality, there remain many questions about the choices Bertolucci makes in developing the three-way grouping of Paul, Jeanne and Tom and the various figures who double these characters. The conclusions drawn by the narrative about the pivotal figure of the woman in that grouping and within the structure of the patriarchy itself point back to a political-psychological rupture that we have seen in other aspects of Bertolucci's work.

This rupture results, in part, from the double discourse of the text. It attempts to speak intensively about the fictional presence of its characters, to give them an immediacy and demand from the viewer a response to them, while at the same time it wants to speak about the connection between the characters and the social order that creates them. The suturing is often loose, though the connections are impossible to ignore. Also impossible to ignore is the fact that, despite the details of investigation and the attempt to deal with the phenomenon of the couple, and all the ideological and emotional baggage brought with it, the text becomes short-circuited. As always, the male figure predominates, centres our attention and focuses our emotions. The woman is his object and ours; she is the body of desire and the object of revenge, until she becomes the agent of revenge, killing the man whose presence has most engaged us. At the same time, it is the male figure who presents the greatest danger. Both Paul and Tom abuse Jeanne in body and spirit, but she is capable of responding only with petulance or murder. Once again we find the woman as defined by Lacan, seeking the fulfilment of desire by yielding herself to the Other, the owner of the phallus, fetishizing that which she does not have, what she is not permitted to have: power, language, self.

The text unravels around the central problem it states without resolving: the conflict between woman as victim and woman as victimizer. I have referred to Paul's speech to Jeanne about what marriage and heterosexual love means to a woman defined by the patriarchy. The speech is central to whatever fragment of a feminist discourse may exist in the film, and it reduces the elaborate and evasive language of Lacan to a clear statement. Paul delivers his analysis in the midst of a moment of tension which he is attempting to resolve. Jeanne has threatened to leave him, and he bathes her as she tells him about her love for Tom. Paul responds:

You want this man that you love to protect you and take care of you . . .? You want this golden, shining, powerful knight* to build a fortress so you can hide in. So you don't ever have to be afraid . . . or you don't have to feel lonely . . . you never have to feel empty. That's what you want, isn't it . . .? Well, you'll never find him. [Jeanne responds that she has found him] . . . then it won't be long until he'll want you to build a fortress for him out of your tits and out of your cunt and out of your hair and your smile and the way you smell . . . someplace where he can feel comfortable enough and secure enough so that he can worship in front of the altar of his own prick . . . No, you're alone, you're all alone and you won't be able to be free of that feeling of being alone until you look death right in the face. I mean, that sounds like bullshit, some romantic crap . . . until you go right up into the ass of death . . . right up in his ass, till you find a womb of fear . . . and then, maybe, maybe then you'll be able to find him.

Jeanne suddenly turns round and claims that she has found this man, and it is Paul. He obliges her by presenting himself as the womb of death, forcing her to put her fingers up his rectum while he reviles her.

Paul denies a central promise of the dominant ideology, that loneliness will be cured by the attachment of a woman to a man; and explicitly states the reality of this promise, that in the attachment the woman will lose her personality, becoming only a 'fortress' in which the male can be secure (in the very next sequence he says to his wife's corpse: 'Our marriage was nothing but a foxhole for you'). He calls for nothing less than the death of the woman's dependence upon phallic authority, for the death of that authority itself (which his own death enacts). But despite his own disclaimer, he cannot help romanticizing his argument. Worse, as in that other sequence where a truth is spoken about male-female relationships and Jeanne tells Paul he hates women, the argument is rapidly deflected as the sequence ends with a sexual act that focuses, once again, upon Paul's agony and places Jeanne in a subordinate and abused position.

Last Tango cannot put its dialectic in balance. Its recognition that a woman is passive in the face of her own lack and the male's ownership of potency is both endorsed and criticized. Situating Paul as its primary signifier and object of the viewer's gaze (thereby reversing the mode of classical American cinema without reversing the oppression of the female that is central to that cinema, for we still are asked to gaze at Jeanne's nude body), it makes the patriarchy attractive at the very time

* Paul actually says 'wife' here, but that makes no sense in the context of the statement.

231

that it attempts to destroy it. Every act and insight of Paul's is mitigated by being presented as a sign of his own suffering. Even his attacks against the patriarchy may be seen merely as statements of someone who has suffered under its cruelty, rather than objective judgments about societal and domestic structures. When Jeanne is abused by Paul, the text manages to turn and indicate a reason for her abuse which *evades* the determining reason – that as a woman she is placed by the social order in a weak and abused position – a fact which, at the same time, the text is aware of.

The male figures dominate Jeanne. Tom, the obsessive film-maker, can only experience Jeanne through a celluloid window. He is not only a surrogate for Bertolucci himself, but through him a surrogate for the spectator, gazing pitilessly at Jeanne. Paul is the complex, multi-faceted, deformed wreck of the history of masculinity; the radioactive waste of the nuclear family. Jeanne remains fool and tool. She is the destroyer. She is the Rosa of the future, the destructive bourgeoise who will first turn Paul into an image of her class (which he has made such a desperate attempt to escape and then an equally desperate attempt to rejoin) and then kill him for his pains. Her role as victim and victimizer is so neutralized by the attention given to Paul that she is denied even the melodrama ordinarily attendant upon such a figure. Paul, not Jeanne, is the melodramatic centre of the film.

The dialectic in *Last Tango* is strained, and so hidden within the film's visual grace and its incessant concentration on the figure of the male that it could be easily missed. Jeanne is so much a victim that her destruction of Paul can be understood as a necessary act. But this recognition is skewed by the fact that it is Paul who suffers most, that Brando and Bertolucci centre all the dynamics of the text on his character so that the other figures – Jeanne, Jeanne's mother, Rosa, Rosa's mother, Tom, Marcel – all become part of his constellation of pain. The only suggestion of a feminine discourse in the film lies within its criticism of the patriarchy, which Bertolucci demonstrates as being destructive to all its members, the male especially. This is an analysis of importance, though weakened by the fact that it is made at the expense of the female character. Any awareness of the particular sufferings of the woman must come from outside the text, glossed in its margins by a reader sensitive to what Bertolucci in fact may not be.

Last Tango may be that exquisite contradiction, a sexist/non-sexist film, attempting to come to terms with its female figure by seeing her through its central male character. In the end both characters lose to the patriarchy against which one of them tried to struggle. Paul becomes the father/lover who must be destroyed; Jeanne the maternal presence, protecting the bourgeois enclave against anarchy. The

Oedipal triangle seems to be secure at the end of the film, though barely coherent. Paul, the demonic parody of the oppressive father, is killed by the daughter, who becomes, in effect, the child of the ghostly couple – her own father and Paul's wife. Oppression appears to be evenly meted out, until we realize that, even in the closing sequences, Bertolucci has turned the tables on his female character. The discovery of her identity is the discovery of her power, which is manifested as violence: as she says her name to Paul she shoots him. The gaining of language for the woman who had none is, in this instance, the gaining of the power of death (indeed, she does look death in the face, as Paul told her she must). Language makes her free; but only of the intolerable demands of a man who has become a demonic parody of the social structure. Language also destroys her, for with it she loses the woman's right of maternity. Paul is the one who cries 'our children' as he dies, and literally assumes the position of an unborn child. Jeanne merely repeats again and again that he tried to rape her, that she did not know his name, that he was a madman. The impasse of violence and violation, the suggestion that the woman uses her language only to perpetuate her fears, only perpetuates her inferiority.

The contradictory forces that make up the figure of Jeanne in *Last Tango* are certainly preferable to the simple-minded disposition of the female in the earlier films: the murdered whore in *The Grim Reaper*; the suffering, sexually insecure Gina of *Before the Revolution*; the women killed by the annihilating force of the double in *Partner*; the mysterious, grasping Draifa, who may be the black widow of *The Spider's Stratagem*. Like all Bertolucci's women, they act as extensions of male fear, insecurity and hatred. Elsewhere, and often when one woman is contrasted with another in the same film, glimmerings of an independent character can occasionally be detected. Finally, one can group together three female characters who attempt to push through the web of male domination to a level of mastery or equality. These are Anna Quadri in *The Conformist*; Anita, Olmo's lover, in *1900*; and Laura, Giovanni's girlfriend, in *Tragedy of a Ridiculous Man*.

Anna Quadri is among the most richly ambiguous figures, male or female, in Bertolucci's films. She gets caught up and divided within the dominant structure of *The Conformist*, whose controlling discourse places the viewer both inside and outside Clerici's perceptions. Often it is difficult to determine who we are seeing, a character functioning independently within the narrative or one formed by the distressed consciousness of the film's central character, posited in the narrative by his own distorting gaze. Anna's opposite, Clerici's wife Giulia, fits his perceptions and needs perfectly. She is the giggling, compliant bourgeoise, whose sexual past (she was the somewhat willing mistress of a family friend) only excites Clerici. Giulia is Clerici's instrument for entering the 'normal' world he desires. Anna is the threat to that desire and simultaneously its obscure object. Her 'difference' attracts Clerici, and she in turn makes use of that attraction in a futile attempt to save herself and her husband from what she understands – more clearly than her husband does – as the purpose of Clerici's presence: their deaths.

I have described how, as part of his perceptual confusion, Clerici seems to see Anna twice before he meets her as the Professor's wife. In each instance she appears to him as a prostitute. Within the temporal, perceptual and psychological dislocations suffered by Clerici, Anna seems to exist in an imaginary realm, as an image he reflects backwards and forwards as madwoman, whore, seductress. Because Clerici only sees himself seeing himself, filtering his perceptions of the world, of the Other, through his own obsessions, Anna becomes what he needs her to be. Therefore, the viewer is forced to infiltrate the narrative beyond Clerici's perceptions in order to distinguish Anna's function outside Clerici's distortions of her.

This task is made more difficult by the fact that in her final incarnation as Quadri's wife she is perceived as a lesbian. But perceived as such by whom? If our own gaze is again blocked by the mask of Clerici's confusions, it would be possible to argue that, as the most powerful threat to his own wilful blindness, Anna is given the attributes of his own worst fears of homosexuality. But two other possibilities exist. One is that Anna's lesbianism is a reflection of Bertolucci's own insecurities, the only way, at this point, he can present a strong woman. The other possibility emerges from the character and her function within the narrative, for she assumes the role of lesbian (or, more accurately, of bisexual seducer of Clerici and Anna) as her only means of saving herself and her husband. In this light, her sexuality counters Clerici's fears of his own. Where he uses his memories of homosexuality to oppress himself, Anna attempts to use her sexuality as a means to free herself.

The difficulty with this is that Anna's strength is *only* allowed to manifest itself in sexual action, which Bertolucci presents as both more powerful than the weak political action of her husband and, at the same time, just as useless. She attempts to seduce the reluctant Giulia, as Clerici peers at them through a doorway in a sequence that seems to have upset even its creator. Bertolucci sees this 'vaguely homosexual seduction scene punctuated by an erotic shiver' as an 'echo of the primal scene'.[39] If this is true, there is no better way Anna could have disturbed Clerici than by confronting him with sexual mysteries that echo the frightening childhood memories of his own sexual initiation.

234

Earlier, she permits herself to be approached sexually by Clerici himself. She bares her breasts to him, begs him to spare her husband and herself in an act that is part self-debasement and part self-assertion. Self-assuredness as well, for it is her knowledge of her self and her knowledge of Clerici's own weakness and cowardice that permits her to attempt a seduction first of him and then of his wife. In neither instance is the seduction climaxed. The desire for self-protection is transferred to the manipulation of sexual desire, which leads only to the destruction of desire. Anna comes to understand the inevitable and joins her husband on his trip to their house in Savoie, during which both are murdered. Clerici is upset that she has accompanied the professor, but when the climactic moment comes he only watches as they are destroyed. Anna's failure – predetermined by the maker of the fiction – is her inability to understand that, for Clerici, sexuality is a stimulus for weakness, a provocation to a collapse into his own emotional and intellectual impotence. Throughout *The Conformist* desire leads only to emotional or, in the case of Anna and her husband, physical annihilation. By using her sexuality as a tool, Anna only brings about her own demise.

In *1900*, Bertolucci performs a clever reversal of roles for the actresses in *The Conformist*. Dominique Sanda, who plays Anna, is given the role of Ada, first Alfredo's lover and then his wife. She is the weak female character of the film, beginning as the decadent haute bourgeoise who would like to be blind to the fascists, ending as the oppressed wife who can confront her husband's political impotence only through drink and, finally, escape. Stefania Sandrelli, who plays Giulia in *The Conformist*, is in *1900* Anita, Olmo's lover, the first female figure in Bertolucci's work who seems able to escape the patriarchy, to act without male guidance or manipulation, without using her sexuality as a tool or by asserting it on her own terms.

But it is a mark of Bertolucci's difficulty in creating an independent female character that he does not quite know what to do with Anita. She works with the other peasants; she teaches Marxism to those few peasants who attend her lessons in the Casa del Popolo; she mourns their death with Olmo; she bears his daughter out of wedlock – a bastard like Olmo himself. Otherwise, in her relatively brief appearances in the film, we learn little else about her. Within the ideological construct of *1900* it seems sufficient, for Bertolucci, that Anita is simply a communist peasant and Olmo's helpmate. He remarks that 'the mothers were the real core of rural communism and the girls were close to their mothers' – a fact, he says, that made it difficult for him to get along with the girls of his childhood.[40] And difficult, one might guess, to fashion a completely formed peasant, communist woman.

235

I must therefore add an important modification to the statement that Anita escapes patriarchal structures. In fact she escapes only the bourgeois patriarchy. Because Bertolucci does not detail the family structure of the peasantry (much beyond showing their communal life), and only suggests the place of the woman within this structure, it is difficult to determine from *1900* precisely how they function and how Anita stands in relation to the rest of them. They are depicted as strong, of course, and brave. In a particularly moving sequence the peasants turn against Attila and his *squadristi*, who shoot them down in an orgy of violence. One old woman defiantly bares her breasts to one of the fascists and is shot instantly. The strength of the peasant women is contrasted to the dependency of the woman of the middle class, like Anna or like Signora Pioppi who, dispossessed of her property by the Berlinghieri family (her husband refused to join the local fascist organization), madly attempts to solve her problem by entrapping Attila and his consort Regina in her home, which they both covet. The result is that Attila murders her by crushing her behind a door.

If Anita stands out from the bourgeois women of the film, it is almost through the ideological given of her class rather than the purposeful construction, within the narrative, of an admirable, free and powerful figure. Ultimately she proves either too powerful or not powerful enough for Bertolucci and his film. She disappears from the narrative. Olmo tells Alfredo that she died in childbirth.

With the character of Laura in *Tragedy of a Ridiculous Man*, Bertolucci finds it possible to create a female figure with the self-assurance of Anna Quadri, independent of conventional social structures and able to survive. Laura is by no means an unambiguous figure, but through that ambiguity her strength is found. Part of the ambiguity arises from the structure of the film's narrative. Laura has to push herself through a film literally dominated by the male voice. Recall that Primo narrates the film, and it is through his gaze that we see most of the action. He is an unregenerate sexist, reactionary in his sexual perceptions as in all others, and does not fail to remark upon female attributes when he looks at Laura's breasts or at a woman's backside through his binoculars. Laura, however, is able to use Primo's sexism as a way to seduce him, not physically, but socially, politically.

She uses her beauty and her sexuality to entice and mislead him. When talking to him about her relationship with his son, she makes a point of saying that there was relatively little sexual activity between them, an idea the ridiculous *homme moyen sensuel* cannot comprehend. He asks if there was a physical problem. Laura responds simply that sex was not the most important thing in their relationship. At the very time she tells him this, she is yielding to his embraces, which he

Sexuality as subversion: Laura and Primo in *Tragedy of a Ridiculous Man* (Ugo Tognazzi, Laura Morante)

pretends to offer as a way of comforting her. The sequence occurs fairly early in the narrative, before the viewer has any concrete notion of Laura's involvement in the presumed kidnapping of Giovanni, and is therefore an unusually enigmatic event in a film where enigmas are presented subtly, quietly. The onus of the apparent seduction is clearly upon Primo, who seems to be 'taking advantage' of this frightened young woman. Yet at the same time the swiftness with which Laura gives in to him is troubling, discouraging, for it seems to point up a weakness in her own character.

Only in retrospect does one suspect that it is a ploy on her part, something akin to the seduction performed by Anna in *The Conformist*, yet without its desperation. The caressing and holding, which she at first resists and then yields to, is not consummated in intercourse. She seems to know that sexuality is a thing Primo cannot resist and is therefore something she can use to get his confidence. This becomes clearer later, after Primo, convincing himself his son is dead, decides to fake the ransom payment that he will then re-collect to refinance his factory. He has Laura write a ransom note; and she pulls off her sweater, confronting Primo with her nakedness. Although he cannot resist making an exclamation about her breasts, he is too involved in the matter at hand to do anything more. His exclamation is both

237

endearing and repulsive. As an expression of masculine discourse – spoken indirectly, as if in a confidential aside to the audience – it is the kind of remark men are meant easily to understand, a statement of camaraderie that is anti-female at its discursive heart. Coming when it does, it is a repellent example of the crudeness of Primo's character. He is so much the patriarchal voice that an exclamation about the most fetishized aspect of a woman's body cannot be repressed. But if we filter the remark through Laura's own discourse, we may suppose that it is purposely elicited to point up Primo's patriarchal self-assertion, which Laura is in the process of undoing. Her act of disrobing is an act of defiance and an act of exposure – not of herself, but of Primo and the sexual-political ideology he represents.

Laura knows that Giovanni is alive. She is a part of the plot, possibly the instigator of the plot, to get Primo's money for the leftists. By exposing herself to Primo she is, in a sense, exposing how he is being used; she is making him ridiculous. Unfortunately, at the same time, she does use her body to make her point. Despite her control of her action within the narrative, the way Bertolucci photographs the sequence makes her an erotic object. Again, Bertolucci can seem to find no other means of allowing his female characters to express themselves. Her breasts are bared to be admired by both Primo *and* the male audience. Her body is the centre of the gaze at that instant. It is not clear whether Bertolucci is implying that the male audience is as ridiculous as the male character.

The sequence raises a number of complex problems. Bertolucci does not define and show the workings of a leftist group, only their results and how these are perceived by Primo, who in turn must be perceived and understood by the viewer. Because of this structure, Bertolucci cannot indicate clearly Laura's role in the plot and may only hint at the plot itself. Like all his other female characters she is not permitted a clear voice – her own discourse. Her actions and purposes may be suggested only. Her cry of 'harakiri' to Primo in the pig barns where the plot is set in motion and her breast-baring are the only outward indications of her knowledge and complicity. She is the film's subversive figure, but her act of subversion is itself subverted by not being clearly defined. Again, this is the strategy of the film's narrative structure, but it is a strategy that also denies full presence to the strong woman and enables Bertolucci to make use of the woman's body as a conventional erotic sign, slightly inflected by the suggestion that she is conscious of the way she uses it. Because she is not permitted to use language, to meet Primo on the level of overt discourse, she must use that other language, the language of the feminine, of sexuality, as a kind of subversive code.[41]

In this, she is much like Primo's wife, Barbara. This character is also quiet and mysterious; as with Laura the spectator is never quite sure what she does and does not know. Like Laura, she cannot *speak*, but can only prod her husband into action – once at the point of the gun. She is the maternal component of Laura. But unlike that other maternal figure, Caterina in *La luna*, she does not transgress her role. She remains firmly within the code of maternity, acting to save her son even if it means killing the father.

Bertolucci's attitude towards the female characters created in his narratives runs parallel to that broader problem I have been discussing: the struggle of the bourgeois intellectual attempting to make Marxist films for a broad bourgeois audience. In both instances, Bertolucci appears unable or unwilling to move through an unambiguous statement of positive, uncompromised change. With all their vitality and political commitment, his films are in the end concerned with the time before the revolution, filled with seductive ambiguities, luxurious spaces for self-indulgence, for moral and political outrage and nostalgia, for bold experimentation in expressive form. For Bertolucci to create a female discourse, a film in which a woman moved definitively beyond the constraints of the patriarchy, would constitute a sign that he was able to break out of the patriarchal prison himself, thereby breaking with all the codes that have structured his work to date.

This statement may appear to burden the film-maker and his work with a demand, a wish that they be other than what they are. If so, it reveals the task of the critic not only to discover the forms and ideas his or her subject has created, but to seek out other forms and ideas, other possibilities; to desire *for* his or her subject – and that subject's audience – what *might* be there, to perceive an extension of the imagination that is already apparent in the existing work. For a film-maker as young as Bertolucci, one of the few still willing to struggle with ideology and discuss within his work left-wing alternatives to the dominant discourse of Western culture, this desire is all the more understandable; perhaps even necessary.

Jacques Lacan wrote the following about images, about self, Other and perception, using the kind of metaphor that endears him to film scholars:

Only the subject – the human subject, the subject of the desire that is the essence of man – is not, unlike the animal, entirely caught up in his imaginary capture. He maps himself in it. How? In so far as he isolates the function of the screen and plays with it. Man, in effect, knows how to play with the mask as that beyond which there is the gaze. The screen is here the locus of mediation.[42]

The 'screen' may be that mediating point between the subject and his or her perception of the Other and the Other's perception of the subject. Or it may be the motion picture screen, upon which the world of the Other is projected, as in Plato's myth of the cave, ready-made, forcing its imaginary presence upon the imagination of the subject. In either case, the subject, in order to be free, must be able to recognize the 'locus of mediation' and understand that what is mediated can be mediated in a variety of ways. Perceptions can be altered: something Bertolucci is keenly aware of, for that is what makes his such a restless cinematic intelligence.

In the end, the *difference* between self and Other, imaginary and symbolic, image and 'reality', desire and possibility is what the cinema is about. The critic as well as the film-maker must 'play with the mask', recognize that the screen is *only* the locus of mediation, and discover what is being mediated, what might be mediated and how. The power of Bertolucci's films lies both in the forms of their mediations and in the substance of idea and emotion created by those forms. To want more from them, to want something different, is not to diminish what is there, but to *desire* more – to meet desire with greater desire.

Notes

Introduction

1. Michel Foucault, 'What is an Author?', trans. D. F. Bouchard, *Screen*, vol. 20, no. 1, 1979, p. 19.
2. Peter Wollen, *Signs and Meanings in the Cinema*, London, Secker & Warburg/BFI, 1969, p. 168.
3. Screenplay in *L'Avant-scène du Cinéma*, no. 82, 1968, p. 35.
4. John Bragin, 'A Conversation with Bernardo Bertolucci', *Film Quarterly*, vol. 20, no. 1, 1966, p. 44.

1 'Versus Godard'

1. *Cahiers du Cinéma*, no. 186, January 1967, p. 29.
2. Enzo Ungari, *Scene madri di Bernardo Bertolucci*, Milan, Ubulibri, 1982, p. 51.
3. See Terry Lovell, *Pictures of Reality*, London, British Film Institute, 1980 pp. 51 and 90.
4. See Enzo Siciliano, *Pasolini*, trans. J. Shepley, New York, Random House, 1982.
5. Quoted in Oswald Stack, *Pasolini on Pasolini*, London, Thames and Hudson/BFI, 1969; Bloomington, Indiana University Press, 1970, p. 39.
6. See David Overbey, *Springtime in Italy*, London, Talisman Books, 1978, pp. 26–9.
7. Cf. Siciliano, *Pasolini*, p. 239.
8. Stack, *Pasolini on Pasolini*, p. 138.
9. Ungari, *Scene madri*, p. 29.
10. Ibid,. p. 31.
11. John Bragin, 'A Conversation with Bernardo Bertolucci', *Film Quarterly*, vol. 20, no. 1, 1966, p. 42.
12. Ungari, *Scene madri*, p. 198.
13. Stack, *Pasolini on Pasolini*, p. 138.
14. *Godard on Godard*, ed. and trans. T. Milne, London, Secker & Warburg; New York, Viking Press, 1972, pp. 213–4.
15. Ungari, *Scene madri*, p. 51.

2 The Search for Form

1. Bertolucci quoted in Enzo Ungari, *Scene madri di Bernardo Bertolucci*, Milan, Ubulibri, 1982, p. 35.
2. Jonathan Culler, *On Deconstruction*, London, Routledge & Kegan Paul, 1983, pp. 120 and 135.
3. Fredric Jameson, *The Political Unconscious*, London, Methuen, 1981, p. 141.

4. Cf. Louis Althusser, *Lenin and Philosophy and Other Essays*, trans. B. Brewster, London, New Left Books, 1971, pp. 127–86.
5. *L'Avant-scène du Cinéma*, no. 82, 1968, p. 7.
6. T. Jefferson Kline, 'The Absent Presence: Stendhal in Bertolucci's *Prima della rivoluzione*', *Cinema Journal*, vol. 23, no. 2, 1984. Kline has undertaken a series of close, psychoanalytical readings of Bertolucci's films. While his approach is different from mine, there are inevitable overlaps in our analyses.
7. Ungari, *Scene madri*, p. 71.
8. P. P. Pasolini, 'Observations on the Long Take', trans. N. MacAfee and C. Owens, in *October*, vol. 13, 1980, p. 6.
9. Cf. Ungari, *Scene madri*, pp. 71–3.
10. *L'Avant-scène du Cinéma*, op. cit., p. 45.
11. G. Baldini, *The Story of Giuseppe Verdi*, ed. and trans. R. Parker, Cambridge, Cambridge University Press, 1980, p. 5.
12. Marilyn Goldin, 'Bertolucci on *The Conformist*', *Sight and Sound*, vol. 40, no. 2, 1971, p. 65.
13. Ungari, *Scene madri*, p. 36.
14. For the references to Pavese, see Kline, 'The Absent Presence'.
15. Cf. Joan Mellen, 'A Conversation with Bernardo Bertolucci', *Cineaste*, vol. 5, no. 4, 1973, p. 22; and Ungari, *Scene madri*, p. 117.
16. *Cineaste*, vol. 7, no. 4, 1976, p. 8. This issue includes two interviews with Bertolucci under the collective title 'Bertolucci's "1900": A Preview'.

3 The Formalist's Strategies

1. Bertolucci quoted in Enzo Ungari, *Scene madri di Bernardo Bertolucci*, Milan, Ubulibri, 1982, p. 21.
2. Ungari, *Scene madri*, p. 129.
3. Terry Eagleton, *Criticism and Ideology*, London, New Left Books, 1976, p. 60.
4. Ibid., pp. 44–63. I have somewhat condensed and modified Eagleton's categories.
5. 'Bertolucci's "1900": A Preview', *Cineaste*, vol. 7, no. 4, 1976, p. 8.
6. Ungari, *Scene madri*, pp. 129–30.
7. Ibid.
8. *Time*, 2 May 1977, pp. 70–1.
9. 'Bertolucci's "1900": A Preview', p. 5.
10. See *Post-Impressionism: Cross-currents in European Painting*, London, Royal Academy of Arts, Weidenfeld and Nicolson; New York, Harper & Row, 1979, pp. 245–6.
11. Ibid., p. 246.
12. C. Vaughan James, *Soviet Socialist Realism*, London, Macmillan, 1973, p. 93.
13. Joan Mellen, 'A Conversation with Bernardo Bertolucci', *Cineaste*, vol. 5, no. 4, 1973, p. 22.
14. 'Bertolucci's "1900": A Preview', p. 3.
15. Fernando Solanas and Octavio Getino, 'Towards a Third Cinema', reprinted in Bill Nichols (ed.), *Movies and Methods*, Berkeley, University of

California Press, 1976, p. 58.
16. Terry Lovell, *Pictures of Reality*, London, British Film Institute, 1980, p. 90.
17. James Monaco, *Alain Resnais*, New York, Oxford University Press, 1979, p. 8.
18. Amos Vogel, 'Bernardo Bertolucci: An Interview', *Film Comment*, vol. 7, no. 3, 1971, pp. 26–7.
19. 'Bertolucci's "1900": A Preview', p. 5.
20. Cf. Bill Nichols, *Ideology and the Image*, Bloomington, Indiana University Press, 1981, pp. 29–42.
21. 'Bernardo Bertolucci Seminar', *Dialogue on Film*, vol. 3, no. 5, 1974, p. 17.
22. Ibid., p. 21.
23. As T. Jefferson Kline suggests in his essay 'The Unconformist' in *Modern European Filmmakers and the Art of Adaptation*, ed. A. Horton and J. Magretta, New York, Frederick Ungar, 1981, p. 225.
24. Ungari, *Scene madri*, p. 63.
25. Ibid., p. 45.
26. Cf. Richard Roud, 'Fathers and Sons', *Sight and Sound*, vol. 40, no. 2, 1971, p. 61.
27. Cf. Nichols, *Ideology and the Image*, p. 23.
28. Ungari, *Scene madri*, p. 217.
29. Quotations from the libretti are from *Seven Verdi Librettos*, trans. W. Weaver, New York, W. W. Norton, 1975.
30. Ungari, *Scene madri*, pp. 117–18.
31. John Russell, *Francis Bacon*, London, Thames and Hudson, 1971, p. 72.
32. Roland Barthes, *S/Z*, trans. R. Miller, London, Cape; New York, Hill & Wang, 1975, pp. 21, 75.
33. Ungari, *Scene madri*, p. 89.
34. See Joan Mellen, *Women and Their Sexuality in the New Film*, New York, Horizon Press, 1973, p. 144.

4 Collapse and Renewal

1. Roland Barthes, *The Pleasure of the Text*, trans. R. Miller, New York, Hill & Wang, 1975, p. 8.
2. Ibid., p. 14.
3. Enzo Ungari, *Scene madri di Bernardo Bertolucci*, Milan, Ubulibri, 1982, pp. 196–7.
4. See Richard Roud, 'Bertolucci on *La Luna*', *Sight and Sound*, vol. 48, no. 4, 1979, p. 237.
5. Ungari, *Scene madri*, p. 191.
6. Roud, 'Bertolucci on *La Luna*', pp. 236–7.
7. Ibid.
8. Gary Crowdus and Dan Georgakas, '*Luna* and the Critics: An Interview with Bernardo Bertolucci', *Cineaste*, vol. 10, no. 1, 1979–80, p. 28.
9. *Dialogue on Film*, vol. 5, no. 4, 1980, p. 37.
10. Ungari, *Scene madri*, p. 36.
11. *Dialogue on Film*, 1980, p. 40.

12. Ungari, *Scene madri*, p. 221.
13. Ibid., p. 31.
14. Ibid., p. 221.
15. Ibid., pp. 221–2.

5   In the Name of the Son, the Father and the Dialectic

1. Bertolucci quoted in Enzo Ungari, *Scene madri di Bernardo Bertolucci*, Milan, Ubulibri, 1982, p. 30.
2. Georg Lukács, *Essays on Thomas Mann*, trans. S. Mitchell, London, Merlin, 1964, pp. 94–5.
3. Georg Lukács, *Studies in European Realism*, New York, Grosset & Dunlap, 1964, p. 171.
4. Cf. Christine Gledhill, 'Recent Developments in Feminist Criticism', *Quarterly Review of Film Studies*, vol. 3, no. 4, 1978, pp. 478–80.
5. Louis Althusser, *Lenin and Philosophy and Other Essays*, trans. B. Brewster, London, New Left Books, 1971, pp. 215–16.
6. Michael Ryan, *Marxism and Deconstruction*, Baltimore, Johns Hopkins University Press, 1982, p. 104.
7. Gilles Deleuze and Félix Guattari, *Anti-Oedipus: Capitalism and Schizophrenia*, trans. R. Hurley, M. Seem and H. R. Lane, Minneapolis, University of Minnesota Press, 1977, pp. 74–5.
8. 'Bertolucci's "1900": A Preview', *Cineaste*, vol. 7, no. 4, 1976, pp. 5, 8–9.
9. Jacques Lacan, *Ecrits*, trans. A. Sheridan, London, Tavistock; New York, W. W. Norton, 1977, p. 40.
10. Ungari, *Scene madri*, p. 221.
11. Sigmund Freud, *Totem and Taboo*, London, Hogarth Press, 1951, p. 150.
12. See S. Hughes, *The Fall and Rise of Modern Italy*, New York, Macmillan, 1967, p. 215.
13. 'Bertolucci's "1900": A Preview', pp. 9, 50.
14. Ungari, *Scene madri*, p. 132
15. Gideon Bachmann, 'Films are Animal Events: Bernardo Bertolucci talks about his new film, *1900*', *Film Quarterly*, vol. 24, no. 1, 1975, pp. 18–19.
16. Antonio Gramsci, *Selections from the Prison Notebooks*, ed. and trans. Q. Hoare and G. Nowell-Smith, London, Lawrence & Wishart, 1971, p. 172.
17. Ibid., p. 177.
18. Ibid, pp. 177–9.
19. 'Bertolucci's "1900": A Preview', p. 3.
20. Quoted in J. C. Franklin, 'The Films of Fassbinder: Form and Formula', *Quarterly Review of Film Studies*, vol. 5, no. 2, 1980, p. 169.
21. P. P. Pasolini, introduction to *Oedipus Rex*, trans. J. Matthews, London, Lorrimer, 1974, p. 7.
22. Ungari, *Scene madri*, p. 131.
23. Ibid., p. 129.
24. Ibid., p. 131.
25. In Marilyn Goldin, 'Bertolucci on *The Conformist*', *Sight and Sound*, vol. 40, no. 2, 1971, p. 66.
26. Ungari, *Scene madri*, p. 87.

27. 'Bertolucci's "1900": A Preview', p. 8.

28. 'Bernardo Bertolucci Seminar', *Dialogue on Film*, vol. 3, no. 5, 1974, p. 19.

29. Quoted in J. M. Cammett, *Antonio Gramsci and the Origins of Italian Communism*, Stanford, University of California Press, 1967, p. 16.

30. Quoted in T. J. Kline, 'The Absent Presence: Stendhal in Bertolucci's *Prima della rivoluzione*', *Cinema Journal*, vol. 23, no. 2, 1984, p. 24.

31. Ungari, *Scene madri*, p. 177.

32. Deleuze and Guattari, *Anti-Oedipus*, p. 97.

33. Roland Barthes, *The Pleasure of the Text*, trans. R. Miller, New York, Hill & Wang, 1975, p. 53.

34. Gramsci, *Selections from the Prison Notebooks*, p. 12.

35. Jacqueline Rose, introduction to Jacques Lacan, *Feminine Sexuality*, London, Macmillan; New York, W. W. Norton, 1982, p. 47.

36. Lacan, *Feminine Sexuality*, p. 84.

37. *Dialogue on Film*, vol. 5, no. 4, 1980, p. 37.

38. Ryan, *Marxism and Deconstruction*, p. 109.

39. Ungari, *Scene madri*, pp. 191–2.

40. Ibid., p. 14.

41. See Annette Kuhn, *Women's Pictures*, London, Routledge & Kegan Paul, 1982, pp. 64–5.

42. Jacques Lacan, *The Four Fundamental Concepts of Psycho-analysis*, ed. J.–A. Miller, trans. A. Sheridan, Harmondsworth, Penguin, 1979.

Filmography

Bernardo Bertolucci, born Parma, 16 March 1941

Abbreviations

P. c.	Production company
P.	Producer
Assoc. p.	Associate Producer
P. man.	Production manager
D.	Director
Asst. d.	Assistant director
Sc.	Screenplay
Ph.	Photography
Ed.	Editor
A. d.	Art Director
M.	Music
M. dir.	Music Director
Sd.	Sound
Cost.	Costumes

1962 **La commare secca** (The Grim Reaper)
P. c: Cinematografica Cervi. P: Antonio Cervi. P. man: Ugo Tucci. D: Bernardo Bertolucci. Asst. d: Adolfo Cagnacci. Sc: Bernardo Bertolucci, Sergio Citti, from a story by Pier Paolo Pasolini. Ph: Gianni Narzisi. Ed: Nino Baragli. A. d/cost: Adriana Spadaro. M: Carlo Rustichelli, Piero Piccioni. Sd: Sandro Fortini.
Francesco Ruiu *(Canticchia)*, Giancarlo De Rosa *(Nino)*, Vincenzo Ciccora *(Mayor)*, Alvaro D'Ercole *(Francolicchio)*, Romano Labate *(Pipito)*, Lorenza Benedetti *(Milly)*, Emy Rocci *(Domenica)*, Erina Torelli *(Mariella)*, Renato Troiani *(Natalino)*, Allen Midgette *(Teodoro, the soldier)*, Marisa Solinas *(Bruna)*, Wanda Rocci *(Prostitute)*, Alfredo Leggi *(Bostelli)*, Carlotta Barilli *(Serenella)*, Gabriella Giorgelli *(Esperia)*, Santina Lisio *(Esperia's mother)*, Clorinda Celani *(Soraya)*, Ada Peragostini *(Maria)*, Silvio Laurenzi *(Homosexual)*, Nadia Bonafede, Ugo Santucci, Santina Fioravanti, Elena Fontana, Maria Fontana.
100 mins.
Distributors: BFI (UK).

1964 **Prima della rivoluzione** (Before the Revolution)
P. c: Iride Cinematografica. P. man: Gianni Amico. D: Bernardo Bertolucci.
Sc: Bernardo Bertolucci, Gianni Amico. Ph: Aldo Scavarda. Ed: Roberto Perpignani. M: Gino Paoli, Ennio Morricone; extracts from *Macbeth* by Verdi.
Sd: Romano Pampaloni.
Adriana Asti *(Gina)*, Francesco Barilli *(Fabrizio)*, Allen Midgette *(Agostino)*, Morando Morandini *(Cesare)*, Cristina Pariset *(Clelia)*, Cecrope Barilli *(Puck)*, Gianni Amico *(The friend)*, Domenico Alpi *(Fabrizio's father)*, Emilia Borghi

246

(Fabrizio's mother), Iole Lunardi *(Fabrizio's grandmother)*, Goliardo Padova *(The painter)*, Guido Fanti *(Enore)*, Evelina Alpi *(Little girl)*, Salvatore Enrico *(Sacrestan)*, Ida Pellegri *(Clelia's mother)*, Antonio Maghenzani *(Antonio)*.
112 mins.
Distributors: Contemporary (UK), New Yorker Films (USA).

1965–6 **La via del petrolio** (documentary in three parts)
P.c: RAI TV/Eni. P: Giovanni Bertolucci. P. man: Giorgio Patara. D: Bernardo Bertolucci. Sc: Bernardo Bertolucci. Ph: Ugo Piccone, Luis Saldanha, Giorgio Pelloni, Maurizio Salvadori. Ed: Roberto Perpignani. M: Egisto Macchi. Speakers: Nino Castelnuovo, Mario Feliciani, Giulio Bosetti, Nino Dal Fabbro, Roberto Cucciolla. Adviser: Alberto Bonchey.
48 mins. (1st part); 40 mins. (2nd part); 45 mins. (3rd part).
Shown on Italian television in January and February 1967.

1966 **Il canale** (documentary)
P: Giorgio Patara. D: Bernardo Bertolucci. Sc: Bernardo Bertolucci. Ph: Maurizio Salvadori, Ugo Piccone (Eastman Colour). Ed: Robert Perpignani. M: Egisto Macchi.
12 mins. (not released).

1967 **Agonia**
P.c: Castoro Film. P: Carlo Lizzani. D: Bernardo Bertolucci. Asst. d: Gianluigi Calderoni. Sc: Bernardo Bertolucci. Ph: Ugo Piccone (Technicolor and Techniscope). Ed: Roberto Perpignani. A. d/cost: Lorenzo Tornabuoni. M: Giovanni Fusco.
Julian Beck *(The dying man)*, Giulio Cesare Castello *(Priest)*, Milena Vukotic *(Nurse)*, Adriano Aprà *(Altar boy)*, Romano Costa, Members of the Living Theatre group.
Made in 1967 under the working title 'Il fico infruttuoso' for the episode film *Vangelo '70*; released in 1969 as the third episode in *Amore e rabbia* (other episodes directed by Pier Paolo Pasolini, Carlo Lizzani, Jean-Luc Godard and Marco Bellocchio).
28 mins.

1968 **Partner**
P. c: Red Film. P: Giovanni Bertolucci. D: Bernardo Bertolucci. Sc: Bernardo Bertolucci, Gianni Amico, adapted from the novel *The Double* by Feodor Dostoevsky. Ph: Ugo Piccone (Technicolor and Techniscope). Ed: Roberto Perpignani. A. d: Francesco Tullio Altan. Cost: Nicoletta Sivieri. M: Ennio Morricone. M. dir: Bruno Nicolai. Sd: Mario Magara.
Pierre Clementi *(Jacob I and II)*, Stefania Sandrelli *(Clara)*, Tina Aumont *(Salesgirl)*, Sergio Tofano *(Petrushka)*, Romano Costa *(Clara's father)*, Giulio Cesare Castello *(Prof. Mozzoni)*, Antonio Maestri *('Tre zampe')*, Mario Venturini *(Professor)*, John Ohettplace *(Pianist)*, Ninetto Davoli, Jean-Robert

Marquis, Nicola Laguiné, Sibilla Sedat, Giampaolo Capovilla, Umberto Silva, Giuseppe Mangano, Alessandro Cane, Sandro Bernardone, David Grieco, Rocchelle Barbieri, Antonio Guerra, Vittorio Fantoni, Giancarlo Nanni, Salvatore Sampieri, Stefano Oppedisano *(Students)*.
105 mins.
Distributors: New Yorker Films (USA).

1970 **Strategia del ragno** (The Spider's Stratagem)
P.c: RAI TV/Red Film. P: Giovanni Bertolucci. D: Bernardo Bertolucci. Asst. d: Giuseppe Bertolucci. Sc: Bernardo Bertolucci, Marilù Parolini, Edoardo De Gregorio, adapted from the story *Theme of the Traitor and Hero* by Jorge Luis Borges. Ph: Vittorio Storaro, Franco De Giacomo (Eastman Colour). Ed: Roberto Perpignani. A. d/cost: Maria Paola Maino. M: extracts from 2nd chamber symphony by Arnold Schönberg and *Rigoletto* by Verdi; song 'Il conformista' by Mina and Martelli. Sd: Giorgio Belloni.
Giulio Brogi *(Athos Magnani, father and son)*, Alida Valli *(Draifa)*, Tino Scotti *(Costa)*, Pippo Campanini *(Gaibazzi)*, Franco Giovannelli *(Rasori)*, Allen Midgette *(Sailor)*.
100 mins.
Distributors: Artificial Eye (UK), New Yorker Films (USA).

1970 **Il conformista** (The Conformist)
P.c: Mars Film (Rome)/Marianne Productions (Paris)/Maran-Film (Munich). P: Maurizio Lodi-Fé. Assoc. p: Giovanni Bertolucci. D: Bernardo Bertolucci. Asst. d: Aldo Lado. Sc: Bernardo Bertolucci, from the novel by Alberto Moravia. Ph: Vittorio Storaro (Technicolor). Ed: Franco Arcalli. A. d: Ferdinando Scarfiotti. Cost: Gitt Magrini. M: Georges Delerue. Sd: Mario Dallimonti.
Jean-Louis Trintignant *(Marcello Clerici)*, Stefania Sandrelli *(Giulia)*, Dominique Sanda *(Anna Quadri)*, Enzo Tarascio *(Luca Quadri)*, Pierre Clementi *(Lino Seminara)*, Gastone Moschin *(Manganiello)*, José Quaglio *(Italo)*, Milly *(Clerici's mother)*, Giuseppe Addobbati *(Clerici's father)*, Yvonne Sanson *(Giulia's mother)*, Fosco Giachetti *(Colonel)*, Benedetto Benedetti *(Minister)*, Christian Alegny *(Raoul)*, Gino Vagni *(Luca)*, Antonio Maestri *(Priest)*, Christian Belègue *(Gypsy)*, Pasquale Fortunato *(Marcello as a boy)*, Pierangelo Civera *(Attendant)*, Marilyn Goldin *(Flower girl)*, Marta Lado, Carlo Gaddi, Franco Pellerani, Claudio Carpelli, Umberto Silvestri.
108 mins.
Distributors: Curzon (UK), Paramount (USA).

1971 **La salute è malata o I poveri muoiono prima** (documentary)
D: Bernardo Bertolucci. Ph: Elio Bisignani, Renato Tafuri. Ed: Franco Arcalli.
35 mins. (16mm.)

1972 **L'ultimo tango a Parigi** (Last Tango in Paris)
P.c: PEA Cinematografica (Rome)/Les Artistes Associés (Paris). P: Alberto

Grimaldi. P. man: Mario Di Biase, Gérard Crosnier. D: Bernardo Bertolucci. Asst. d: Fernand Moszkowics, Jean-David Lefèbvre. Sc: Bernardo Bertolucci, Franco Arcalli. Ph: Vittorio Storaro (Technicolor). Ed: Franco Arcalli. A. d: Ferdinando Scarfiotti. Cost: Gitt Magrini. M: Gato Barbieri. Sd: Antoine Bonfanti.

Marlon Brando *(Paul)*, Maria Schneider *(Jeanne)*, Jean-Pierre Léaud *(Tom)*, Massimo Girotti *(Marcel)*, Maria Michi *(Rosa's Mother)*, Giovanna Galletti *(Prostitute)*, Catherine Allégret *(Catherine)*, Darling Legitimus *(Concierge)*, Marie-Hélène Breillat *(Monique)*, Catherine Breillat *(Mouchette)*, Veronica Lazare *(Rosa)*, Luce Marquand *(Olimpia)*, Gitt Magrini *(Jeanne's mother)*, Rachel Kesterber *(Christine)*, Armand Ablanalp *(Prostitute's client)*, Mimi Pinson *(President of tango jury)*, Catherine Sola *(TV script-girl)*, Mauro Marchetti *(TV cameraman)*, Dan Diament *(TV sound engineer)*, Peter Schommer *(TV assistant cameraman)*, Ramon Mendizabal *(Tango orchestra leader)*, Stéphane Kosiak, Gérard Lepennec.

129 mins.
Distributors: Rank (UK), United Artists (USA).

1976 **Novecento** (1900)
P.c: PEA Cinematografica (Rome)/Les Artistes Associés (Paris)/Artemis (Berlin). P: Alberto Grimaldi. P. man: Mario Di Biase. D: Bernardo Bertolucci. Asst. d: Gabriele Polverosi, Peter Shepherd. Sc: Bernardo Bertolucci, Franco Arcalli, Giuseppe Bertolucci. Ph: Vittorio Storaro (Technicolor). Ed: Franco Arcalli. A. d: Ezio Frigerio. Cost: Gitt Magrini. M: Ennio Morricone. Sd: Claudio Maielli.

Burt Lancaster *(Alfredo Berlinghieri)*, Robert De Niro *(Alfredo Berlinghieri, grandson)*, Sterling Hayden *(Leo Dalco)*, Gérard Depardieu *(Olmo Dalco)*, Dominique Sanda *(Ada Fiastri Paulhan)*, Stefania Sandrelli *(Anita Foschi)*, Laura Betti *(Regina)*, Donald Sutherland *(Attila)*, Francesca Bertini *(Desolata, sister of the elder Alfredo)*, Werner Bruhns *(Ottavio Berlinghieri)*, Romolo Valli *(Giovanni Berlinghieri)*, Anna-Maria Gherardi *(Eleonora, Giovanni's wife)*, Ellen Schwiers *(Amelia, Eleonora's sister)*, Alida Valli *(Signora Pioppi)*, Pippo Campanini *(Don Tarcisio)*, Paolo Branco *(Orso Dalco)*, Giacomo Rizzo *(Rigoletto)*, Antonio Piovanelli *(Turo Dalco)*, Liù Bosisio *(Nella Dalco)*, Maria Monti *(Rosina Dalco, Olmo's mother)*, Anna Henkel *(Anita, Olmo's daughter)*, Paolo Pavesi *(Alfredo as a child)*, Roberto Maccanti *(Olmo as a child)*, Tiziana Senatore *(Regina as a child)*, José Quaglio *(Aranzini)*, Edoardo Dallagio *(Oreste Dalco)*, Stefania Cassini *(Neve, laundrywoman)*, Salvator Mureddu *(Chief of Guards)*, Allen Midgette *(Vagabond)*.

320 mins. (English version, 248 mins.)
Distributors: Harris Films (UK), Paramount and (full-length version) Films Incorporated (USA).

1979 **La luna** (Luna)
P.c: Fiction Cinematografica. P: Giovanni Bertolucci. P. man: Mario Di Biase. D: Bernardo Bertolucci. Asst. d: Gabriele Polverosi, Clare Peploe, Jirges Ristum. Sc: Giuseppe Bertolucci, Bernardo Bertolucci, Clare Peploe, from a

story by Franco Arcalli, Giuseppe Bertolucci, Bernardo Bertolucci. Ph: Vittorio Storaro (Eastman Colour). Ed: Gabriella Cristiani. A. d: Gianni Silvestri, Maria Paula Maino. Cost: Lina Nerli Taviani. M: extracts from *Il trovatore, Rigoletto, La traviata* and *Un ballo in maschera* by Verdi, and from *Così fan tutte* by Mozart. Sd: Mario Dallimonti.

Jill Clayburgh *(Caterina)*, Matthew Barry *(Joe)*, Fred Gwynne *(Douglas)*, Veronica Lazar *(Marina)*, Renato Salvatori *(Communist)*, Tomas Milian *(Giuseppe)*, Alida Valli *(Giuseppe's mother)*, Elisabetta Campeti *(Arianna)*, Stephane Barat *(Mustafa)*, Peter Eyre *(Edward)*, Julian Adamoli *(Julian)*, Franco Citti *(Mario)*, Pippo Campanini *(Innkeeper)*, Shara Di Nepi *(Caterina's maid)*, Roberto Benigni *(Upholsterer)*, Carlo Verdone and Ronaldo Bonacchi *(Directors of Caracalla opera)*, Rodolfo Lodi *(Maestro Giancarlo Calo)*, Iole Silvani *(Wardrobe mistress)*. Francesco Mei *(Barman)*, Mimmo Poli *(Furniture remover)*, Massimiliano Filoni *(Small boy)*, Alessandro Vlad *(Caracalla orchestra conductor)*, Enzo Siciliano *(Orchestra conductor in Rome)*, Iole Cecchini *(Opera hair stylist)*, Nicola Nicoloso *(Tenor in 'Il trovatore')*, Mario Tocci *(Count di Luna in 'Il trovatore')*, Franco Magrini *(Doctor)*, Liana del Balzo *(Maestro's sister)*, Fabrizio Polverini *(Driver)*.

142 mins.

Distributors: Harris Films (UK), 20th Century-Fox (USA).

1981 **La tragedia di un uomo ridicolo**   (The Tragedy of a Ridiculous Man)
P.c: Fiction Cinematografica, for the Ladd Company. P: Giovanni Bertolucci. P. man: Mario Di Biase. D: Bernardo Bertolucci. Asst. d: Antonio Gabrielli, Fiorella Infascelli. Sc: Bernardo Bertolucci. Ph: Carlo Di Palma (Eastman Colour). Ed: Gabriella Cristiani. A. d: Gianni Silvestri. Cost: Lina Nerli Taviani. M: Ennio Morricone. Sd: Mario Dallimonti.

Ugo Tognazzi *(Primo Spaggiari)*, Anouk Aimée *(Barbara Spaggiari)*, Laura Morante *(Laura)*, Victor Cavallo *(Adelfo)*, Olympia Carlisi *(Signora Romola, fortune-teller)*, Riccardo Tognazzi *(Giovanni Spaggiari)*, Vittorio Caprioli *(Marshal Angrisani)*, Renato Salvatori *(Colonel Macchi)*, Don Backy *(Crossing keeper)*, Cosimo Cinieri *(Magistrate)*, Margherita Chiari *(Maid)*, Antonio Trevisi *(Bank Manager)*, Gaetano Ferrari *(Guard)*, Gianni Migliavacca, Ennio Ferrari, Pietro Longari Ponzoni *(Money lenders)*.

116 mins.

Distributors: Columbia-EMI-Warner (UK), Warner Bros. (USA).

Bertolucci has also worked on the following films as scriptwriter:

1966   *Ballata da un miliardo* (co-sc: Bruno Baratti, Gianni Puccini; directed by Gianni Puccini)
1968   *C'era una volta il West* (story by Bertolucci, Dario Argento, Sergio Leone; directed by Sergio Leone)
1971   *L'inchiesta* (co-sc: Gianni Amico; directed by Gianni Amico)

In 1983, Bertolucci was the producer on *Io con te no ci sto più*, directed by Gianni Amico.

Select Bibliography

This bibliography includes works referred to in the text and background material.

Althusser, Louis, *For Marx*, trans. B. Brewster, London, New Left Books, 1970.
    Lenin and Philosophy and Other Essays, trans. B. Brewster, London, New Left Books, 1971.
Artaud, Antonin, *The Theatre and its Double*, trans. M. C. Richards, New York, Grove Press, 1958.
Bachmann, Gideon, 'Every Sexual Relationship is Condemned: An interview with Bernardo Bertolucci apropos *Last Tango in Paris*', *Film Quarterly*, vol. 26, no. 3, 1973.
    'Films are Animal Events: Bernardo Bertolucci talks about his new film, *1900*', *Film Quarterly*, vol. 29, no. 1, 1975.
Baldini, G., *The Story of Giuseppe Verdi*, trans. R. Parker, Cambridge, Cambridge University Press, 1980.
Barthes, Roland, *S/Z*, trans. R. Miller, London, Cape; New York, Hill & Wang, 1975.
    The Pleasure of the Text, trans. R. Miller, New York, Hill & Wang, 1975.
Bazin, André, *What is Cinema?*, trans. H. Gray, 2 vols., Berkeley, University of Calforina Press, 1968 and 1971.
Beck, Julian, 'Tourner avec Bertolucci', *Cahiers du Cinéma*, no. 194, 1967.
Beressford, S., 'Italy: Divisionism', in *Post-Impressionism: Cross-currents in European Painting*, London, Royal Academy of Arts/Weidenfeld and Nicolson; New York, Harper & Row, 1979.
'Bernardo Bertolucci Seminar', *Dialogue on Film*, vol. 3, no. 5, 1974.
Bertolucci, Bernardo, 'Versus Godard', *Cahiers du Cinéma*, no. 186, 1967.
    'Le monde entier dans un chambre', *Cahiers du Cinéma*, no. 194, 1967.
    'L'Ambiguité et l'incertitude au miroir' and screenplay of *Prima della rivoluzione*, *L'Avant-scène du Cinéma*, no. 82, 1968.
Bondanella, Peter, *Italian Cinema from Neorealism to the Present*, New York, Frederick Ungar, 1983.
Borges, Jorge Luis, *Theme of the Traitor and Hero*, in *Fictions*, trans. A. Kerrigan, New York, Grove Press, 1962.
Bragin, John, 'A Conversation with Bernardo Bertolucci', *Film Quarterly*, vol. 20, no. 1, 1966.
Brooks, Peter, *The Melodramatic Imagination*, New Haven, Yale University Press, 1976.
Cammett, J. M., *Antonio Gramsci and the Origins of Italian Communism*, Stanford, University of California Press, 1967.
Casetti, Francesco, *Bernardo Bertolucci*, Florence, La Nuova Italia, 1974.
Crofts, Stephen, 'Authorship and Hollywood', *Wide Angle*, vol. 5, no. 3, 1983.
Crowdus, Gary, and Georgakas, Dan, '*Luna* and the Critics', *Cineaste*, vol. 10, no. 1, 1979–80.
Culler, Jonathan, *On Deconstruction*, London, Routledge & Kegan Paul, 1983.

Deleuze, Gilles, and Guattari, Félix, *Anti-Oedipus: Capitalism and Schizophrenia*, trans. R. Hurley, M. Seem, H. R. Lane, Minneapolis, University of Minnesota Press, 1977.

'Dialogue on Film', *American Film*, vol. 5, no. 4, 1980.

Di Bernardo, Giovanna, 'Bertolucci's "*1900*": A Preview: Red Flags and American Dollars', *Cineaste*, vol. 7, no. 4, 1976.

Di Vico, Fabio, and Degni, Roberto, 'Bertolucci's "*1900*": A Preview: The Poetry of Class Struggle', *Cineaste*, vol. 7, no. 4, 1976.

Eagleton, Terry, *Criticism and Ideology*, London, New Left Books, 1976.

Eco, Umberto, *A Theory of Semiotics*, Bloomington, Indiana University Press, 1976.

Foucault, Michel, 'What is an Author?', trans. D. F. Bouchard, *Screen*, vol. 20, no. 1, 1979.

Franklin, J. C., 'The Films of Fassbinder: Form and Formula', *Quarterly Review of Film Studies*, vol. 5, no. 2, 1980.

Frayling, Christopher, *Spaghetti Westerns*, London, Routledge & Kegan Paul, 1981.

Freud, Sigmund, *Totem and Taboo*, London, Hogarth Press, 1951.

Civilization and Its Discontents, London, Hogarth Press, 1963.

Gledhill, Christine, 'Recent Developments in Feminist Criticism', *Quarterly Review of Film Studies*, vol. 3, no. 4, 1978.

Godard, Jean-Luc, *Godard on Godard*, ed. and trans. T. Milne, London, Secker & Warburg; New York, Viking Press, 1972.

Goldin, Marilyn, 'Bertolucci on *The Conformist*', *Sight and Sound*, vol. 40, no. 2, 1971.

Gramsci, Antonio, *Selections from the Prison Notebooks*, ed. and trans. Q. Hoare and G. Nowell-Smith, London, Lawrence and Wishart, 1971.

Harvey, Sylvia, *May '68 and Film Culture*, London, British Film Institute, 1980.

Hughes, S., *The Fall and Rise of Modern Italy*, New York, Macmillan, 1967.

James, C. Vaughan, *Soviet Socialist Realism*, London, Macmillan, 1973.

Jameson, Fredric, *The Political Unconscious*, London, Methuen, 1981.

Kline, T. Jefferson, 'Orpheus Transcending: Bertolucci's *Last Tango in Paris*', *International Review of Psycho-Analysis*, no. 3, 1976.

'Father as Mirror: Bertolucci's Oedipal Quest and the Collapse of Paternity', *Psychocultural Review*, 1979.

'Doubling *The Double*', in *Fearful Symmetry: Doubles and Doubling in Literature and Film*, Tallahassee, University Presses of Florida, 1981.

'The Unconformist', in *Modern European Filmmakers and the Art of Adaptation*, eds. A. Horton and J. Magretta, New York, Frederick Ungar, 1981.

'The Absent Presence: Stendhal in Bertolucci's *Prima della rivoluzione*', *Cinema Journal*, vol. 23, no. 2, 1984.

Kogan, N., *A Political History of Postwar Italy*, New York, Praeger, 1981.

Kolker, Robert Phillip, 'Angle and Reality: Godard and Gorin in America', *Sight and Sound*, vol. 42, no. 3, 1973.

The Altering Eye: Contemporary International Cinema, New York, Oxford University Press, 1983.

Kuhn, Annette, *Women's Pictures*, London, Routledge & Kegan Paul, 1982.

Lacan, Jacques, *Ecrits*, trans. A. Sheridan, London, Tavistock; New York, W. W. Norton, 1977.

The Four Fundamental Concepts of Psycho-analysis, ed. J.-A. Miller, trans. A. Sheridan, Harmondsworth, Penguin, 1979.

Feminine Sexuality, ed. J. Mitchell and J. Rose, trans. J. Rose, London, Macmillan; New York, W. W. Norton, 1982.

Leprohon, Pierre, *The Italian Cinema*, trans. R. Greaves and O. Stallybrass, London, Secker & Warburg, 1972.

Lopez, Daniel, 'The Father Figure in *The Conformist* and in *Last Tango in Paris*', *Film Heritage*, vol. 9, no. 4, 1976.

Lukács, Georg, *Studies in European Realism*, New York, Grosset & Dunlap, 1964.

Essays on Thomas Mann, trans. S. Mitchell, London, Merlin, 1964.

MacCabe, Colin, *Godard: Images, Sounds, Politics*, London, Macmillan, 1980.

Mellen, Joan, 'A Conversation with Bernardo Bertolucci', *Cineaste*, vol. 5, no. 4, 1973.

Women and Their Sexuality in the New Film, New York, Horizon Press, 1973.

Metz, Christian, *Language and Cinema*, trans. D. J. U.-Sebeok, The Hague, Mouton, 1974.

The Imaginary Signifier, trans. C. Britton, A. Williams, B. Brewster, A. Guzzetti, Bloomington, Indiana University Press, 1982.

Mulvey, Laura, 'Visual Pleasure and Narrative Cinema', *Screen*, vol. 16, no. 3, 1975.

Nichols, Bill, 'Il Conformista', *Cineaste*, vol. 4, no. 4, 1971.

Ideology and the Image, Bloomington, Indiana University Press, 1981.

Overbey, David (ed. and trans.), *Springtime in Italy: A Reader on Neo-Realism*, London, Talisman Books, 1978.

Pasolini, Pier Paolo, *Oedipus Rex*, trans. J. Matthews, London, Lorrimer, 1974.

'The Cinema of Poetry', in *Movies and Methods*, ed. Bill Nichols, Berkeley, University of California Press, 1976.

'Observations on the Long Take', trans. N. MacAfee and C. Owens, in *October*, vol. 13, 1980.

Poulantzas, Nicos, *Fascism and Dictatorship*, trans. J. White, London, New Left Books, 1974.

Roud, Richard, 'Fathers and Sons', *Sight and Sound*, vol. 40, no. 2, 1971.

'Bertolucci on *La Luna*', *Sight and Sound*, vol. 48, no. 4, 1979.

Russell, John, *Francis Bacon*, London, Thames and Hudson, 1971.

Ryan, Michael, *Marxism and Deconstruction*, Baltimore, Johns Hopkins University Press, 1982.

Siciliano, Enzo, *Pasolini*, trans. J. Shepley, New York, Random House, 1982.

Silverman, Kaja, *The Subject of Semiotics*, New York, Oxford University Press, 1983.

Soby, James T., *René Magritte*, New York, Doubleday, 1965.

Solanas, Fernando, and Getino, Octavio, 'Towards a Third Cinema', in B. Nichols (ed.), *Movies and Methods*, Berkeley, University of California Press, 1976.

Stack, Oswald, *Pasolini on Pasolini*, London, Thames and Hudson/BFI, 1969; Bloomington, Indiana University Press, 1970.

Tannenbaum, E. R., *The Fascist Experience*, New York, Basic Books, 1972.

Tannenbaum, E. R., and Noether, E. P. (eds.), *Modern Italy*, New York, New York University Press, 1974.

Time magazine, 'A messy fight for the final cut', 2 May 1977.

Togliatti, Palmiro, *On Gramsci and other writings*, ed. D. Sassoon, London, Lawrence and Wishart, 1979.

Ungari, Enzo, *Scene madri di Bernardo Bertolucci*, Milan, Ubulibri, 1982.

Vogel, Amos, 'Bernardo Bertolucci: An Interview', *Film Comment*, vol. 7, no. 3, 1971.

Weaver, William (trans.), *Seven Verdi Librettos*, New York, W. W. Norton, 1975.

Wollen, Peter, *Signs and Meaning in the Cinema*, London, Secker & Warburg/BFI, 1969.

Index

255